CRITIQUE OF CREATIVITY

Today, at one and the same time, scholarly publishing is drawn in two directions. On the one hand, this is a time of the most exciting theoretical, political and artistic projects that respond to and seek to move beyond global administered society. On the other hand, the publishing industries are vying for total control of the ever-lucrative arena of scholarly publication, creating a situation in which the means of distribution of books grounded in research and in radical interrogation of the present are increasingly restricted. In this context, MayFlyBooks has been established as an independent publishing house, publishing political, theoretical and aesthetic works on the question of organization. MayFlyBooks publications are published under Creative Commons license free online and in paperback. MayFlyBooks is a not-for-profit operation that publishes books that matter, not because they reinforce or reassure any existing market.

1. Herbert Marcuse, *Negations: Essays in Critical Theory*
2. Dag Aasland, *Ethics and Economy: After Levinas*
3. Gerald Raunig and Gene Ray (eds), *Art and Contemporary Critical Practice: Reinventing Institutional Critique*
4. Steffen Böhm and Siddhartha Dabhi (eds), *Upsetting the Offset: The Political Economy of Carbon Markets*
5. Peter Armstrong and Geoff Lightfoot (eds), *'The Leading Journal in the Field': Destabilizing Authority in the Social Sciences of Management*
6. Carl Cederström and Casper Hoedemaekers (eds), *Lacan and Organization*
7. Félix Guattari and Antonio Negri, *New Lines of Alliance, New Spaces of Liberty*
8. Gerald Raunig, Gene Ray and Ulf Wuggenig (eds), *Critique of Creativity: Precarity, Subjectivity and Resistance in the 'Creative Industries'*

Critique of Creativity:
Precarity, Subjectivity and Resistance in the 'Creative Industries'

Gerald Raunig, Gene Ray and Ulf Wuggenig (eds)

www.mayflybooks.org

First published in English by MayFlyBooks in paperback in London and free online at www.mayflybooks.org in 2011.

Printed by the MPG Books Group in the UK

ISBN (Print) 978-1-906948-13-9
ISBN (PDF) 978-1-906948-14-6

This work has been published in conjunction with the European Institute for Progressive Cultural Policies (www.eipcp.net) and with support of Wien Kultur.

Contents

Contributors

Brigitta Kuster is a cultural producer primarily active as video-maker and author. She has dealt with the themes of migration and transnational space, the representation of labor, gender and sexual identity. She has also collaborated with Pauline Boudry, Renate Lorenz and others in a long-term interdisciplinary research project on labor and sexuality. She received the Swiss Art Award in 2006 and 2010.

Maurizio Lazzarato is a sociologist, philosopher and independent researcher specialized in studies of relationships of work, economy and society. He works at the University of Paris I. His recent publications include *Le gouvernement des inégalités: critique de l'insécurité néolibérale* (2008); with Antonella Corsani, *Intermittents et précaires* (2008); *Etude statistique, économique et sociologique du régime d'assurance chômage des professionnels du spectacle vivant, du cinéma et de l'audiovisuel* (2005); *Les révolutions du capitalisme, Les empêcheurs de penser en rond* (2004), and *Les mutations du travail sur le territoire de la Plaine St. Denis* (2003).

Esther Leslie is Professor of Political Aesthetics in the School of English and Humanities at Birkbeck, University of London. She is the author of *Walter Benjamin* (Reaktion, 2007), *Synthetic Worlds: Nature, Art and the Chemical Industry* (2005), *Hollywood Flatlands: Animation, Critical Theory and the Avant Garde* (2002) and *Walter Benjamin: Overpowering Conformism* (2000). She is on the editorial boards of the journals *Historical Materialism*, *Radical Philosophy* and *Revolutionary History*.

Isabell Lorey is a political scientist, Visiting Professor at the Humboldt University, Berlin (2010 and 2011), Visiting Professor for Gender

Studies, Biopolitics and Postcolonial Studies at the Faculty for Social Science, Vienna University (2009), and previously Assistant Professor for Gender & Postcolonial Studies at the University of the Arts Berlin (2001-2007). She has published on: feminist and political theory, biopolitical governmentality, critical whiteness studies, political immunization, and precarization. *Figuren des Immunen: Elemente einer politischen Theorie*, her habilitation on Roman struggles of order, the Plebeian, concepts of community and immunization, was published with diaphanes in 2011.

Angela McRobbie is Professor of Communications at Goldsmiths College, London. Her special topics of research are: gender and feminist theory and cultural studies, and 'precarious labour' in art worlds and in the new culture industries. She is the author of *In the Culture Society: Art, Fashion and Popular Music* (1999), *The Uses of Cultural Studies: A Textbook* (2005), *The Aftermath of Feminism* (2008) and *Sexuality, Gender and Generation: Postfeminist Art and Culture* (2010). Her current research on the 'new culture industry' will be published as *Be Creative: Precarious Labour in Art and Cultural Worlds, London, Berlin, Glasgow*.

Raimund Minichbauer has conducted a wide range of studies and research projects in the cultural sector since 1995. He works with the European Institute for Progressive Cultural Policies (eipcp), where he was member of the coordinating teams of the transnational projects republicart (2002-2005), translate (2005-2008) and transform (2005-2008). He is currently working on the multi-year research project Creating Worlds (2009-2012). He is co-editor, with Maria Lind, of *European Cultural Policies* (2005).

Monika Mokre is a Researcher of the Institute for European Integration Research (EIF), Austrian Academy of Sciences. She is a board member of FOKUS, the Austrian Association for Cultural Economics and Policy Studies, a member of eipcp, and a Lecturer at the Universities of Innsbruck, Salzburg and Vienna. Her research focuses on European democracy and the public sphere, cultural politics and financing of the arts, media politics, and gender studies. Her most recent publications in English are *Exchange and Deception: A Feminist Perspective* (2010, co-edited with Caroline Gerschlager) and *Culture and External Relations: Europe and Beyond* (2011, with Jozef Batora).

Stefan Nowotny is a philosopher based in Vienna. He has collaborated in the eipcp's transnational projects transform and translate (2005-2008) and Europe as a Translational Space: The Politics of Heterolinguality (2010-2012). He has done research or taught at universities in Belgium, Germany and Austria (since 2001), alongside other project involvements and collaborations. He has published various essays especially on philosophical and political topics, co-edited several anthologies, translated a number of texts from both French and English into German, and co-authored the volumes *Instituierende Praxen: Bruchlinien der Institutionskritik* (with Gerald Raunig, 2008) and *Übersetzung: Das Versprechen eines Begriffs* (with Boris Buden, 2008) and co-edited *Kunst der Kritik* (2010, with Birgit Mennel and Gerald Raunig).

Marion von Osten is Professor at the Academy of Fine Arts, Vienna, and works as an artist, author and curator. Her projects focus on the changed conditions of the production of cultural work in neo-liberal societies, technologies of the self and the governance of mobility. Her most recent publication in English is *Colonial Modern: Aesthetics of the Past Rebellions for the Future* (2010, with Tom Avermaete and Serhat Karakayali). She has edited or co-edited *Projekt Migration* (2005), *Norm der Abweichung* (2003), *MoneyNations* (2003), and *Das Phantom sucht seinen Mörder: Ein Reader zur Kulturalisierung der Ökonomie* (1999).

Gerald Raunig is philosopher and art theoretician. He teaches at the Züricher Hochschule der Künste (Departement Kunst und Medien) where he coordinates the specialization Theory. He is co-founder of the eipcp (European Institute for Progressive Cultural Policies) and co-ordinator of the transnational eipcp research projects republicart (2002-2005), transform (2005-2008) and Creating Worlds (2009-2012). His recent books include *Art and Revolution. Transversal Activism in the Long Twentieth Century* (2007), and *A Thousand Machines* (2010) both published by Semiotext(e)/MIT Press.

Gene Ray teaches critical studies in the CCC research-based Master Program at Geneva University of Art and Design. He is the author of *Terror and the Sublime in Art and Critical Theory* (2005, 2010) and co-editor, with Gerald Raunig, of *Art and Contemporary Critical Practice: Reinventing Institutional Critique* (2009).

Suely Rolnik is a cultural critic, curator, psychoanalyst and full professor at the Universidade Católica de São Paulo, where she conducts a transdisciplinary doctoral program on contemporary subjectivity. She is co-author with Félix Guattari of *Micropolítica: Cartografias do desejo* (1986) and of *Molecular Revolution in Brazil* (2008). She is author of a research project about Lygia Clark, in which she realized 63 films of interviews, exhibited at the Musée de Beaux-arts de Nantes (Nantes, 2005) and the Pinacoteca do Estado de São Paulo (São Paulo, 2006). She lives in Brazil where she has a private practice in psychoanalysis.

Vassilis Tsianos teaches theoretical sociology and migration studies at the University of Hamburg. He is a research fellow with the project 'Transit Migration' (Johann Wolfgang Goethe-University, Frankfurt) investigating the border regimes in southeast Europe. His research interests and publications include contemporary political theory, labor studies and the concept of the autonomy of migration. He is co-author of *Escape Routes: Control and Subversion in the Twenty-First Century* (2008) and co-editor of a book on 'Empire and the biopolitical turn'. He is active member of *kanak attak* and of the *Society for Legalization*.

Paolo Virno is a philosopher living in Rome and teaching at the Università degli Studi Roma Tre. He was active as a member of the Italian political group *Potere Operaio* during the 1970s, where he was imprisoned for three years before being acquitted. Virno is author of *Convenzione e materialismo* (1986), *Mondanità* (1994), *Parole con parole* (1995), *Il ricordo del presente: Saggio sul tempo storico* (1999), *Grammatica della moltitudine* (2001), *Esercizi di esodo* (2002), *Quando il verbo si fa carne: Linguaggio e natura umana* (2003), *Motto di spirito e azione innovativa* (2005), *E così via, all'infinito. Logica e antropologia* (2010). Books in English are *A Grammar of the Multitude* (2004), *Multitude Between Innovation and Negation* (2008) and *Radical Thought in Italy: A Potential Politics* (1996, co-edited with Michael Hardt). He is a contributor to the philosophical review *Forme di vita*.

Ulf Wuggenig is a sociologist at Leuphana University of Lüneburg, Germany, where he is also director of the contemporary visual art gallery of this university ('Kunstraum'). Among his more recent publications in English are the co-*edited* catalogue books *Dierk Schmidt. The Division of the Earth – Tableaux on the Legal Synopses of the Berlin Africa*

Conférence (2010), *Moirés. Andreas Fogarasi, Katya Sander, Urtica* (2008, with Astrid Wege) and *Next Flag. The African Sniper Reader* (2005, with Heike Munder and Fernando Alvim). He co-edited (with Gerald Raunig) *Kritik der Kreativität* (2007) as well as *Publicum* (2005) and (with Beatrice von Bismarck and Therese Kaufmann) *Nach Bourdieu: Kunst, Visualität, Politik* (2008).

Acknowledgements

We wish to extend our warm thanks to all those who have contributed to the realization of this book, and who have participated in the conception and organization of the 2006 conferences which stimulated many of the essays in this volume: 'Critique of Creative Industries' took place at the Museum of Contemporary Art Kiasma in Helsinki as a collaboration between eipcp, Vienna and frame, Helsinki; 'Creating Effects' took place in Lüneburg and was co-organized by eipcp and the Kunstraum of Leuphana University Lüneburg. We would like to express special thanks to Bernhard Hummer, Yvonne Mattern, Birgit Mennel, Raimund Minichbauer, Marita Muukkonen, Jenny Nachtigall, Stefan Nowotny, Steffen Rudolph, Marketta Seppälä, Bettina Steinbrügge, Diethelm Stoller and Ingo Vavra.

Introduction: On the Strange Case of 'Creativity' and its Troubled Resurrection

Gerald Raunig, Gene Ray and Ulf Wuggenig

Creativity is astir: reborn, re-conjured, re-branded, resurgent. The old myths of creation and creators – the hallowed labors and privileged agencies of demiurges and prime movers, of Biblical world-makers and self-fashioning artist-geniuses – are back underway, producing effects, circulating appeals. Much as the Catholic Church dresses the old creationism in the new gowns of 'intelligent design', the Creative Industries sound the clarion call to the Cultural Entrepreneurs. In the hype of the 'creative class' and the high flights of the digital bohemians, the renaissance of 'the creatives' is visibly enacted. On the resonant conceptual ground of creativity, new social functions are unfolding – or are projected. In the tradition of the aesthetics of genius and charismatic imagination, a social selection is performed: the truly creative social actors, the designated elect who generate and release innovations, are marked apart – and marked up for symbolic ascension.

At the same time, powerful populist impulses are mobilized. Radical cultural-political demands – encapsulated in the slogan 'Culture for all' and Joseph Beuys's dictum 'Everyone an artist' – are perverted into a logic of the total creative imperative. In this social and semantic recoding, old notions of art and 'the artistic' are being replaced, even as they are absorbed, by the new concepts of creativity and creative industry. The claims made in the name of the latter rose up in the skies of metropolitan capital in pace with the bubbles of real estate, stock and derivatives markets. For the gurus of the rising creative class, not even global economic meltdown should shake the faith of the new elect and their backers. For Richard Florida, one of the main promoters of the new discourse, the full flowering of creativity and entrepreneurship actually requires the stimulus of crisis. Not to worry, we are told, investments in creativity always pay off; the 'Great Reset' and the era of 'post-crash prosperity' are on the way.[1]

The essays collected here analyze this complex resurgence of creation myths and formulate a critique of creativity. The concept of critique in this context should perhaps be clarified. The theoretical orientations of the authors contributing to this volume are not identical; important differences in approach and position will emerge from the texts themselves. But all the critical practices deployed here can agree on one point: critique should be more than a gesture of global negation or a predictable ritual of rejection. Beyond this shared minimum, an attempt to re-conceptualize critique more precisely is also legible. Its outlines are indicated by 'Transform', the three-year (2005-8) research project of the European Institute for Progressive Cultural Policies (eipcp) that forms the context for these essays. The Transform project set out explicitly to rethink the modalities of critique and contemporary critical practices. Emerging from those inquiries, discussions and textual exchanges was a willingness to re-conceive critique as a capacity for differentiation and for the embodiment of difference.[2] In this spirit, the problem of a resurgent creativity is approached through a rich diversity of critical practices and interpretations of contemporary social processes. We hope readers will find these inter-textual tensions and differences as stimulating and productive as we have.

In order to shape this abundance into an emerging critique of creativity, we have structured the book into four sections. In the first section, 'Creativity', the sources and exemplary forms of the new discourses of creativity are traced and deconstructed. In his essay, Stefan Nowotny leads us into the genealogy of critique as 'cre-activity' and into the question of the immanent effects of critique. This perspective performs a de-theologization of creativity and with Bakhtin leads back from the mythically individualist quality of creativity to its foundational sociality. In her text here, the Brazilian psychoanalyst and art theorist Suely Rolnik takes a Deleuzean approach to the changing cultural field. She argues that the openings of transformation have been accompanied by a capturing geopolitics that Rolnik calls 'pimping': the taking over of struggles and creativity from 1968 by cognitive capitalism, but also the movements of exodus that came out of 1968.

Next, Maurizio Lazzarato scrutinizes the notion of 'artistic critique', a keyword in the French debates that continue to flare around the work of Luc Boltanski and Ève Chiapello. While Boltanski and Chiapello's theses have become known to English readers through the translation of their *Le nouvel esprit du capitalisme*, Pierre-Michel Menger's analyses of cultural employment are relatively unknown beyond the borders of France. Lazzarato, who has made decisive interventions into these debates, aims to show exactly how both Boltanski and Chiapello and Menger have gotten it wrong. In his essay, Ulf Wuggenig investigates the current Anglophone discourse on innovation and creativity and presents a critique of the reinterpretations of the history of nineteenth-century art by network theoretical sociologist Harrison C. White. Along the way, the figure of the art dealer as heroic entrepreneur who paved the way of modernist avantgarde art is brought down from his pedestal.

The second section explores the ambivalences of 'Precarization', the placeholder in critical discourses of what the jargon of creativity celebrates as 'flexibility' and freedom. Isabell Lorey's work on the relations between biopolitical governmentality and the self-precarization of cultural producers has stimulated much discussion. In her text for this volume, Lorey brings her theses to bear on debates in the German feuilletons around the 'dependent precariat'. In their essay, Brigitta Kuster and Vassilis Tsianos consider Spinoza as the 'pre-thinker' of precarity and borrow Paolo Virno's phenomenology of fear and anxiety in order to explore *The Village*, the feature film by M. Night Shyamalan. At film's end, Kuster and Tsianos uncover the possibility of a destroying grin of precarity. With another co-author (namely Dimitris Papadopolous) and in another context (that of political sociology), Tsianos had reconnoitered the macro-political side of this grin, the problem of the place and reemergence of a political subject moved by fear. The section ends with 'Wit and Innovation', by Paolo Virno, an author whose texts on virtuosity, culture industry and the ambivalence of the multitude have contributed much to the formation of the background shared by many of the writers in this volume.

The third section, 'Creativity Industries', offers detailed studies of the creative industries as they are actually developing in four concrete fields of practice. Angela McRobbie, who has been investigating the British creative industries for more than ten years, reports on the 'Los Angelesation' of London since the 1990s. McRobbie parses the three successive 'short-waves' that have transformed the micro-economies in

3

which young women bring their creative work to market. Against this background of Blairite cultural politics and its miserable consequences, Monika Mokre thematizes the confusion of Austrian cultural politics in the face of the new cultural-political subject. She investigates the exemplary failure of 'Quartier 21', the would-be flagship advertisement of the Creative Industries in Vienna. In her essay, Marion von Osten analyzes the concrete and heterogeneous developments of cultural labor in the self-organized design and multi-media sector in Zurich. Her work leads her to the surprising thesis that the so-called Creative Industries in fact have yet to appear. Raimund Minichbauer offers a critical analysis of creativity discourses, as these have taken hold in the cultural policies of the European Union. Reviewing the official programs and positions since the implementation of the so-called Lisbon strategy, he finds a clear and accelerating economization of cultural policy.

The fourth and last section, 'Culture Industry', focuses on the famous arguments of Max Horkheimer and Theodor W. Adorno. As many of the writers in this book note, the revalorizations of the 'creative industries' enact a neutralizing recoding of Horkheimer and Adorno's critical category. In his contribution, Gene Ray re-reads Adorno's culture industry arguments against the alarming background of the national security-surveillance state and the planetary 'war on terror'. Arguing that theories of subjectivation must give due weight to the objective tendencies of a global capitalist process, he proposes that the Lacanian notion of 'enjoyment' mobilized by the culture industry entails the category of 'enforcement' epitomized by state terror. In her essay, Esther Leslie tracks the twists and turns of the current recoding of 'culture industry', which she sees reflected in the 'segue' from cultural populism to the rhetoric of choice within the field of cultural studies. In the new cultural policies, she finds a contemporary form of that 'aestheticization of politics' which Walter Benjamin identified as a strategy of fascism. Finally, Gerald Raunig analyzes four elements of Horkheimer and Adorno's concept of culture industry. Bringing post-structuralist theory to bear on the problems of precarity and subjectivation, he deconstructs the contemporary Creative Industries and also offers some critical reflections on Horkheimer and Adorno's manipulation thesis.

In sum, the essays collected here advance a critique of contemporary creative industries both as ideology and as specific material relations of exploitation. From numerous theoretical perspectives, the authors expose and analyze the forms and modalities of precarity and subjectivation, as well as the potentials and actual practices of resistance operative in the current cultural field.

Notes

1   Florida, 2002, was a landmark in the establishment of the discourse of creativity among urban policymakers and branders. The title of his new sequel (2010) indicates the self-affirming circuits of this discourse: *The Great Reset: How New Ways of Living and Working Drive Post-Crash Prosperity.*

2   See especially 'Critique' and 'Do You Remember Institutional Critique?', the relevant issues of the multi-lingual eipcp web journal *transversal*, online at <http://transform.eipcp.net/tranversal/0806>   and   <http://transform. eipcp.net/tranversal/0106>; and Raunig and Ray, 2009.

PART ONE: CREATIVITY

1

Immanent Effects: Notes on Cre-activity

Stefan Nowotny
translated by Aileen Derieg

In the preface to the first edition of his cycle *Monsieur Teste*, written in 1925, Paul Valéry recalled writing the first text that he devoted to the figure of Teste thirty years before:

> It seemed necessary to me to strive for the sensation of effort, and I did not appreciate the happy results that are merely the natural fruits of our innate abilities. In other words, the results in general – and consequently the works – were far less important to me than the energy of the creator – the essential core of the things to which he aspires. This proves that a little theology is to be found everywhere. (Valéry, 1978: 8, trans. Derieg)

My intention here is basically to start from these sentences, or at least remain in their field of resonance, to circle around the question of a possible critique of creativity. In doing so, as will become evident, there is no easy way past theology: as soon as one speaks of something like the 'energy of the creator' – cipher for so many designations of what is presumed to be at work in creativity – a reality is already invoked that rises above all other reality; a reality that surpasses the 'natural fruits', as Valéry says with a certain irony, indeed the results and works in general. It is obvious that Valéry immediately attributes this surpassing to a certain youthful enthusiasm, a youthful presumptuousness, which seeks exertion, but has not yet been overcome by the results of its exertions. Yet exactly this – being overcome by the results of one's own exertions – describes the situation of an author, who finds himself accompanied throughout his life by a figure (Monsieur Teste) created in his younger years and reflects on this figure thirty years after its creation. And as it initially appears, this also exactly describes the situation and perspective of a critique of creativity, as it is to be treated here.

The Question of a Critique of Creativity and How Boltanski and Chiapello Do Not Answer It

In comparison with critical investigations of a number of other objects, the peculiarity of a 'critique of creativity' is undoubtedly its confidence in a certain critical capability on the part of its object. As a critique of the object 'creativity' ('critique of creativity' as *genitivus obiectivus*), it aims to distinguish the possibilities and limitations of a creativity that is ultimately characterized by its own inherent critique or critical capacity ('critique of creativity' as *genitivus subiectivus*). Hence we are dealing with a critique that aims less to reject its object (as idols, ideologies, false gods, and so forth) than to achieve an enlightening understanding of it, which seeks to separate what is idolatrous, ideological, false about this object from what may appear all the more legitimate about it, the more it is purified through critique from all that is idolatrous, and so forth. In this sense, the task of a critique of creativity could additionally be understood in a certain analogy to the Kantian project of a critique of reason. Just as in Kant's critique of the various capacities of reason, reason is not only the object of the critique, but is also actualized in some of its capacities at the same time in the course of carrying out this critique, in the same way it could be possible that a certain capacity of creativity is actualized in the procedure of a critique of creativity. Indeed this capacity would then assume an irrevocable difference to that which could ever come into view as the 'object' of creativity – and every object named 'creativity' would conversely always already be an immanent effect of a certain creative activity.

Let us first consider an argument that must at first glance appear as a possible elaboration of this kind of approach, at least in its initial aspect: the idea that a critique of creativity has to do with a critique and critical capacity inherent to creativity itself also seems to be a principle point of departure in the recently much discussed study *The New Spirit of Capitalism* by Luc Boltanski and Ève Chiapello. One of the central motifs of this book is the critique of what the authors call 'artistic critique', that is of a critique that one might suspect derives from creativity or at least from a special relationship to creativity. The study

10

suggests that this artistic critique has turned primarily against the 'disenchantment', the 'lack of authenticity', the 'loss of meaning' and the 'oppression' proceeding from the hollowness and the standardization of the bourgeois commodity society, raising instead demands for 'freedom', for 'autonomy' and 'mobility' (Boltanski and Chiapello, 1999: 83). However, this form of critique, which entered into history above all in the context of May 1968 in Paris, inspired (and this is where Boltanski and Chiapello's 'critique of creativity' starts in the form of a critique of the 'artistic critique') new strategies of business management and in this way ultimately resulted in effects that were accompanied by new forms of exploitation and precarization and thus, not least of all, forestalled the equality and security demands of the other main strand of the critique, which the authors call 'social critique' (and with which the 'artistic critique' connected in a hitherto unknown way in May 1968).

In light of this line of argument, two points are immediately conspicuous: one is the alleged reference of the critique of creativity (*genitivus obiectivus*) to a creativity of critique (or 'critique of creativity' as *genitivus subiectivus*) subsumed under the name 'artistic critique'; the other is the theme of an effect of critique, which becomes the actual object of Boltanski and Chiapello's 'critique of critique', because it ultimately undermines the concern and intention of the critique that engenders it to criticize capitalism, partly due to a certain blindness that blocks its motives, partly due to the way these motives are appropriated and taken over by exploitative capitalist interests. In terms of the first point, it is quickly evident that despite expectations of Boltanski and Chiapello's book, it is not really addressed at all: creativity or the specific experience of creativity play no role whatsoever where the concept of an artist critique is introduced; the artist critique is rooted much more 'in the way of living of the Boheme', shares 'individualism' with bourgeois modernity from the start, and finds its 'epitome in the figure of the dandy in the mid-19th century' (Boltanski and Chiapello, 1999: 83, 86 and 84). The only – and certainly significant – indication of something like a question of creativity that Boltanski and Chiapello offer in this context is found in an insertion, which at least acknowledges that the dandified stylization of 'non-production' involves a specific exception: the 'exception of self-production' (Boltanski and Chiapello, 1999: 84) – In other words a form of self-engendering in the sense of engendering a certain way of living.

11

With regard to the second point – the question of the effectiveness of critique – it is worth taking a closer look at Boltanski and Chiapello's concept of critique:

> The idea of critique [...] only makes sense if there is a discrepancy between a desirable and an actual state of things. To make as much room for critique as it deserves in the social world, issues of justice cannot be simply reduced to power. However, one must also not be so blinded by the norm of justice as to lose sight of the actual circumstances of power. To claim validity, critique must be able to justify itself. In other words, it must clarify its normative relational system, especially if it has to react to justifications that those criticized produce for their actions. (Boltanski and Chiapello, 1999: 69)

As frequently as the link between the concept of critique and the necessity of clarifying a 'normative relational system' may be encountered, this link cannot claim to be self-evident.[1] It is based on a fundamental distance between the subject exercising critique and what is being criticized, or more precisely: on a flexible ability to take a distance, which is carried out in the space opened up by the discrepancy between the 'actual' and the 'desirable' state. However, the idea of taking a distance in this way is not only in danger of misjudging the very involvement in the existing circumstances of power which applies to the criticizing subject her/himself in their activity (and which is by no means covered simply by keeping an eye on the 'actual circumstances of power'). In conjunction with the demand to indicate a 'normative relational system', this idea is also in danger of repeating an exclusion, which could virtually be called a leitmotiv in the history of political conceptions, and which was already clearly formulated by Aristotle. I refer here to the separation of 'mere voice' that is only capable of expressing 'pleasure or pain' from the power of speech 'intended to set forth the expedient and inexpedient, and therefore likewise the just and the unjust'. (Aristotle, 1988: 3) The demand that criticism must clarify a 'norm of justice' is thus linked not only with an implicit fundamental privileging of verbal expression, it also establishes a hierarchy among the modes of speaking and hence largely forestalls access to the – even though never consistently expressed – origin of criticism in the affective (experiences of violence, overexertion, displeasure, and so on, but also desire, experiences of pleasure, and so on).[2]

At the same time, the aforementioned emphasis on distance does not solely determine Boltanski and Chiapello's perspective of the subject exercising criticism. It also fixes the question of the effects of critique to a thinking of exteriority, thus missing the second aspect of the implications of a critique of creativity outlined above, which allows the question of effects to appear as a question of immanent effects. This thinking of exteriority is manifested in Boltanski and Chiapello at several levels: exteriority (distance), which determines the relationship of the subject exercising critique in reference to 'actual' and 'desirable' states; mutual exteriority (fundamental disconnectedness and even incompatibility) of 'artistic critique' and 'social critique'; exteriority of the intentions of critique in reference to its effects (the misery of the artist critique that Boltanski and Chiapello object to is based on a certain blindness with regards to demands for equality, which is inherent to its critical intentions; the actual effects of this critique, however, first become tangible in networked capitalism driven by entirely different interests and projects of legitimation).

Critique as Cre-activity

A critique of creativity in the aforementioned sense is thus hardly to be found in the described approach. Nevertheless, I think it is important to avoid two misunderstandings: on the one hand my point is not at all to principally disparage or discredit the analyses presented in the book by Boltanski and Chiapello, which I consider important on many points. On the other, it is even less my intention to defend any kind of 'artistic critique' – a category that I generally find of dubious use in contexts of social analysis – and thus end up in the waters of an overly familiar emphasis on art. For this reason, in the following the question of the connection between critique and creativity is initially not to be treated from the perspective of any kind of 'artistic critique', but rather with a view to what Boltanski and Chiapello call 'social critique' and qualify as being 'inspired by the socialists and, later, the Marxists' (Boltanski and Chiapello, 1999: 84).

Whereas Kant's critical philosophy summarizes the theoretical implications of critique as a theoretical procedure (the explication of which forms the project of the post-Kantian idealists in many respects), something similar could be said about Marx when it is a matter of accounting for critique as a practical activity in the sense of changing politics and society. Even the first of Marx's 'Theses on Feuerbach' speaks of the 'significance of "revolutionary", of "practical-critical", activity' (Marx, 1975: 422) and locates the problem, to a certain extent, in between idealism and materialism. Whereas the former 'does not know real, sensuous activity as such' and therefore has an abstract concept of practice, materialism so far (primarily that of Feuerbach) has not yet come to an understanding of practice at all and thus considers reality 'only in the form of the *object or of contemplation*' (Marx, 1975: 421). Marx's central example, explained in his fourth thesis, relates to Feuerbach's criticism of religion. If religion, as Feuerbach writes, is nothing other than a projection of earthly human condition, then it is not sufficient to unmask this projection at a purely theoretical level for the criticism to take effect; 'the secular basis' of this projection must indeed 'be both understood in its contradiction [or, to disentwine Marx's idea from its dialectical grounding, let us say: in its circumstances of power] and revolutionized in practice' (Marx, 1975: 422). And this revolutionizing cannot be reduced, as noted already in the third thesis, to the general formula of 'the changing of circumstances', but instead implies a 'coincidence of the changing of circumstances and of human activity or self-changing' (Marx, 1975: 422).

What is most remarkable about the concept of critique formulated in the Marxian Feuerbach theses is initially that they sketch an image of a fundamental involvement in an operative structure ('circumstances') that the notion of external 'conditions' only insufficiently covers, and which applies equally to critical and uncritical subjects. In short, it is not enough to fix 'objects' worthy of criticism or to strive for their 'change', if an operative structure is reproduced at the same time, which persistently produces precisely these objects in their reality. This form of criticism resembles a race dog chasing a fake rabbit attached to its own neck with a pole: it keeps running, yet it never comes any closer to its goal. For this reason there can be no change without self-change, a self-change that is by no means an individual private matter, but rather starts from the subjective (as Marx calls it: sensuous, practical) mode of reproducing the structure. The concept of self-change thus occupies the intersection between the first named aspect of the Marxian emphasis on involvement in the criticized circumstances and a third characteristic of the concept of criticism articulated in the Feuerbach theses: contrary to a widely held understanding in relation to Marx (and equally in relation to the question of critique in a more general sense, as seen in Boltanski and Chiapello), this concept of critique needs no clarification of its 'norm references' and no orientation to a 'desirable state'; it needs no purpose orientation at all, with the specific exception perhaps of the destitutive purpose of a 'dispossession' of the criticized operative structure, but such a purpose can ultimately only be resolved through a self-changing practice – and is therefore not exterior to this practice.

A clear echo of this practical concept of criticism formulated by Marx is found in Walter Benjamin's essay 'Critique of Violence' from 1921, specifically where Benjamin compares the 'political' to the 'proletarian general strike': whereas the first form of the general strike is simply to achieve certain purposes or ends that remain exterior to the action itself and hence only achieve external modifications of the circumstances of action (or work), the second form is like 'a wholly transformed work... an upheaval that this kind of strike not so much causes as consummates' (Benjamin, 1978: 292) – in other words, an overthrow that ultimately makes the strike appear not only abstract as a cessation of work, but as a release of a different, self-changing activity (assemblies, processes of exchange beyond the functionality of work, and so forth). And in reference to activities of art, a similar direction is also indicated by Benjamin's shifting of the question 'What is the *attitude* of a work to the relations of production of its time?' in the direction of the question: 'What is its *position* in them?', as formulated in 'The Author as Producer' (Benjamin, 1978: 222). Involvement, self-change, the lack of a definition of purpose – these three aspects determine Benjamin's reflection on a practical critique as well as Marx's.

Especially the last of these three aspects finally reveals an unmistakable link to the question of creativity. This is not primarily in the sense that the usually vague and indeterminate talk of art as non-purposed or as 'an end in itself' suggests – an idea that cannot be regarded outside of any connection with the problem posed here, but one that belongs primarily to the history of the ideas of artistic autonomy from the nineteenth century. What is more crucial is that the lack of a purpose indicates a certain shift of the question of creation or creativity, in which this question begins to detach itself from the onto-theological schema to which the opening quotation from Paul Valéry alludes, and in which it was held over the course of centuries or even millennia. This schema perpetually tied the 'purpose' or 'end' (final cause) of a creation to a primary, sovereign primal reality removed from the causal connection of the world and grounding this purpose, to a reality ontologically superior to every possibility, the prototype of which is found in the 'unmoved mover' of Aristotle's *Metaphysics*, Book XII: demiurge, prime cause and creator of the world, which Christian scholastic theology was to adapt as the *actus purus*. Valéry's allusion to the 'energy of the creator' (following a long tradition of translation, the Aristotelian term *enérgeia* is translated into German as 'reality'; the corresponding Latin term is *actus*) is to be understood against this background particularly as an indication that this construction has been less replaced by modern ideas of creativity relating to 'creating art' than it has been assimilated by them – at least in a certain presumptuousness of these ideas that is still in effect today, which insists on the artist subject as a reality of creating that is removed from the world, 'drawing from itself'.

In this kind of construction the world always appears as a secondary reality, and yet at the same time it finds itself fixed on being 'reality', which is always posited in a more or less distinctive opposition to possibility (the 'results in general', the 'natural fruits' or even the 'innate abilities' in Valéry's words). Exactly at this point, however, a shift becomes recognizable in the movement leading to modernism and, not least of all, to the ideas of Karl Marx and others. In a text entitled 'On Creation', Jean-Luc Nancy sees this shift expressed primarily in the works of Descartes, Spinoza and especially Leibniz. This shift sees the world as 'something possible, before it is something real' (Nancy, 2002: 81). In other words, it is real precisely in that it is possible, at stake, 'capable of being perfected' (Leibniz) or 'capable of being revolutionized' (according to Marxian logic). And this real possibility, in which the field of possibilities is limited neither to an existing nor to a presupposed reality, always refers at the same time to an inalienable involvement in the world (another world is only possible by virtue of changing this world and not as a castle in the clouds) and to the necessity of a self-change, which opens up new fields of possibility (the former 'creatures' become themselves potential 'creators', specifically and not least of all – and not only among dandies – as creators of themselves).[3]

'That there is in the world or even as the world (under the name "human" or "history", "technology", "art", "existence") a putting at stake of its origin and its end, its being-possible and hence its being and being in general' – in this, according to Nancy, a 'hitherto unknown problem of "creation"' becomes evident, which can neither be broken down to the register of 'production', nor refers to one prior subject of creation, but rather to a 'multiplicity of existences' that are involved in this problem (Nancy, 2002: 83). Nancy's list of the various names under which this problem can be recognized should be taken seriously, not only because 'art' is only one element of a series in it; we should also append the name 'critique' to this list, especially in the sense of the practical critique articulated by Marx or Benjamin, for example. In this sense, critique is a manner (but not the only one) of carrying out an activity, which I would like to call cre-activity here – to refrain from continuing the problematic and charged name of 'creativity'. The effects of critique are accordingly to be regarded as immanent effects of this cre-activity, which means that the 'cause' of these effects is not exterior to them, but is instead actualized in them, especially through the modes of subjectivation, which the cre-active activity (or the cre-active critique as one of its forms) engenders.

Consequently, Walter Benjamin's point could be taken up again, this time in reference to the question of critique: the question is not where one stands vis-à-vis the effects of critique, but where one stands within them.

The Perspectives of a Genealogy of Cre-activity

Against this background referring to the question of critique, art has no special privileges at all. Nevertheless, it is one of its modern names, one of the forms under which cre-activity is carried out. At the same time, to recall Valéry's allusion again, the history of modern forms of accounting for 'art' is not free from continuations and secularized adaptations of the onto-theological construction of creation mentioned above. The reservation of 'secular' crea(c)tivity for art issues usually corresponds to an isolated and isolating view of the artistic subject, which does justice to its situation amongst a multiplicity of cre-active existences at best in certain styles of biography, which are then again concerned with detaching a special subject from its surrounding reality. Robert Walser's text 'Poetenleben' (Poet's Life) might perhaps be read as a kind of counter-sketch to this. Its humorous concise prose speaks of nothing but contingencies and also of the many 'prosaic' historical-social localizations of the poet's life, seeing the poet's work as no more ennobled than any other 'work carried out with determination' (Walser, 1986: 121); this prose text fades out in the end in sentences that lay the question of the poet's secret to rest with gentle irony, because they have begun to speak of one life – and that means whatever life in the midst of a multiplicity of lives:

> In this way he lived on.
>
> What became of him, what may have happened to him later is outside the scope of our knowledge. For the time being, we have not been able to discover any further traces. Perhaps we may be able to some other time. We will see what endeavors might yet be undertaken. We will wait and see, and as soon as something new might have come to light, assuming that sufficient new interest will have kindly been made known, we will be happy to convey it. (Walser, 1986: 130)

Walser's text takes its place among countless documents that work towards a de-theologization of 'creativity' in the modern history of the arts themselves, thus articulating, to a certain extent, a cre-active critique of creativity. Antonin Artaud's protest against the 'European ideal of art', which aims to 'cast the mind [*esprit*] into an attitude distinct from force but addicted to exaltation' (Artaud, 1958: 10), is as much a part of this history as, for example, the anarchisms of Dada, the interventionist practices of the Situationists, the techniques of a 'Theater of the Oppressed' initiated by Augusto Boal, among many other examples. On a theoretical level, the use of these cre-active critiques can be comprehended, not least of all, in Mikhail Bakhtin's theory of the novel, which contends that conventional stylistics of genre overlook 'the social life of the word outside the artist workshop, in the squares and streets, in cities and villages, in groups, generations and eras', in turn defining the novel drawing from this manifold life as 'artistically organized diversity of speech' (Bakhtin, 1975: 154, 157). All these critiques, as well as Robert Walser's 'Poetenleben', are concerned with making the 'crucial social tone' (Bakhtin) heard, which makes the question of 'creativity' understandable as the problem of cre-activity in a multiplicity of existences (instead of attributing and subordinating it to the individualism of a Boheme, as Boltanski and Chiapello do, the final effect of which – indeed, the effect of this critique – only ends up burying the history of the cre-active critique of 'creativity' once again).

For this reason, there would also be little use in starting from the aforementioned and other names of the existing canonizations to append yet another one denoting a certain 'tendency' in art history (histories). It would be far more propitious to develop the perspective of a necessarily interminable genealogy of cre-activity, not as a new art-specific discipline, but instead equally in reference to the history of forms of social protest, the emergence and various uses of technologies, and so forth.

Two elements that this kind of genealogy of cre-activity must inevitably take into consideration are outlined here in conclusion:

1) The history of what is here called cre-activity cannot be considered independent from the institutions and forms of governmentality in which it takes place and which it engenders. In terms of art, this applies not only to obviously institutional structures such as museums, but also, for example, to ideas of artistic autonomy, which from a historical perspective – far removed from expressing an actual 'self-regulation' – basically reflect little other than the battle over a certain cultural policies model in the formational phase of something generally like cultural policies as a separate field of political administration.[4] And this applies not only to the forms of government and self-government, in which 'art', 'culture' and other areas of social life are situated, but naturally also to how they have been re-formed in times of neo-liberalism and the corresponding individual and collective self-practices in project-based contexts.[5] These re-formulations have also generated a new type of institution, namely the project institution, which has no stable institutional structure at its disposal at all, which allows it a certain flexibility, but is on the other hand also linked with new forms of instrumental purpose-orientation and with the fact that this type of institution has little to counter the current spread of individual and social precarity.

2) This last point brings us back to Paul Valéry's words quoted at the beginning: the 'effort' that Valéry speaks of and the 'sensation' of it that his youthful theological caprice sought, is still found in Valéry's distancing gesture as the effort of an isolated artist subject able to 'autonomously' decide on its creation techniques. Yet this subject is as little neutral and general, or conversely: it is as presupposed and predetermined as its predecessors from the theological tradition and their secular counterparts. We need only place a brief statement from a different voice, the voice of Virginia Woolf, next to Valéry's words to see this, a statement that was made only three years after Valéry's preface was written, namely in 1928: '[…] a woman must have money and a room of her own if she is to write fiction' (Woolf, 2004: 4). It is

not a coincidence that this statement appears again in a central position in one of the programmatic texts emerging from the struggles and solidarity movements of the French Intermittents (Précaires Associés de Paris, 2003). It refers to a discriminating policy and social practice, which continues to attribute certain activities (particularly symbolically valued ones such as 'creativity') to a certain preferred type of presupposed (gendered, racialized, or otherwise qualified) subjects, and which should not be lost sight of in the perspective of a genealogy of cre-activity or in any contemporary cre-active critique. For cre-activity in the sense developed here has nothing to do with an ordering of subjects, but rather with the multiplicity of existences and the subjectivation processes that take place in them.

Notes

1   Cf. the criticism of Michel Foucault in Habermas, 1985 and 1987, which includes reference to similar criticism by Nancy Fraser.

2   Boltanski and Chiapello's mention of 'sources of indignation' or 'motives of indignation' forms only a weak reflection of this origin, for their validity as critique remains constantly tied to the presence of 'norm references'.

3   In the 'monadological' thinking of Leibniz, which ultimately remains framed in theology, the three aspects of the Marxian concept of critique developed above are already very clearly presaged: involvement – every monad is embedded in a monad universe and thus a 'reflection of the world' (for which reason it also needs no 'window', because it is *perceptio* per se of this embeddedness); self-change – change is unthinkable without an 'inner principle of change', in other words without the monad's self-changing; lack of a defined purpose – the world is not the 'best of all worlds' because it is perfect (final cause), but because it is perfectible.

4   On this, see Georg Bollenbeck's relevant remark about the 'class [meaning the nineteenth-century German *Bildungsbürgertum*] that barred any intervention in culture on the part of the authoritarian state by invoking the "state of culture", assigning to this authoritarian state at the same time the responsibility for supporting "culture"' (Bollenbeck, 1999: 16).

5   It is one of the unfortunate curtailments of some more recent discourses in the cultural field that 'governmentality' appears to have begun with neo-liberalism; it is sufficient, and not only in more recent times, to go into any museum and analyze one's own self-restraint, in order to grasp the governmentality – embedded in specific historical political formations – that has been inscribed in 'culture' and the cultural field from the beginning.

That political economy is governmentality's 'most important form of knowledge' (Foucault, 2004a: 162) does not mean that it is its only form of knowledge or that the forms of symbolic socialization historically circulating under the term 'culture' are not in need of separate attention. On this, see Bennett, 1995. On the differentiation of liberal and neoliberal governmentality at the economic level, see Lorey, 2009.

2

The Geopolitics of Pimping

Suely Rolnik
translated by Brian Holmes

Powerful winds of critique have begun shaking the territory of art again since the mid-1990s. With different strategies, from the most activist to the most strikingly aesthetic, this movement in the air of the times finds one of its origins in an unease with the politics that govern the processes of subjectivation, and especially the place of the other and the destiny of the power of creation: a politics characteristic of the finance capitalism that established itself across the planet from the mid-1970s onward.

It is curious to notice that in Brazil this movement only began to take shape at the turn of the century, among elements of the new generation of artists who were beginning to express themselves publicly, frequently organized as 'collectives'. Still more recent is the participation of this local movement in the discussion that has long been maintained outside the country.[1] Today, this type of theme has even begun to enter the Brazilian institutional scene, in the wake of what has been happening outside the country for some time, where artistic practices involving these questions have been transformed into a 'trend' within the official circuit – a phenomenon characteristic of the media, with its market-based logic, which orients a great deal of artistic production today. In this migration the critical density of those questions is often dissolved, in order to constitute a new fetish that feeds the institutional art system and the voracious market that depends on it.

A certain number of questions arise concerning the emergence of these themes in the territory of art. What are such preoccupations doing here? Why have they become increasingly recurrent in artistic practices?

And in the case of Brazil, why have they appeared so recently? What interest do the institutions have in incorporating them? What I will do here is to sketch out a few prospective pathways of investigation, in order to confront these questions.

At least two presuppositions orient the choice of those pathways. The first is that theoretical questions always arise on the basis of problems that present themselves within a singular context, insofar as those problems affect our bodies, provoking changes in the tissue of our sensibility and a resultant crisis of meaning in our references. It is the uneasiness of the crisis that triggers the work of thinking, a process of creation that can be expressed in different forms: verbal (whether theoretical or literary), visual, musical, cinematographic, and so on, or again in a purely existential form. Whatever the means of expression, we think/create because something in our everyday lives forces us to invent new possibilities, in order to incorporate into the current map of meaning the sensible mutation that is seeking passage in our day-to-day experience. All of this has nothing to do with the narcissistic demand to align oneself on the 'trend' of the moment, in order to obtain institutional recognition and/or media prestige.

The specificity of art as a mode of the production of thought is that the changes of the sensible texture are embodied in artistic action and they present themselves alive within it. Hence the power of contagion and transformation this action potentially bears: it puts the world to work and reconfigures its landscape. Thus it is hardly surprising that art should investigate the present and partake of the changes that are occurring in actuality. If we grasp the use of thinking from this perspective, and if we accept art as a way of thinking, then the insistence on this type of theme in the artistic territory can indicate to us that the politics of subjectivity – and especially of the relation to the other and of cultural creation – is in crisis, and that a transformation in these fields is surely underway. So, if we want to answer the questions posed above we cannot avoid the problematization of this crisis and the process of changing it involves.

The second presupposition is that to think this problematic field requires us to summon up a transdisciplinary gaze, for innumerable layers of reality are interwoven there, whether on the macropolitical plane (facts and lifestyles in their formal, sociological exteriority) or on the micropolitical one (the forces that shake reality, dissolving its forms

24

and engendering others in a process that involves desire and subjectivity). What will be proposed next are some elements for a cartography of this process, sketched essentially from a micropolitical point of view.

In Search of Vulnerability

One of the problems of the politics of subjectivation that artistic practices face has been the anesthesia of our vulnerability to the other – an anesthesia all the more devastating when the other is represented by the ruling cartography as hierarchically inferior, because of his or her economic, social or racial condition, or on any other basis. But vulnerability is the precondition for the other to cease being a simple object for the projection of pre-established images, in order to become a living presence, with whom we can construct the territories of our existence and the changing contours of our subjectivity. Now, being vulnerable depends on the activation of a specific capacity of the sensible, which has been repressed for many centuries, remaining active only in certain philosophical and poetic traditions. These traditions culminated in the artistic vanguards of the late nineteenth and early twentieth century, whose activity produced effects that have left their mark on art across the twentieth century. More broadly, they propagated throughout the social tissue, ceasing to be a privilege of the cultural elites, particularly from the 1960s on. Neuroscience itself, in recent research, corroborates this observation that each of our sense organs is the bearer of a double capacity: cortical and subcortical.[2]

The former corresponds to perception, allowing us to apprehend the world in terms of forms, in order to then project upon them the representations we have available, so as to give them meaning. This capacity, which is the most familiar to us, is associated with time, with the history of the subject and with language. With it arise the very figures of subject and object, clearly delineated and maintaining a relationship of exteriority to each other. The cortical capacity of the sensible is what allows us to preserve the map of reigning representations, so that we can move through a known scenario where things remain in their due places with a minimum of stability.

The second, subcortical capacity, which is less known to us because of its historical repression, allows us to apprehend the world as a field of forces that affect us and make themselves present in our bodies in the form of sensations. The exercise of this capacity is disengaged from

25

the history of the subject and of language. With it, the other is a living presence composed of a malleable multiplicity of forces that pulse in our sensible texture, thus becoming part of our very selves. Here the figures of subject and object dissolve, and with them, that which separates the body from the world. In the 1980s, in a book, which has recently been reissued (Rolnik, 2006a), I began referring to this second capacity of our sense organs as the 'resonant body'. It is our body as a whole that has this power of resonating with the world.

Between the capacity of our body to resonate and its capacity of perception there is a paradoxical relation, for these are modes of apprehending reality that work according to totally distinct logics, irreducible to each other. It is the tension of this paradox that mobilizes and galvanizes the potential of thought/creation, to the extent that the new sensations that incorporate themselves in our sensible texture carry out mutations that are not transmittable by our available representations. For this reason they throw our references into crisis and impose on us the urgency of inventing new forms of expression. Thus we integrate into our body the signs that the world gives us, and through their expression, we incorporate them to our existential territories. In the course of this operation a shared map of references is reestablished, with new outlines. Moved by this paradox, we are continually forced to think/create, as suggested above. The exercise of thought/creation therefore has a power to intervene in reality and to participate in the orientation of its destiny, constituting an essential instrument for the transformation of the subjective and objective landscape.

The weight of each of these modes of knowledge of the world, as well as the relation between them, is variable. Which is also to say that the place of the other varies, along with the politics of relation to him or her. The latter in its turn defines a mode of subjectivation. The politics of subjectivation are known to change along with historical transformations, since each regime depends on a specific form of subjectivity in order to become viable in the daily life of everyone. It is on this terrain that a regime acquires existential consistency and concreteness; hence the very idea of differing 'politics' of subjectivation. Yet in the specific case of neoliberalism, the strategy of subjectivation, of relation with the other and of cultural creation takes on essential importance, because it holds a central role in the very principle that governs the contemporary version of capitalism. For this regime feeds primarily on subjective forces, and especially on those of knowledge and creation, to the point where it has recently been described as 'cultural' or 'cognitive' capitalism.[3] Considering what has been indicated above, I will now propose a cartography of the changes that have led art to engage with this kind of problem. To do so, I will take the departure point of the 1960s and 70s.

Birth of a Flexible Subjectivity

Until the early 1960s we lived beneath a disciplinary Fordist regime that reached its height in the 'American way of life' triumphant in the postwar period, when a politics of identity reigned in subjectivity, along with a rejection of the resonant body. These two aspects are in fact inseparable, because only to the extent that we anesthetize our vulnerability can we maintain a stable image of ourselves and the other, that is, our supposed identities. Without this anesthesia, we are constantly deterritorialized and led to reconfigure the outlines of our selves and our territories of existence. Until the early 1960s, the creative imagination operated mainly by sneaking away to the fringes. That period came to an end in the course of 1960s-70s as a result of cultural movements that problematized the governing regime of the time, calling for *l'imagination au pouvoir*. Those movements brought the dominant mode of subjectivation into crisis, and it soon collapsed along with the entire structure of the Victorian family and its Hollywood apogee – a structure which had been fundamental for the regime whose hegemony began to fade at that moment. A 'flexible subjectivity'[4] was then created, accompanied by radical experimentation with modes of existence and cultural creation which shattered the 'bourgeois' lifestyle and its politics of desire, with its logic of identity, its relation to otherness and its culture.

In the resulting 'counter-culture', as it was called, forms were created to express that which was indicated by the resonant body affected by the otherness of the world, at grips with the problematics of its time. The forms thus created tend to transmit subjectivity's incorporation of the forces that shake up the environment and deterritorialize it. The advent of such forms is inseparable from a becoming-other of the self, but also of the environment. It can be said that the creation of these new territories has to do with public life, in the strong sense of the phrase: the collective construction of reality moved by the tensions that destabilize the reigning cartographies, as these affect the body of each person singularly, and as they are expressed on the basis of that singular affect. In other words, what each person expresses is the current state of the world – its meaning, but also and mainly, its lacks of meaning – as it presents itself within the body. So, the singular expression of each person participates in the endless tracing of a necessarily collective cartography.

Today these transformations have consolidated themselves. The scenario of our times is completely different: we are no longer beneath the regime of identity, the politics of subjectivation is no longer the same. We all now have available a flexible and processual subjectivity as instituted by the counter-cultural movements, and our force of creation in its experimental freedom is not only favorably viewed and welcomed, but is even stimulated, celebrated and frequently glamorized. However, in all this there is a 'but', which is hardly negligible. In the present, the most common destiny of flexible subjectivity and of the freedom of creation that accompanies it is not the invention of forms of expression motivated by an attention to sensations that signal the effects of the other's existence within our resonant body. What guides us in this creation of territories for our post-Fordist flexibility is an almost hypnotic identification with the images of the world broadcast by advertising and mass culture.

By offering ready-made territories to subjectivities rendered fragile by deterritorialization, these images tend to soothe their unrest, thus contributing to the deafness of their resonant body, and therefore to its invulnerability to the affects of the time that are presented within it. But that may not be the most deadly aspect of this politics of subjectivation, which instead is the very message that such images invariably convey, independently of their style or their target-public. At stake here is the idea that there exist paradises, that these are now in this world and not beyond it, and above all, that certain people have the privilege of inhabiting them. What is more, such images transmit the illusion that we could be one of these VIPs, if we simply invested all our vital energy – our desire, affect, knowledge, intellect, eroticism, imagination, action, etc. – in order to actualize these virtual worlds of signs in our own existence, through the consumption of the objects and services they propose to us.

What we are faced with here is a new élan for the idea of paradise developed by Judeo-Christian religions: the mirage of a smoothed-over, stable life under perfect control. This kind of hallucination has its origin in the refusal of one's vulnerability to the other and to the deterritorializing turbulence that he or she provokes; and also in the disdain for fragility that necessarily derives from such an experience. This fragility is nonetheless essential because it indicates the crisis of a certain diagram of sensibility, its modes of expression, its cartographies of meaning. By disdaining fragility, it does not call up the desire for creation anymore; instead it provokes a sentiment of humiliation and shame whose result is the blockage of the vital process. In other words, what the Western idea of a promised paradise amounts to is a refusal of life in its immanent nature as an impulse to continuous processes of creation and differentiation. In its terrestrial version, capital has replaced God in his function as keeper of the promise, and the virtue that makes us worthy of it now becomes consumption: this is what constitutes the fundamental myth of advanced capitalism. In such a context, it is at the very least mistaken to consider that we lack myths today: it is precisely through our belief in this religious myth of neoliberalism, that the image-worlds produced by this regime turn into concrete reality in our own existence.

Flexible Subjectivity Surrenders to Its Pimp

In other words, the 'cultural' or 'cognitive' capitalism that was conceived as a solution to the crisis provoked by the movements of the 1960s and 1970s absorbed the modes of existence that those movements invented and appropriated their subjective forces, especially that of the creative potential, which at the time was breaking free in social life. The creative potential was in effect put into power, as was called for by those movements. Yet we know now that this rise of the imagination to power is a micropolitical operation that consists in making its potential into the major fuel of an insatiable hypermachine for the production and accumulation of capital – to the point where one can speak of a new working class, which some authors call the 'cognitariat.'[5] This kind of pimping of the creative force is what has been transforming the planet into a gigantic marketplace, expanding at an exponential rate, either by including its inhabitants as hyperactive zombies or by excluding them as human trash. In fact, those two opposing poles are interdependent fruits of the same logic; all our destinies unfold between them. This is the world that the imagination creates in the present. As one might expect, the politics of subjectivation and of the relation to the other that predominates in this scenario is extremely impoverished.

Currently, after almost three decades, it is possible to perceive this logic of cognitive capitalism operating within our subjectivity. Yet in the late 1970s, when its installation began, the experimentation that had been carried out collectively in the decades before in order to achieve emancipation from the pattern of Fordist and disciplinary subjectivity was quite difficult to distinguish from its incorporation into the new regime. The consequences of this difficulty are that the cloning of the transformations proposed by those movements was experienced by a great many of their protagonists as a signal of recognition and inclusion: the new regime appeared to be liberating them from the marginality to which they had been confined in the 'provincial' world that was now fading away. Dazzled by the rise to power of their transgressive and experimental force of creation which was now thrusting them beneath the glamorizing spotlights of the media, launching them into the world and lining their pockets with dollars, the inventors of the transformations of earlier decades frequently fell into the trap. Many of them surrendered themselves voluntarily to their pimp, becoming the very creators and constructors of the world fabricated by and for the new-style capitalism.

This confusion undoubtedly stems from the politics of desire that characterizes the pimping of subjective and creative forces – a kind of power-relation that is basically exerted through the sorcery of seduction. The seducer conjures up a spellbinding idealization that leads the seduced to identify with the seducer and submit to him: that is to say, to identify with and submit to the aggressor, impelled by an inner desire, in hopes of being recognized and admitted into the seducer's world. Only recently has this situation become conscious, which tends to break the spell. This transpires in the different strategies of individual and collective resistance that have been accumulating over the last few years, particularly through the initiative of a new generation which does not in any way identify with the proposed model of existence and understands the trick that has been played. It is clear that artistic practices – through their very nature as expressions of the problematics of the present as they flow through the artist's body – could hardly remain indifferent to this movement. On the contrary, it is exactly for this reason that these questions emerged in art from the early 1990s onward, as mentioned at the outset. Using different procedures, these strategies have been carrying out an exodus from the minefield stretching between the opposite and complementary figures of luxury and trash subjectivity, the field in which human destinies are confined in the world of globalized capitalism. Amidst this exodus, other kinds of worlds are being created.

Profitable Wound

But the difficulty of resisting the seduction of the serpent of paradise in its neoliberal version has grown even greater in the countries of Latin America and Eastern Europe which, like Brazil, were under totalitarian regimes at the moment when financial capitalism took hold. Let us not forget that the 'democratic opening' of these countries, which took place during the 1980s, was partially due to the advent of the post-Fordist regime, whose flexibility could only encounter the rigidity of the totalitarian systems as an obstacle.

If we approach the totalitarian regimes not by their visible or macropolitical side, but instead by their invisible or micropolitical side, we can see that what characterizes such regimes is the pathological rigidity of the identity principle. This holds for totalitarianisms of the Right and the Left, since from the viewpoint of the politics of subjectivation such regimes are not so different. In order to hold on to power, they do not content themselves with simply ignoring the expressions of the resonant body – that is, the cultural and existential forms engendered in a living relation with the other, which continually destabilize the reigning cartographies and deterritorialize us. As a matter of fact, the very advent of such regimes constitutes a violent reaction to destabilization, when it exceeds a threshold of tolerability for subjectivities in a state of servile adaptation to the status quo. For them, such a threshold does not summon up an urgency to create, but on the contrary, to preserve the established order at any price. Destructively conservative, the totalitarian states go much further than a simple scorn or censorship of the expressions of the resonant body: they obstinately seek to disqualify and humiliate them, to the point where the force of creation, of which such expressions are the product, is so marked by the trauma of this vital terrorism that it finally blocks itself off, and is thereby reduced to silence. A century of psychoanalysis has shown that the time required to confront and work through a trauma of this scope can extend to as much as thirty years.[6]

It is not hard to imagine that the meeting of these two regimes makes up a scenario even more vulnerable to the abuses of pimping: in its penetration to totalitarian contexts, cultural capitalism took advantage of the experimental past which was exceptionally audacious and singular in many of those countries; but above all, it took advantage of the wounds inflicted on the forces of creation by the blows they had suffered. The new regime presented itself not only as the system that could welcome and institutionalize the principle of the production of subjectivity and culture by the movements of the 1960s and 1970s, as had been the case in the United States and in the countries of Western Europe. In the countries under dictatorships it gained an extra power of seduction: its apparent condition as a savior come to liberate the energy of creation from its bonds, to cure it of its debilitated state, allowing it to reactivate and manifest itself again.

Power by seduction, characteristic of the worldwide governance of finance capital, is no doubt 'lighter' and subtler than the heavy hand of local governments commanded by the military states that preceded; yet its effects are no less destructive, though with entirely different strategies and ends. It is therefore clear that the combination of these two historical factors, as occurred in these countries, has considerably aggravated the state of pathological alienation of subjectivity, especially with respect to the politics that governs the relation to the other and the destiny of the force of creation.

Anthropophagic Zombies

If we now focus our micropolitical gaze on Brazil, we will discover an even more specific feature in the process of neoliberalism's installation, and of its cloning of the movements of the 1960s and 1970s. In Brazil those movements had a particularity, because of a reactivation of a certain cultural tradition of the country, which had come to be known as 'anthropophagy'. Some of the characteristics of this tradition are: the absence of an absolute and stable identification with any particular repertory and the non-existence of any blind obedience to established rules, generating a plasticity in the contours of subjectivity (instead of identities); an opening to the incorporation of new universes, accompanied by a freedom of hybridization (instead of a truth-value assigned to a particular repertory); an agility of experimentation and improvisation to create territories and their respective cartographies (instead of fixed territories authorized by stable and predetermined languages) – all of this carried out with grace, joy and spontaneity.

The tradition had initially been circumscribed and named in the 1920s by the Brazilian modernists gathered around the Anthropophagic Movement. Like all the cultural vanguards of the early twentieth century, the visionary spirit of the local modernists already pointed critically to the limits of the politics of subjectivation, of relation to the other and of cultural production that characterized the disciplinary regime, taking its logic of identity as a major target. But whereas the European vanguards tried to create alternatives to this model, in Brazil there was already another model of subjectivation and cultural creation inscribed in people's memory since the very foundation of the country. Maybe this was the reason why Oswald de Andrade, the major reference of the Anthropophagic Movement, could glimpse in the national tradition a 'program for the reeducation of the sensibility' that could function as a 'social therapy for the modern world'.[7] The service that the Brazilian modernist movement did for the country's culture by highlighting and naming this politics was to lend it value, making possible a consciousness of cultural singularity. It could then be asserted against the idealization of European culture, a colonial heritage that marked the intelligentsia of the country. It's worth noting that even today this submissive identification affects a great deal of Brazil's intellectual production, which in some sectors has merely replaced its former object of idealization with North American culture, as is especially the case in the field of art.

In the 1960s and 1970s, as we have seen, the inventions of the early part of the century ceased to be restricted to the cultural vanguards; after a few decades, they had contaminated the politics of subjectivation, generating changes that would come to be expressed most strikingly by the generation born after the Second World War. For the members of this generation, the disciplinary society that attained its apogee at that moment became absolutely intolerable, which made them launch upon the process of rupture with this pattern as manifested in their own everyday existence. Flexible subjectivity thus became the new model, the model of a counter-culture. It was in the course of this process that the ideas of anthropophagy were reactivated in Brazil, reappearing most explicitly in cultural movements such as Tropicalismo, taken in its widest sense.[8] By calling up the traits of a tradition that was deeply inscribed in the Brazilians' bodies, the counter-culture of the country attained an especially radical freedom of experimentation, generating artistic proposals of great force and originality.

Now, the same singularity that gave such strength to the counter-cultural movements in Brazil also tended to aggravate the cloning of those movements carried out by neoliberalism. The anthropophagical savoir-faire of the Brazilians gives them a special facility for adapting to the new times. The country's elites and middle classes are absolutely dazzled by being so contemporary, so up-to-date on the international scene of the new post-identity subjectivities, so well-equipped to live out this post-Fordist flexibility (which, for example, makes them international champions in advertising and positions them high in the world ranking of media strategies).[9] But this is only the form taken by the voluptuous and alienated abandonment to the neoliberal regime in its local Brazilian version, making its inhabitants, especially the city-dwellers, into veritable anthropophagic zombies.

Predictable characteristics in a country with a colonial history? Whatever the response, an obvious sign of this pathetically uncritical identification with finance capital by part of the Brazilian cultural elite is the fact that the leadership of the group that restructured the Brazilian state petrified by the military regime, and that made the process of re-democratization into one of alignment on neoliberalism, was composed to a great extent of leftist intellectuals, many of whom had lived in exile during the period of the dictatorship.

The point is that anthropophagy itself is only a form of subjectivation, one that happens to be distinct from the politics of identity. But that doesn't guarantee anything, because any form can be invested with different ethics, from the most critical to the most execrably reactive and reactionary, as Oswald de Andrade already pointed out in the 1920s, designating the latter as 'base anthropophagy'.[10] What distinguishes between the ethics is the same 'but' that I mentioned above, when I referred to the difference between the flexible subjectivity invented in the 1960s and 1970s and its clone fabricated by post-Fordist capitalism. The difference lies in the strategy of the creation of territories and, implicitly, in the politics of the relation to the other. In order for this process to be oriented by an ethics of the affirmation of life it is necessary to construct territories with a basis in the urgencies indicated by the sensations – that is, by the signs of the presence of the other in our resonant body. It is around the expression of these signals and their reverberation in subjectivities that breathe the same air of the times that possibilities open up in individual and collective existence.

34

Now, that is emphatically not the politics of the creation of territories that has predominated in Brazil. Instead, neoliberalism mobilized only the worst of this tradition, the basest anthropophagy. The 'plasticity' of the border between public and private and the 'freedom' of private appropriation of public goods – taken with derision and exhibited with pride – is one of its worst facets, clearly imbued with the colonial heritage. Indeed, this is exactly the facet of anthropophagy to which Oswald de Andrade had called attention when he designated its reactionary side. And this lineage is so intoxicating for Brazilian society, especially for its political and economic elites, that it would be naïve to imagine it could simply disappear as though by magic.

There have been five centuries of anthropophagic experience, and almost one of reflection upon it, since the moment when the modernists circumscribed it critically and made it conscious. Against this backdrop the Brazilians' anthropophagic savoir-faire – especially as it was actualized in the 1960s and 1970s – can still be useful today, but not to guarantee their access to the imaginary paradises of capital; on the contrary, to help them problematize the disgraceful confusion between the two politics of flexible subjectivity and to separate the wheat from the chaff, essentially on the basis of the place or non-place that is attributed to the other. This knowledge would offer the conditions for fertile participation in the debate that is gathering internationally around the problematization of a regime that has now become hegemonic, and also in the invention of strategies of exodus outside the imaginary field whose origins lie in its deadly myth.[11]

Art has a special vocation to carry out such a task, to the extent that by bringing the mutations of sensibility into the realm of the visible and the speakable, it can unravel the cartography of the present, liberating life at its points of interruption and releasing its power of germination – a task utterly distinct from and irreducible to macropolitical activism. The latter relates to reality from the viewpoint of representation, denouncing the conflicts inherent to the distribution of places established in the reigning cartography (conflicts of class, race, gender, etc.) and struggling for a more just configuration. These are two distinct and complementary gazes on reality, corresponding to two different potentials of intervention, both participating in their own ways in the shaping of its destiny. Nonetheless, problematizing the confusion between the two politics of flexible subjectivity so as to intervene effectively in this field and contribute to breaking the spell of the seduction that sustains the neoliberalism power at the very heart of its politics of desire, necessarily entails treating the illness that arose from the unfortunate confluence in Brazil of the three historical factors that exerted a negative effect on the creative imagination: the traumatic violence of the dictatorship, the pimping by neoliberalism and the activation of a base anthropophagy. This confluence clearly exacerbated the lowering of the critical capacity and the servile identification with the new regime.

Here we can return to our initial inquiry into the particular situation of Brazil within the geopolitical field of the international debate that has been gathering in the territory of art for over a decade, around the destiny of subjectivity, its relation to the other and its potential of invention under the regime of cultural capitalism. The unfortunate confluence of these three historical factors could be one of the reasons why the debate is so recent in this country. It is clear that there are exceptions, as is the case of the Brazlian artist Lygia Clark, who just one year after May 1968 already foresaw this situation. As she described it at the time:

> In the very moment when he digests the object, the artist is digested by the society that has already found a title and a bureaucratic occupation for him: he will be the future engineer of entertainment, an activity that has no effect whatsoever on the equilibrium of social structures. The only way for the artist to escape co-optation is to succeed in unleashing a general creativity, without any psychological or social limits. This creativity will be expressed in lived experience.[12]

What Are the Powers of Art?

From within this new scenario emerge the questions that are asked of all those who think/create – and especially artists – in the attempt to delineate a cartography of the present, so as to identify the points of asphyxiation of the vital process and to bring about, at exactly those points, the irruption of the power to create other worlds.

A first bloc of questions would relate to the cartography of pimping exploitation. How does the tourniquet that leads us to tolerate the intolerable, and even to desire it, come to take hold of our vitality? By means of what processes is our vulnerability to the other anesthetized? What mechanisms of our subjectivity lead us to offer our creative force for the fulfillment of the market? And our desire, our affects, our

36

eroticism, our time? How are all of the potentials captured by the faith in the promise of paradise by the capitalist religion? Which artistic practices have fallen into this trap? What allows us to identify them? What makes them so numerous?

Another bloc of questions, which is in fact inseparable from the former, would relate to the cartography of the movements of exodus. How to liberate life from its new dead ends? What can our force of creation do in order to confront this challenge? Which artistic devices are succeeding in that confrontation? Which of them are treating the territory of art itself, a territory that is increasingly lusted for and at the same time undermined by the pimping that takes it as a bottomless well for the extortion of the surplus value of creativity, in order to increase its seductive power? In short, how to reactivate in our times, in each situation, the political potential inherent in artistic activity, its power to unleash possibilities? By which I mean, its power to embody the mutations of the sensible, and thereby, contribute to reconfiguring the contours of the world.

Answers to these and other questions are being constructed by different artistic practices, along with territories of all kinds that are being reinvented every day, outside the imaginary field whose origins lie in the deadly myth proposed by cultural capitalism. It is impossible to foresee the effects of these subtle perforations in the compact mass of dominant brutality that envelops the planet today. The only thing we can say is that by all indications, the geopolitical landscape of globalized pimping is no longer exactly the same; molecular currents would be moving the earth. Could this be a mere hallucination?

Notes

1   Translator's note: Here the author refers to a number of political art collectives that have significantly multiplied in recent years primarily in the region of São Paulo Contra Filé, including Bijari, Cia Cachorra, Catadores de Histórias, c.o.b.a.i.a., A revolução não será televisionada, TrancaRua, Frente 3 de Fevereiro. If some of the most 'visible' and 'institutional' moments of the articulation of this 'local movement' are compared with similar activities taking place outside Brazil – a concatenation to which Suely Rolnik refers without going into detail – this results in an interesting diagram of contemporary forms of a transnational articulation of artistic and politicized practices that have occurred in these years. Their

characteristics are, above all, a progressive connection with local and translocal social and political practices (e.g. the movement Sem Teto do Centro) and a 'flexible', ideologically unbiased relationship to the art institution with fluid entries into and exits from the institutions. See for example the participation of 13 collectives in the IX Biennial of Havana under the title Territorio São Paulo (http://www.bienalhabana.cult.cu/protagonicas/proyectos/proyecto.php?i db=9&&idpy=23), the exhibition Kollektive Kreativität in Kassel, organized by the collective What, How & For Whom (WHW) (http://www.fridericianum-kassel.de/ausst/ausstkollektiv.html#inter funktionen_english), the group Etcétera (http://www.exargentina.org/ participantes.html) and the exhibition Self-Education in the National Center for Contemporary Art Moscow, coordinated by Daria Pirkyna and the St. Petersburg collective Chto Delat? (What is to be done?) (http://transform.eipcp.net/calendar/1153261452). On Collective Creativity, WHW, Etcétera, Ex Argentina, Grupo de Arte Callejero (GAC), see *Brumaria* 5, Arte: la imaginación política radical, Summer 2005, http://www.brumaria.net.

2 See Hubert Godard, 'Regard aveugle', in Diserens and Rolnik, 2005: 73-8. The text is the transcription of a filmed interview I conducted with Godard in the context of a project I have been developing since 2002, seeking to construct a living memory of the experimental practices proposed by Lygia Clark and of the Brazilian and French cultural context within which they originated.

3 The notions of 'cognitive' or 'cultural' capitalism, proposed from the early 1990s onward, chiefly by the researchers now associated with the French journal *Multitudes*, represent a further elaboration of Gilles Deleuze and Félix Guattari's ideas relative to the status of culture and subjectivity in the contemporary capitalist regime.

4 I derive 'flexible subjectivity' from Brian Holmes's notion of the 'flexible personality' in Holmes 2002. In recent texts I have developed from the viewpoint of the process of subjectivation; see Rolnik 2005a and 2006b.

5 See note 3 above.

6 At the outset of the military dictatorship in Brazil, the cultural movement persisted with all its vigor. With the promulgation of Institutional Act no. 5 in December of 1968, the regime reasserted itself and the movement faltered, tending toward paralysis. Like any totalitarian regime, its deadliest effects may not have been the palpable and visible ones of prison, torture, repression and censorship, but other more subtle and invisible ones: the paralysis of the force of creation and the subsequent frustration of the collective intelligence, these being associated with the terrorizing threat of a punishment that could extend even to death. One of the most tangible

effects of such a blockage was the significant number of young people who underwent psychotic episodes at that time. Many of them were interned in psychiatric hospitals and not a few succumbed to the 'psychiatricization' of their suffering, never again returning from madness. Such psychotic manifestations, partly stemming from the terror of the dictatorship, also occurred in relation with the 'extreme experiences' characteristic of the counter-culture movement, consisting in all kinds of sensory experimentation, generally including the use of hallucinogenics, in a posture of active resistance to the bourgeois politics of subjectivation. The diffuse presence of terror and paranoia that this engendered no doubt contributed to the pathological destiny of these experiences of the opening of sensibility to its capacity for resonance.

7 See Oswald de Andrade's 1953 text 'A marcha das utopias' in Andrade, 1990.

8 The counter-cultural movement in Brazil was especially radical and broad, Tropicalism being one of the major expressions of its singularity. The active youth of the period were divided into the counter-culture and the political militants, both of which suffered equal violence from the dictatorship: prison, torture, assassination, exile, in addition to those who succumbed to madness, as already noted. Nonetheless, the counter-culture was never recognized for its political potency, unless it was by the military regime that fiercely punished those who participated, placing them in the same jails as the official political prisoners. Brazilian society projected a pejorative image on the counter-culture, originating in a conservative vision that in this specific aspect was shared by both Right and Left (including the militants of the same generation). Such a negation, even today, persists in the memory of the period, which on the contrary preserves and elevates the militant past.

9 Brazilian television occupies an important place on the international scene. A sign of this is the fact that the telenovelas of the Globo network are now broadcast in over 200 countries.

10 See Andrade's 1928 text 'Manifesto Antropófago' in Andrade, 1990.

11 In the early 1990s I began to work on the question of anthropophagy in the sense whereby it is problematized here. See Rolnik, 1998a, 1998b and 2005b.

12 Clark, 1997; this text originally appeared in 1971, in the Paris journal *Robho* no. 5-6.

3

The Misfortunes of the 'Artistic Critique' and of Cultural Employment

Maurizio Lazzarato
translated by Mary O'Neill

In the work of sociologists and economists who are concerned with the transformations in capitalism and more specifically the changes in the artistic and cultural labor market, there is a tendency to use artistic activity and those conditions of professional practice as the model from which, they argue, neoliberal economics draws its inspiration. This is an ambiguous discourse and it deserves to be examined more closely. Luc Boltanski and Ève Chiapello's *Le nouvel esprit du capitalisme* (1999; in English as *The New Spirit of Capitalism*, 2005) has the merit of making the so-called 'artistic critique' one of the economic, political and social actors of the century just past, and of the post-1945 period in particular. But both the exact definition of this 'artistic critique' and the role the authors assign to it in contemporary capitalism are puzzling in many respects.

The thesis that runs throughout *The New Spirit of Capitalism* is the following: the 'artistic critique' (based on and demanding freedom, autonomy and authenticity) and the 'social critique' (based on and demanding solidarity, security and equality) 'are most often developed and embodied by different groups' and are 'incompatible'.[1]

The torch of the 'artistic critique', which was handed over by the artists to the students in May 1968, was then apparently taken up by 'trendy' individuals working in the sectors of media, finance, show-business, fashion, the internet and so on – that is, the 'creatives' at the 'top of the socio-cultural hierarchy'. The 'social critique', on the other hand, developed and embodied by the workers of May '68, was taken up by the 'little people', subordinates, those excluded by liberalism. 'Artistic critique' and 'social critique' are therefore 'largely incompatible'.

The 'artistic critique' provokes in the authors an unease, even a kind of contempt, which they have difficulty hiding. Seen from their point of view, this is entirely understandable since the 'artistic critique [...] is not naturally egalitarian; indeed it always runs the risk of being reinterpreted in an aristocratic sense' and 'untempered by considerations of equality and solidarity of the 'social critique', [it] can very quickly play into the hands of a particularly destructive form of liberalism, as we have seen in recent years'. Besides, the 'artistic critique' is

> not in itself necessary to effectively challenge capitalism, a fact demonstrated by the earlier successes of the workers' movement without the support of the artistic critique. From this point of view, May '68 was exceptional. (Boltanski and Chiapello, 2000)

Reading it, one also feels that the book is pervaded by a certain resentment against May 1968 that for some years now has been prevalent among the French intellectual elites. Michel Foucault, Gilles Deleuze and Félix Guattari, who (it is argued) as the key thinkers of 1968 inadvertently sowed seeds of liberalism in people's minds, are bearing the brunt of that resentment in this text, as well as in the mind of the former Minister of Education.

So not only is the 'artistic critique' not necessary, other than to 'moderate the excess of equality in the social critique' that is in danger of 'treating freedom with disdain'[2], but what is more, it acts like a Trojan Horse for liberalism, to which it is related by the aristocratic taste for freedom, autonomy and authenticity, which the artists supposedly handed on to 'the students' and which then went into circulation via 'the trendy, left-wing *bobos*'.[3] Here Boltanski and Chiapello give us a re-run of the opposition between freedom and equality, between autonomy and security. This opposition dates from another era and, it must be said, has resulted in the failure of socialism as well as communism.

'No Culture Without Social Rights'

The concept of 'artistic critique' doesn't hold up for theoretical as well as political reasons:

a) As far as this last aspect goes, Boltanski and Chiapello's theses were roundly refuted four years after publication. The misfortunes of their 'artistic critique' are many, but the greatest of these befell it with the emergence of the 'Coordination des Intermittents et Précaires'[4] and the resistance movement among the 'artists' and the 'technicians' in the performing arts sector of the cultural industry (*l'industrie du spectacle*); indeed this coordinating group constitutes the most successful expression of that resistance. The six words of one of this movement's slogans 'No culture without social rights' are more than enough grounds on which to base a criticism of Boltanski and Chiapello's book and to highlight all the weaknesses in their analysis of contemporary capitalism. If the slogan 'No culture without social rights' is translated into Boltanski and Chiapello's terms, what is considered to be potentially aristocratic-liberal and incompatible with social justice will, as a result, become a battleground, perhaps the only one, where the neo-liberal logic can be thwarted: 'no freedom, autonomy, authenticity (culture) without solidarity, equality, security (social rights)'.

Le nouvel esprit du capitalisme was published in 1999, but it ceased to apply both theoretically and politically on the night of 25 June 2004, when the Coordination des Intermittents et Précaires was founded at the Théâtre Nationale de la Colline. When, developed and embodied as it was by 'artists and technicians in the show-business industry', by cultural workers, the 'artistic critique' became organized and adopted a name, it brought together what the authors held to be incompatible: the artist and the temporary worker, the artist and the intermittent (or casual) worker, the artist and the unemployed person, the artist and the *Rmiste*[5] living on minimum benefit payments.

The strongest and fiercest resistance (the conflict has been going on for three years) to the French employers' liberal scheme of 'social reconstruction' comes from cultural workers in the performing arts sector. It was the individual Coordinations des Intermittents et Précaires, and not just the cultural workers, who developed and put forward a model of indemnification for 'workers in discontinuous employment', based on solidarity, security and justice. It was again these representative groups who indicated the battlegrounds for a system of unemployment insurance that is based on both security and autonomy and is capable of functioning even in the mobile labor market.

b) From a theoretical point of view, the concept of 'artistic critique' introduces a whole host of misunderstandings. Only the top three have been taken into consideration here:

1. The divisions which liberal policies have created in society have nothing to do with the caricature of the social composition and the mapping of inequalities described in this book. Let us look again at the description of the social groups embodying the 'artistic critique', according to Boltanski and Chiapello, and try to see why indeed it is such a caricature (bordering on populism):

> Moreover, it must be said that the artistic critique is today embodied by people at the top of the socio-cultural hierarchy, university graduates, often working in the creative sectors (marketing, advertising, media, fashion, internet, etc.) or in the financial markets or in consultancy firms; their awareness of what, at the other end of the social scale, the life of a temporary worker or the life of someone who has no interest whatsoever in mobility is like, is virtually non-existent. (Boltanski and Chiapello, 2000)

The divisions that the neo-liberal policies outline are not divisions between the new liberal professions and the new proles, between the trendy types and the unemployed, between a new 'creative class' working in the 'creative industries', and an old working class employed in the traditional industries. The inequalities exist within the so-called creative professions that, according to Boltanski and Chiapello, embody the 'artistic critique'. Each of the professions that they cite as being engaged in the 'artistic critique' is not a homogeneous entity but rather a collection of situations that are highly differentiated internally by status, salaries, social cover, workload, and job. You can work in the same profession, enjoy wealth and job security or be poor and in highly precarious employment. Between these two extremes, there is an almost infinite gradation and modulation of situations and statuses.

The divisions are not between individuals who work in the media, advertising, theatre, and photography on the one hand, and the workers, employees, casual and unemployed workers on the other. The divisions cut across the new liberal professions because, quite simply, a certain proportion of the people working in these professions are poor, with little or no guarantee of secure employment.

Exactly the same could be said of almost all the professions cited by the authors, particularly in research and in the university sector, areas with which these authors ought to be more familiar. It is a situation that the movement of 'casual-contract research staff' helped to bring to public attention, some months after the intermittent workers' movement.

Let us take an example for which there is supporting data. With Antonella Corsani and Jean-Baptiste Olivo and the various Coordinations des Intermittents et Précaires, we carried out a survey on a representative sample of more than 1000 intermittent workers, artists and technicians in the sectors of TV, radio and live performance. Let us look at the internal distribution of employment (the hours worked) and of salaries (without unemployment benefit):

Table 1: Relationship between NHW[6] and annual salary (based on the SMIC, the French guaranteed minimum wage; numbers in the cells in %)

Salaries /NHW	507hrs-520hrs	520hrs-550hrs	550hrs-600hrs	600hrs-650hrs	650hrs-700hrs	700hrs-750hrs	750hrs-800hrs	800hrs-1000hrs	≥1000hrs	Total:
0-0.3	3.56%	0.78%	0.67%	0.00%	0.14%	0.12%	0.00%	0.00%	0.00%	5.26%
0.3-0.4	3.64%	2.26%	1.06%	0.81%	0.39%	0.00%	0.00%	0.00%	0.00%	8.16%
0.4-0.5	3.16%	3.21%	2.07%	1.01%	0.19%	0.14%	0.14%	0.47%	0.41%	10.78%
0.5-0.6	3.39%	2.84%	2.23%	1.18%	0.40%	0.47%	0.48%	0.52%	0.15%	11.66%
0.6-0.8	3.93%	2.51%	1.79%	1.61%	2.20%	0.93%	0.90%	1.30%	0.81%	15.96%
0.8-1.1	2.85%	2.99%	0.87%	2.27%	1.95%	1.37%	0.60%	2.68%	2.42%	18.02%
1.1-1.25	0.91%	0.59%	0.83%	0.75%	0.75%	0.88%	0.47%	1.43%	0.77%	7.37%
1.25-1.5	0.44%	0.78%	0.30%	0.81%	0.19%	0.46%	0.60%	1.47%	3.20%	8.26%
1.5-2	0.66%	0.68%	0.25%	0.32%	0.26%	0.26%	0.13%	2.00%	0.75%	5.30%
2-3	0.37%	0.23%	0.33%	0.12%	0.53%	0.23%	0.23%	1.10%	3.94%	7.07%
3-4	0.00%	0.00%	0.12%	0.00%	0.00%	0.00%	0.00%	0.00%	1.12%	1.24%
4-5	0.00%	0.00%	0.00%	0.00%	0.00%	0.11%	0.00%	0.10%	0.29%	0.49%
5+	0.00%	0.00%	0.00%	0.00%	0.00%	0.00%	0.00%	0.13%	0.29%	0.42%
Total:	22.91%	16.86%	10.51%	8.89%	6.98%	4.96%	3.55%	11.19%	14.15%	100%

What comes across very clearly is that the majority of intermittent workers (56.4 percent) earn an annual salary of between half the guaranteed minimum wage in France – known as the SMIC, this stands at around 1,200 euros gross – and just above that minimum wage. However, at either end of the spectrum, 9.1 percent earn a sum equivalent to more than twice the minimum wage, while 13.1 percent earn less than 0.3 of that minimum wage.

So the majority of intermittent workers barely live above the threshold for indemnification (507 hours), but there is an unspecified number of 'artists' who are not indemnified and who live in a state of even greater precarity, juggling casual work, RMI and other benefit payments for those on the lowest incomes. Remember that, in Paris, 20 percent of those in receipt of minimum benefit payments state their profession as 'artist'. If what we call 'visual artists' are included in that group, then the 'artists' are a highly diverse category, not amenable to classification within those 'molar' and all-embracing categories of artists, individuals working in the media, etc.

Table 2: Average salary, median salary and standard deviation by profession

Professional Activity	Average salary (euros):	Median salary (euros):	Standard deviation:
Circus/Music Hall performer	15159	10448	127592
Stylist - Make-up artist	17709	16438	71202
Communications	9100	7904	37003
Actor	10765	7689	101514
Costume designer - Dresser	11542	9389	57531
Dancer	9353	7900	33525
Set designer	16750	14853	101121
Lighting Technician	13526	12428	52904
Photographer	16970	13794	81601
Production Designer	12192	12400	52237
Film Editor	17334	16769	77318
Musician - Singer	8582	7353	43683
Producer	16682	13791	101455
Director	16128	14254	82724
Sound Technician	14966	14137	63197
Other	8231	8253	10489

2. Boltanski and Chiapello have taken the artist and artistic activity as the model of the liberal economy, whereas this model was constructed on (the idea of the individual) as 'human capital', as an entrepreneur of her/himself. We are going to use Foucault's work *Naissance de la biopolitique* (2004b) to account for the misconception according to which it is claimed that the model of contemporary economic activity is to be found among artists.

As Foucault reminds us, neoliberalism needs to reconstruct a model of *homo oeconomicus* but, as we shall see shortly, this has very little to do with either the artist or artistic 'creativity'. Neoliberalism does not seek its model of subjectivation in the 'artistic critique' since it already has its own model: the entrepreneur, a figure that neoliberalism wants to extend across the board to everyone, artists included, as in the case of the French intermittent workers. In the 'reform' of intermittent employment, the new period of indemnification for intermittent workers is considered 'a capital' derived from indemnified days, which the individual has to manage as 'capital'.

What is this little word 'capital' doing among wage earners? How does it work? It states that unemployment benefits are part of the multiplicity of 'investments' (in education and training, mobility, affectivity, etc.) that the individual (the 'human capital') has to make in order to optimize his performance. Foucault's analysis can help us to see the 'positive' target of neoliberal logic, what it encourages people to aim for through its model of 'human capital'. Capitalization is one of the techniques that must contribute to the worker's transformation into 'human capital'. The latter is then personally responsible for the education and development, growth, accumulation, improvement and valorization of the 'self' in its capacity as 'capital'. This is achieved by managing all its relationships, choices, behaviours according to the logic of a costs/investment ratio and in line with the law of supply and demand. Capitalization must help to turn the worker into 'a kind of permanent, multipurpose business'. The worker is an entrepreneur and entrepreneur of her/himself, 'being her/his own capital, being her/his own producer, being her/his own source of revenue' (Foucault, 2004b: 232). Individuals are expected to deliver not the productivity of labor, but the profitability of a capital investment (of their own capital, a capital that is inseparable from their own selves). The individual has to regard her/himself as a fragment of capital, a molecular fraction of capital. The worker is no longer simply a factor of production; the individual is not strictly speaking a 'workforce' but rather a 'capital-competence', a 'machine of competences'.

This idea of the individual as an entrepreneur of her/himself is the culmination of capital as a machine of subjectivation. For Gilles Deleuze and Félix Guattari (1980: 571; and 1987: 457), capital acts as a formidable 'point of subjectivation that constitutes all human beings as subjects; but some, the "capitalists", are subjects of enunciation [...], while others, the "proletarians", are subjects of the statement, subjected to the technical machines'. We can talk about the fulfillment of the process of subjectivation and exploitation since, in this case, it is the

47

same individual who splits in two, becoming both the subject of enunciation and the subject of the statement. On the one hand, s/he brings the subjectivation process to its pinnacle, because in all these activities s/he involves the 'immaterial' and 'cognitive' resources of her/his 'self', while on the other, s/he inclines towards identification, subjectivation and exploitation, given that s/he is both her/his own master and slave, a capitalist and a proletarian, the subject of enunciation and the subject of the statement.

If we continue to take Foucault as a point of departure, the claim that freedom was introduced into capitalism by the events of May 1968 and by the students can be strongly criticized. According to Foucault, liberalism is a mode of government that consumes freedom; to be able to consume freedom, it is first of all necessary to produce and promote it. Freedom is not a universal value, the enjoyment of which ought to be guaranteed by government; rather, it is the freedom (freedoms) that liberalism needs in order to function. Freedom is quite simply 'the correlative of devices of security' that Foucault describes in *Naissance de la biopolitique*. The great difference from Keynesian liberalism is that this freedom, which must be created and organized, is above all the freedom of business and of the entrepreneur, while the freedom of 'labor', of the 'consumer', of politics, elements which were at the heart of the Keynesian intervention, must be radically subordinated to it. It is always about the freedom of the entrepreneurs.

3. The problem is that the concept of the 'artistic critique' refers us to a notion of artistic activity that belongs to the past and one that, in the terms outlined by Boltanski and Chiapello, may never really have existed:

> But we know very well that, since the eighteenth and above all the nineteenth centuries, the artistic critique, allied as it was with conceptions of art as 'sublime' and the artist as a 'genius', has often been accompanied by a contempt for the 'commonplace', for the 'petty bourgeois', for the narrow-minded, middle-class *beaufs*, and so on. Admittedly, the 'people' or the 'proletariat' might appear protected from such contempt, but that was only because the critics nurtured an idealized, purely abstract image of it. The 'people', as an entity, was seen as 'admirable'. However, when the supporters of the artistic critique chanced upon real representatives of the 'people' with their 'mundane',

'reactionary', etc. concerns, these could only have been a disappointment. (Boltanski and Chiapello, 2000)

This image of the artist corresponds perfectly to the image imposed on intermittent workers by the Culture Minister through the cultural employment policies. It is the liberal members of the French Ministry of Culture who have this image of the artist today.

4. Boltanski and Chiapello, again:

Since the mobility of 'little people' is most often something imposed on them, it is not really likely to generate a network. Buffeted by circumstances that are dictated by the end of their contracts, they run from one employer to the next so as not to drop off the radar completely. They circulate like goods in a network whose links they have no control over. They are then exchanged by others, who use them to maintain their own connections. As we explain when we refer to the nature of exploitation within the network, the mobility of the great person, the source of fulfilment and of profit, is the exact opposite of the mobility of the little person, which is nothing but poverty and precarity. Or, to use one of our formulas: the mobility of the exploiter is counterbalanced by the flexibility of the exploited. (Boltanski and Chiapello, 2000)

It is the poorest, the most minor 'little people' who have carried the intermittent workers' movement. It is the most minor 'little people' who have shown themselves to be a great deal more 'creative', more 'mobile', more 'dynamic' than the employees' trades unions developing and embodying the social critique. Among their numbers, the coordinating groups count not only intermittent workers, but casual workers, unemployed people and people living on the RMI minimum benefits too, and it is this group of 'little people' which has initiated and managed one of the most innovative conflicts of recent years.

Proof that Boltanski and Chiapello's theory is very limited comes from the fact that liberalism has not extended more widely the working conditions of intermittent workers, the only artists with the status of wage-earners. And yet it has imposed on them the economic constraints borne by that model of human capital, the entrepreneur of her/himself. Indeed it is the cultural workers – the artists and technicians of live performance – who have to adopt the behaviours and lifestyles associated with 'human capital'.

Menger and the Misfortunes of Permanent Employment in the Culture Industry

By advocating a policy of permanent employment in the culture industry, Pierre-Michel Menger establishes the limits of possible and reasonable action in the cultural labor market: the 'regulation' of the 'excess' of intermittent artists and technicians. Menger's work clearly shows the complicity, the interweaving, the complementarity and the convergence of the 'right' and 'left' around the battle for employment. His latest book (2005a) is entirely based on the 'disciplinary' opposition between normal and atypical, as the title clearly indicates: *Les intermittents du spectacle: sociologie d'une exception*. For Menger,

> it is not about ordinary unemployment any more than it is about ordinary work [...] The regulation of unemployment among intermittent workers is the regulation of atypical cover against atypical risk. But flexibility beyond the norms has very serious consequences. (Menger, 2005b)

Extraordinary unemployment and employment, atypical risk and atypical cover against risk, flexibility 'beyond the norms': we are at the very heart of disciplinary 'exception'. Menger frames his arguments on the cultural sector and the system of intermittent employment within an elaborate conceptual structure designed to enclose the questions posed by the intermittent workers' movement within the reassuring framework of what is abnormal, exceptional, atypical.[7] The employment policies to be implemented must eradicate the exceptional and ensure that the labor market functions normally again, allowing for both the reconstruction of the entrepreneur's function (her/his autonomy) and the re-imposition of the wage-earner's function (her/his subordination), so that rights and duties can be assigned to each of them.

To express it in the Durkheimian terms of the scholar, a 'direct, organized hierarchy' must be re-established in a labor market deregulated by behaviours that do not conform to the normality of the capital/work relationship. We know that these functions are not natural; they must be created and reproduced through the continuous intervention of employment policies. That is precisely what the reform has been used to do.

While Menger's analysis of intermittent employment seems to be the opposite of the neoliberal version, his conclusions fit perfectly with theirs. Given that 'the number of individuals who enter the system of intermittent employment is increasing far more rapidly than the volume of work they have to share among themselves' (Menger, 2005a), the cultural labor market is characterized by an extreme level of flexibility that leads to increased competition between intermittent workers. The increase in competition between workers has negative consequences for their conditions of employment (shorter and increasingly fragmented contracts), for their pay (a downward trend in salaries) and for their bargaining power with companies.

The 'assessment' that there are too many intermittent workers for it to be possible for all of them to be guaranteed good conditions of employment and indemnification imposes the same solution as the reform does. The numbers of intermittent workers must be reduced by making access to the system of unemployment insurance more difficult, but also by selecting candidates for entry into the performing professions via a series of restrictions on that entry (qualifications, state-controlled education and training). The primary consequence of the fight against extreme flexibility, against underemployment and against the low wages of intermittent workers, and of the fight too to guarantee stable, continuous employment, 'good' pay and 'good' indemnifications for a minority of intermittent workers is that the 'excess' of these workers is redirected to the system of minimum benefit payments,[8] of courses and short-term work placements, to precarity, to basic survival, to poverty.

The initial data on the effects of the reform demonstrate the triumph of neo-liberal policy and the complete subordination of the cultural employment policies.[9] What is being played out here once again is precisely what has been happening in other sectors of the economy for the past 30 years. In its disregard for the current conditions of production, the cultural employment policy – aimed at creating 'real', stable, full-time jobs – actually divides and fragments the labor market by creating an increasing disparity in jobs. All it does is fuel the differentiation, multiply the number of inequalities and thus pave the way for the neoliberal management of the labor market to become established and widespread. Cultural employment policies are subordinated to the liberal logic because, with their aim of reducing competition in the 'corporation', they only segment and differentiate further down the line, and increase the competition between workers who are 'guaranteed' and those who are 'not guaranteed', between stable jobs and casual employment. In this way, they facilitate the policy of 'optimizing differences', the differential management of inequalities in the governing of behaviours in the labor market.

Unemployment and Invisible Work

The analysis of unemployment results in the same disciplinary distinction between the normal (unemployment insurance as it was introduced in the post-war period) and the atypical (unemployment insurance as it has been used, diverted, appropriated by intermittent workers). Menger, like all experts on cultural employment policies, wants to return the unemployment-benefits system, distorted by intermittent employment (since it also finances the activities, cultural and artistic projects and long-term plans of intermittent workers), to its so-called 'natural' function of simple cover against the risk of job loss. But, like the experts, Menger seems to ignore the fact that, in a system of flexible accumulation, the meaning and function of unemployment is altered. The distinct, clear-cut separation between employment and unemployment (unemployment being viewed as the reverse of employment), having been established in a very different system of flexible accumulation (standardization and continuity of production and therefore stability and continuity of employment), has been transformed into an ever tighter interweaving of periods of employment, periods of unemployment and periods of education and training.

If one analyzes the cultural sector, what is first of all striking – indeed it cannot be missed – is the disjunction between work and employment. The length of employment only partially describes the actual work, which in fact goes beyond it. The 'work' habits of intermittent workers (education and training, apprenticeship, the circulation of knowledge and experience, conditions of cooperation, and so forth) are routed through employment and unemployment, but they are not to be reduced to this simple opposition.[10] Since the early 1970s, the time spent in a job only partially encompasses practices of work, education and training, and cooperation by intermittent workers; unemployment cannot simply be reduced to a period of time spent out of work. Unemployment insurance is not limited to covering the risk of job loss. It guarantees the continuity of income that facilitates the interweaving of all these practices and temporalities and allows it to be reproduced; this is income that is not completely the wage-earner's responsibility here as it is in other sectors.

Employer/Wage-Earner

The statements – slogans of employment – prevent Menger from grasping the significance of another transformation that not only disrupts the clear-cut distinction between work and unemployment, but also disrupts the functions that the 'Code of work' allocates to wage-earners (subordination) as well as those it assigns to entrepreneurs (autonomy). Menger is unable to distinguish between the 'legal definition of wage-earners as a body' and the real transformations in wage-earners' activities. So the fact that 'some 86 percent of current jobs today are permanent contracts'[11], means he is exempted from asking questions about what [wage-earners] do and how they go about doing it.

The distinct, clear-cut separation between wage-earner and entrepreneur is increasingly irrelevant, particularly in the system of intermittent employment in which, over the years, a figure neglected by statistics and sociological analyses has emerged. In our research, we have referred to this figure as an 'employer/employee'. This hybrid figure has been established and managed by intermittent workers to adapt to the new demands of cultural production and at the same time bring their own personal projects to a successful conclusion. The employers/employees elude the traditional codifications of the labor market. They are neither wage-earners, nor entrepreneurs, nor freelancers. They combine their different functions without necessarily being confined to any single one of these categories.

This development of hybrid statuses creates many problems for the governing of the labor market. The Latarjet report on the live performance sector identifies it as the main factor in the poor functioning of that sector. It recommends a return to a 'normal' functioning of professional relations, which would end this 'exception' by re-establishing the subordination of the wage-earner (with her/his rights) and the autonomy of the entrepreneur (with her/his duties and responsibilities). This obsession with a return to normality is quite simply a disciplinary mechanism that seeks to suppress and devalue these new forms of activity.

In contrast, our survey on intermittent workers means we can entirely subscribe to a comment in the CERC[12] report on 'Job Security' that does not seek to turn all these hybridizations, exposed by the system of intermittent employment, into an exception or an anomaly – indeed far from it.

> In place of a clear separation between work and unemployment, between salaried employment and freelance work, we find a sort of "halo" of employment with an unspecified status – someone is both unemployed and a wage-earner, for example, or a freelancer and a wage-earner – while the various types of temporary contracts (short-term and intermittent contracts, temporary work) are on the increase. (CERC, 2005)

The alleged 'exception' of intermittent employment is becoming the 'norm' in the wage-earning system, something the groups representing intermittent workers have been claiming since 1992. The 'ordinary' or 'classic' categories that Menger wishes to reinstate within the system of intermittent employment are difficult to apply even in the 'normal' sectors of the economy. Contrary to what he maintains, the difference between intermittent unemployment and the unemployment found in other sectors is a difference of degree, not of kind.

Notes

1 This and subsequent quotations are from Boltanski and Chiapello, 2000, an interview with Yann Moulier Boutang for the journal *Multitudes*. Online at http://multitudes.samizdat.net/Vers-un-renouveau-de-la-critique.html.

2 Translator's note: the use of *faire fi à* rather than *faire fi de* is a grammatical error noted by Lazzarato.

3 Translator's note: *bobos* is an abbreviation for *bourgeois-bohèmes*.

4 Translator's note: The *Coordination des Intermittents et Précaires* is an organization established to coordinate intermittent and casual workers and represent their claims for indemnification due to the precarity of their employment.

5 Translator's note: A *Rmiste* is a person living on RMI, or *Revenu minimum d'insertion*, a form of income support.

6 Translator's note: NHW is the Number of Hours Worked, a translation of NHT or *Nombre d'heures travaillées*.

7   Menger compares the extreme flexibility of intermittent employment (abnormality) with a relative stability in the other sectors of the economy (normality). This assessment is highly debatable because it has been arrived at by contrasting data on intermittent employment, evaluated in terms of flow, with data relating to the rest of the economy, which is measured in terms of stocks. If we also interpret the latter in terms of flow, as an Insee study (Insee Première, N° 1014, May 2005) and the 2005 CERC report on 'Job Security' have done, it is obvious that flexibility (of employment) is far from being a specific exception within the system of intermittent employment:

> Every year the number of wage-earners rises in many companies and falls in others without a corresponding rise or fall in the balance of total employment figures. These gross trends in corporate employment cannot be compared with the net variations in total employment. So, in seven years, in the period between 1995 and 2001, it is possible to calculate 17.6 million annual employment transactions for a net balance of 1.6 million jobs.

Every year, millions of people lose their job and millions more find another (there are 33,753 transactions in and out of the job market daily). In its 2002 report on 'Job Security', the CERC draws the same conclusions from its survey of the private sector alone:

> In 2002, the total employment figure (for metropolitan France and its overseas territories) stood at around 25 million people, with 23 million in salaried employment. From 2001 to 2002, the number of those in employment grew by around 170,000 people. But this rise is the result of a flow in appointments and departures, both of which reached extraordinarily high levels. Thus, in a field of around 13 million private-sector wage-earners, companies made 5.2 million appointments during 2002 (excluding temporary contracts and non-renewable contracts of less than a month's duration to cover absences due to wage-earners' annual leave). So the rate of recruitment is close to 40 percent. At the same time, around 40 percent of wage-earners left their jobs.

8   Translator's note: Lazzarato refers here to the RMI and a raft of other benefits available to those on the lowest incomes.

9   None of the objectives of the 'regulation' proposed by Menger has been achieved. Since 2003, the salaries of intermittent workers, who have remained within the system and who constitute the culture industry's 'human capital', have fallen while unemployment benefit has gone up, in particular for those categories working directly for the culture industry (cinema and television). The rise in income (salary plus allowances) of intermittent workers who have not left the system and who constitute the culture industry's 'human capital' is financed by inter-professional solidarity;

yet the CFDT [French trade union], Medef [representative body of the majority of French employers' interest groups] and the official experts do not find fault with any of this.

10 Menger claims to have studied this field for thirty years, yet he blithely and systematically confuses these two temporalities. His analyses and recommendations are concerned with 'employment' exclusively, while the concept of 'work' is never considered.

11 Translator's note: In a CDI or *contrat à durée indéterminée*, the duration of employment is not contractually specified.

12 Translator's note: CERC is the abbreviation for the Conseil de l'emploi, des revenus et de la cohésion sociale, French government institution researching the links between employment, income and social cohesion.

4

'Creativity and Innovation' in the Nineteenth Century: Harrison C. White and the Impressionist Revolution Reconsidered

Ulf Wuggenig
translated by Larissa Buchholz, Aileen Derieg and Karl Hoffmann

According to interpretations in the dominant hagiographic literature on art, as well as in the writings of some well known critics and intellectuals, the Impressionists of the 1860s and 1870s in Paris challenged and overthrew the artistic orthodoxies and thus paved the way for aesthetic modernism.[1] According to Clement Greenberg (1993), Edouard Manet's paintings became the first Modernist ones, as they stressed flatness and two-dimensionality. Michel Foucault echoes this formalist interpretation and goes even further when he declares that the way in which Manet's paintings represented the material aspects of the surface has made possible the whole art of the twentieth century (Foucault, 2010). Social historians of art such as T. J. Clark, by contrast, understand the emergence of modernist painting in Paris primarily as a response to the experience of modernity – of the dehumanizing aspects of life under capitalism associated with a loss of certainty about the very act of representation (See Clark, 1984).

Despite all the differences in interpretation there is a tendency to particularly highlight the role of Manet, who is credited with having set painting upon a new course. This is also true for Pierre Bourdieu, one of the few sociologists whose work refers to this artistic movement: 'The revolutionary hero, the liberator, is evidently Manet. Understanding the revolution brought about by Manet is also understanding the birth of the modern artist and of modern painting' (Bourdieu, 1987: 4). Bourdieu interprets this revolution as a symbolic one, that is, as a fundamental change of mental structures, of the hierarchy of signifier and signified and the manner of representing it, of the function of painting. On the other hand, he outlines that the Impressionist revolution led by Manet brought about a different understanding of the artist: he ceases to be a master and becomes an artist in the modern sense with an extraordinary biography, the object of outstanding and celebrated singularity. For Bourdieu, Manet invented the position of the autonomous artist and imposed it on a field of art that was itself in a state of attaining relative autonomy.

Yet what Bourdieu emphasizes as well is that historical figures can gain important functions in contemporary debates: 'The works of the past, whether literary or pictorial, are always a matter of struggles in the present' (Bourdieu, 1987: 5). Bourdieu's eulogy on Manet was presented shortly after the opening of the Musée d'Orsay in Paris in 1986. This 'presidential museum' initiated by Giscard d'Estaing was dedicated to the art of the second half of the nineteenth century. Among French cultural leftists at that time, it was interpreted as an attempt to rehabilitate academic art – *art pompier* – marginalized by formalist as well as revisionist art history and criticism. Among these academic painters were, just to mention a few, Jean-Louis-Ernest Meissonier, hardly known anymore today, yet of the painters still living at the time in the nineteenth century, the one who achieved the highest prices on the market; Jean-Leon Gérome, Academy member who fought against Impressionism up into the 1890s; and also Alexandre Cabanel, whose *Naissance de Venus* was personally purchased by Napoleon III straight from the Salon of the year 1863, from which Manet's *Déjeuner sur l'herbe* had been banned (See Zola, 1867: 107ff.).

The academism that dominated the Academy, the École des Beaux Arts, the Salon, the art sections, and the taste of the broader public, were oriented toward producing copies, toward conformity in regard to tradition, and a clear hierarchy of legitimate subjects and objects to be depicted. Painting was generally oriented toward precision, perfection and consummation; the artists were therefore more or less exchangeable. Bourdieu thus classified the academic artist type, following Max Weber's sociology of religion, as 'priestly' rather than 'prophetic'.

In view of the classification of academism and impressionism, as well as of the importance of historical figures and positions for contemporary discourses, I want to draw attention to the writings of an American author, Harrison C. White. He is well known in the field of Impressionism research as well as in the social sciences, where he is 'regarded by some as the greatest living sociologist' (Collins, 2005: ix). In art discourse Harrison C. White is particularly known for a study of the institutional changes in the nineteenth century French art world, written together with art historian Cynthia White in the early 1960s. This study is recognized for having established the concept of the 'dealer and critic system' and having described and explained the emergence of the modern institutional system of art or rather the beginnings of an art market in today's sense, largely separated from the state (White and White, 1993).

In sociology, White is regarded as having inaugurated network analysis and a school of talented followers, among them Mark Granovetter and Ronald S. Burt, famous for their work on 'weak ties' and 'structural holes', notions also used in a study on the artworld by Katherine Guiffre (1999), another pupil of White. His major theoretical work *Identity and Control* was published in 1992 and in a revised and expanded version in 2008. Especially the first edition was written in such an idiosyncratic and technical style that hardly anyone was able to understand it; it gained the status of an intelligence test for sociologists. A spin-off of this work is White's second book on art, which was published in 1993. Even its title, *Careers and Creativity*, already demonstrates that it can be seen as belonging to the social science literature that is interested in innovation and creativity and their role and function for economic processes. A flood of literature on 'creative industries', 'creative cities', 'creativity and innovation' and so on emerged in the late 1990s, after this theme had been taken up in the political field by Tony Blair and the 'third way' spin-doctors in Great Britain (see Schlesinger, 2007). White's book on the arts was thus published ahead of this wave of literature, and long before writers such as Richard Florida (2002) made this theme popular.

Although White is not at all reducible to the pop sociology and economy of the usual creative industries literature, his scientific approach bears similarities with this literature in several respects, for example in regard to: a) the supposed economic importance of creativity; b) the uncritical use of this term; c) the position towards the differentiation of high and low art, for which in his view the same social and economic laws regarding innovations apply; d) the treatment of the opposition between art and economy, which in contrast e.g. to Bourdieu (1993) is explicitly or implicitly denied. Some of the theoretical features of his approach also resemble other aspects of the creative industries type of literature, for instance, the use of general theory and the reliance on the notion of 'art world' in the tradition of Howard S. Becker (1982). This concept implies that the different actors involved in the production, distribution and reception of art are principally more or less of similar importance; it thus decenters the author or artist. In White's approach this presupposition leads to a revaluation and celebration of the role of economic actors in the history of art, who appear to be as significant for artistic innovations as the artists themselves. This idea is reflected in a series of propositions on innovation in art. I will only mention and comment on three of them:

> Innovation in style involves change in social organization coordinated with cultural change across art worlds. (White, 1993: 72)

Artistic innovation itself is thus far from sufficient for major changes of conventions in art. Whereas in art history and philosophy most often aesthetic or purely symbolic aspects of domains are regarded as decisive for changes of style, the approach of the Whites in *Canvases and Careers*, to which this more recent proposition refers, already emphasises that stylistic and institutional changes have to go hand in hand for radical innovations to occur. In *Careers and Creativity*, White discusses this thesis mainly in regard to Impressionism and Abstract Expressionism, but also with some examples from music, dance and theatre.

White stresses that a radical shift in 'style' requires many and prolonged efforts. It presupposes social and economic support as well as changes in the social organization of art, that is, its institutional frame. This argument already constituted the central theme of *Canvases and Careers*, which was essentially the story of an old system being replaced by a new one after a period of hybridity in which the two systems were merged. White's general 'process' proposition for innovation in the arts reads as follows:

> A new style results from an intermediate period of overlay and melding between one style and another in both social and cultural infrastructures; the new style is followed by rejection of the separate

styles that went into its formation and then again became separate. (White, 1993: 82)

This hypothesis emphasises the overlapping and the phase of coexistence between an earlier and a newly emerging system in processes that include both social and artistic aspects. One indication of the novelty of a style is its rejection and denunciation by established criticism. The old one was the 'academic system', wrongly interpreted as a system under peer group control by Wijnberg and Gemser (2000), since it was not a relative autonomous field but an authoritarian system under state control (cf. Bourdieu, 1987; 1993: 238ff.). This hierarchical institution according to the Whites was unable to react in a flexible way to changes in its environment, especially the dramatic rise of artists in Paris in the nineteenth century and the flood of pictures to be handled in the central exhibition and art market space, the Salon. At a time when visual mass media like television and film did not yet exist, this Salon attracted hundreds of thousands of visitors.[2] According to the morphological hypothesis of White and White (1993), the crisis into which the Academy and the Salon had slid resulted from the success of the system itself, because the profession of painter had become increasingly attractive in symbolic and economic terms. Thanks to Andrée Sfeir-Semler's study, meanwhile we know much more about details of the morphological changes in the artworld in Paris than at the time when *Canvases and Careers* was first published. While at the beginning of the nineteenth century the number of painters at the Salons was around 200, it had increased to around 1,300 by 1863. The number of pictures submitted to the Salon rose to between 4,000 and 6,000 in the 1860s and 1870s. (See figure 1)

This development – documented by the curve of artists applying to the Salon showing an exponential growth from 1791 to 1880[3] – exerted – at least that's how White and White specify the necessary precondition for changes – enormous pressure on an organizational and economic frame that had been conceived for merely a few hundred painters. From the perspective of Bourdieu (1987, 1993) it was an 'overproduction crisis', which had the effect of creating a large precarious artistic 'lumpenproletariat', being a decisive step in the development of the artist in the modern sense. This morphologically induced crisis from his point of view was used by some artists – first of all Manet – for realizing a symbolic and an institutional revolution.

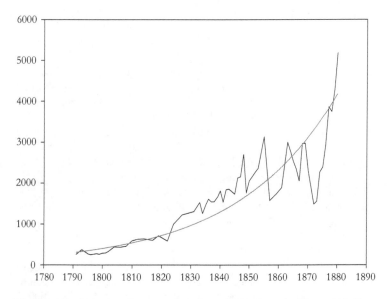

Figure 1: Number of applicants (artists) for the Salon in Paris 1791 - 1880 (data source: Sfeir-Semler, 1992: 40-43; exponential curve – fit $R^2 = 0,79$ – added with SigmaPlot TableCurve 2D).

Against the background of the academic system in crisis, its failure in supporting and guiding the careers of painters due to its lack of flexibility, and the dissatisfaction of the artists being rejected on account of the system's rigid concept of art, the beginnings of Impressionism are to be dated in the 1860s. As a movement, it appeared from 1874 on with the offensive measure of organizing its own exhibitions and breaking the monopoly of the state-run Salons, a strategy that ultimately succeeded (See Rewald, 1961; Denvir, 1993).

These ideas most likely sprung from the 'Circle of Batignolles', to which Fantin-Latour's famous group portrait from 1870 refers, depicting Manet in his studio in the middle of a group of artists who obviously admire him – a nucleus of the future Impressionists with, among others, Bazilles, Monet and Renoir. The idea of a self-organized group exhibition probably came up for first time in this studio in 1869. In the the end, Manet did not participate in any of the eight

Impressionist exhibitions between 1874 and 1886, because he shunned the image of a rebel and didn't want to see himself associated too closely with the Impressionists (Cachin, 1995; and Brombert, 1996).

The Whites emphasized that this bureaucratic and monopolist system was successfully attacked by a network of artists, dealers, critics and collectors. They added a lot of sociological insights to the well-known heroic art history stories that highlight the Salon des Refusés, Manet's Pavilion and the series of self-organised group exhibitions outside the Salon in the 1870s and 1880s as the decisive events in a struggle between academic art and the revolutionary 'painters of modern life'.

The new system, according to the Whites, was supported by a highly functional new ideology in intellectual as well as in economic respect, namely individualism, or, to be more precise, charismatic individualism. Instead of single pictures, as it was in the old system influenced by the Salon, the new system shifted the artist to the centre of attention. For both the newly emerging type of dealers – real entrepreneurs for the first time – and for the increasingly important art criticism, highlighting a personality and the entire oeuvre of a painter seemed obvious. As an isolated object a single work was too transient to serve as the focus of a system of trade or advertising. Conversely, the concept of the 'genius' developed in the Romantic era, which implies being unrecognised and – in its Kantian version – not following any rules, proved especially suitable for concentrating on the artist. In about twenty years, according to Emile Zola, one of the numerous writers who sought to distinguish themselves as intellectuals through art criticism at that time, one would be able to see the unrecognised and derided Manet in the Louvre. A view like this enabled not only unrecognised artists to maintain their motivation despite a lack of acknowledgement. At the same time it also opened up the possibility for speculations in taste in an economic sense and for the development of an ultimately highly speculative art market as we know it today (See Watson, 1992; Moulin, 2009).

For the development of a new system, however, still other factors were important, such as the change in the type and formats of artistic production. A greater number of smaller, often quickly painted pictures were produced, which was facilitated by technical progress in the field of paints. These took the place of the larger, planned 'machines' of academism. In addition, accessing new classes of buyers assumed a central significance. A potential market for art was to be found in the expanding middle class and in the more prosperous bourgeoisie, if one was capable of accessing this market.

Another central proposition from White refers to this in a general form, by seeking to specify a necessary context for artistic innovations:

> The key to innovation in arts is flexibility in reception; that is, a field of alternative reception must be feasible not only culturally but also in material and social technology. (White, 1993: 81)

This hypothesis referring to demand and consumption shifts attention away from artistic practice to those protagonists who are capable of influencing desires and preferences and thus generating or opening up a demand for innovative art. In principle there are various art-world protagonists who could be considered for this – the artists themselves, critics, dealers, collectors and museum representatives. White sets flexible reception in opposition to the notion of individual creation widespread in art historical hagiography, which isolates it from its acceptance in a 'field' in the sense of systems theoretical psychology of creativity (Csíkszentmihályi, 1999), where this notion is used for the aggregate of actors, who evaluate, select, conserve and transmit artefacts produced in 'domains', not to be confounded with a field in the sense of Bourdieu (1993).

And in this context White's attention undergoes a remarkable reorientation from the first to the second study on impressionism, a symptomatic transformation from the 1960s to the 1990s. As the conscious use of the term 'dealer and critic system' in the first work shows, where the dealer is the first protagonist named, at that time White already regarded the dealers as the central actors of the new system. It was not until the 1990s, however, that White went as far as using formulations that virtually amounted to an apotheosis of one dealer in particular, namely Paul Durand-Ruel. White notes that the concept of the 'dealer-critic system' introduced in *Canvases and Careers* in the early 1960ies, since then often taken up in literature, was conceived as an homage to Durand-Ruel. It deserves to be pointed out that in this way the roles of both the producers and the collectors in the art field are implicitly lowered in value.

From White's new perspective Durand-Ruel now appeared just as important for the recognition and establishment of Impressionism as those who had carried out the innovation on the level of symbolic production. In White's view, Durand-Ruel created a new role for the dealer, the dealer as an entrepreneur in the modern Schumpeterian sense. White writes in regard to him, that he recognised the speculative potential of purchasing unknown or unrecognised painters and persuaded others that this could be a profitable investment. He was generous toward initially unsuccessful artists, sometimes assuming the role of their patron. And finally, he also made use of new strategies, such as seeking control over all the works by an artist to gain a monopoly, or making informal contracts with the artists to bind them to him. In the end he introduced solo exhibitions for artists, similar to those that dominate the 'dealer and critic system' today. According to White, he was also aware of the high value of publicity and advertising.

These observations take White substantially beyond the conventional remarks in art historical literature that Durand-Ruel was the central dealer of the Impressionists. White even chooses formulations in which Durand-Ruel is elevated to the 'father' of the entire new system and ultimately even to a 'genius' with a significance homologous to that of Paul Cézanne:

> The real core of a new style however is always dual. [...] Durand-Ruel was central to just such dual realization of the Impressionists. In so doing, he can be called the father of a whole new system of art world. (White, 1993: 75)

And in his response to the question of who the impressionists actually were artistically, White himself takes recourse to the charismatic individualist ideology of the 'dealer and critic system'.

The dealers of the nineteenth century were supposed to remain entirely in the background in light of what is perhaps best described by Bourdieu (1993) as the anti-economism of the art field. Witness to this is borne by, for example, the well-known group portraits in the anti-academic milieu of the 1860s and 1870s such as Frédéric Bazille's *L'Atelier de la rue de la Condamine* (1870) and Henri Fantin-Latour's *Hommage à Delacroix* (1864) and *Un atelier aux Batignolles* (1870). In addition to painters, there are indeed depictions of writers and critics such as Baudelaire and Zola, who among other critics on the path to the autonomy of the art field were important allies (see Bourdieu, 1996), and in one case also that of a befriended collector, but never dealers.

They were never included in these portraits of artistic networks, as little as Berthe Morisot and Mary Cassatt – the female members of the Impressionist movement with the highest reputation today. (Table 1 below gives their contemporary Artfacts. Net ranks.)

Whereas the Whites still described the role of the dealers dispassionately and analytically in the 1960s, already speaking of a 'dealer-critic system', in the 1990s we find that Durand-Ruel is supposed to have been the 'genius' that ultimately brought forth the impressionists. Indeed, according to him the Impressionists were not the first to make use of Impressionist painting techniques, they did not really invent the new style but rather the Barbizon artist Charles-François Daubigny:

> My own answer to this question of who the Impressionists were artistically centers on Paul Durand-Ruel, who to a sociologist seems as predominant a genius in one way as was Cézanne in the painterly dimension among the Impressionists-to-be. Subsequent recognition of 'them' as the impressionists, I argue, was accomplished by Durand-Ruel's agency, not by some immanent painterly style. (White, 1993: 75)

White especially emphasises that Durand-Ruel, driven by his weak and vacillating success in France, came to prominence in the 1880s when he succeeded in finding a new audience, particularly in the USA, where there were no comparable blockades the way academism had created them in France. He opened a gallery in New York after organising a first major Impressionist exhibition in 1887. Durand-Ruel thus exemplified the proposition of flexible reception with the ability to reach new relevant groups of the public, namely collectors, and win them over for a more than merely symbolic appropriation of the new French art.

Against the backdrop of the demise of the academic system, the needs of painters, dealers and critics were united in this way with the wishes of buyers and collectors for pictures that were suitable for bourgeois households. Through a complex process a new system emerged by the end of the nineteenth century, which took the control over the status and rewarding of artists out of the hands of the academic system. The prices paid for academic painters fell abruptly, professorships at academies and art schools lost their significance for the selection of art works and for constructing the status of artists, which was henceforth increasingly determined by non-state expert and market forces.

Whereas Bourdieu, in line with such diverse authors as Clement Greenberg, André Malraux, Michael Fried and Michel Foucault, is inclined toward an heroisation of Manet in conjunction with the Impressionist revolution, Harrison C. White tends to emphasize a single protagonist from the relational constellation of fields and networks, namely Durand-Ruel. In a turn that seems symptomatic for a new thought-syle regarding cultural production, it is not an artist like Manet, but rather a dealer like Durand-Ruel who is celebrated as a radically innovative 'genius'.

What evidence is there for the emergence of the new system and the role of Durand-Ruel in particular? David Galenson and Robert Jensen (2007), who refer only to the previous study by White and White, have stressed that it took far longer than is assumed in this study for the Salon system to be replaced by a gallery system centred on the one-man show ascribed to the initiative of Durand-Ruel. As an intermediate step, a system of a plurality of Salons emerged in Paris, which finally gave way to the modern system, heavily based on an art market beyond state control. According to their analysis, a commercial gallery show devoted to a single artist – the dominant format in the twentieth century – was no option for young or unrecognised artists until the end of the nineteenth century. Durand-Ruel only presented Impressionist artists in solo shows whose reputation was already established. White is perhaps right in emphasising that of all the major dealers of the time only Paul Durand-Ruel bought advanced art in quantity. Yet Galenson and Jensen have shown that he bought from the Impressionists primarily only during two brief and widely separated periods, in 1872 and 1873, and in the early 1880s. Since the independent exhibitions of the Impressionists took place from 1874 to 1886, they received almost no financial support from him during the most important period of their struggle against the Salon. Durand-Ruel only began to buy the work of Impressionists again after they had gained substantial symbolic capital through their self-organized exhibitions. Thus he did not provide effective, continuous support for his artists. Furthermore, the French art historian Anne Distel (1990) has identified just over two-dozen collectors who bought paintings by the Impressionists in Paris during the 1870s and early 1880s. Only two of them, the opera singer Jean-Baptiste Faure and the merchant Ernest Hoschedé, both collectors of the speculative type, appear to have become acquainted with the work of the Impressionists through Durand-Ruel. Most of the others bought directly from the artists, having become acquainted with them through other artists or writers.

Although White, in his 1993 study, drew special attention to the importance of Durand-Ruel's role in opening the US-American market for the Impressionists, the truth is that the most important US collectors became acquainted with Impressionism through the painter Mary Cassatt. She came from the upper class family of an investment banker in Pittsburgh and went to Paris as an artist, where she rose to become one of the dozen Impressionist artists later regarded as the core of the movement in mainstream art history (See Callen, 2000; and Thomson, 2000). There Cassatt became part of the circle of Degas, who was himself from the upper class and had a background of bankers with network links (family connections) that also reached to the USA. Prior to Durand-Ruel's New York venture, Mary Cassatt had already found a small, but crucial number of American collectors who were part of her social network, her upper class social capital. Thus she was able to convince some of her family members and close friends to buy paintings by Manet, Degas, Cézanne and other painters associated with Impressionism. Among them was Louisine Elder, who was to marry Henry Havemeyer, the future 'sugar king' in the USA. Based on consultation with Cassatt, the Havemeyers and also Potter Palmer and his wife – owners of a big hotel chain – began to build up the collections that would become the most important collections of Impressionism in the USA. The initial acquaintance with the work of the Impressionists, however, was due to an artist, not a dealer. Of course, the Havemeyer collection would not have gained such importance, had a large part of it not been donated by the widowed Louisine Havemeyer, who had meanwhile become a well-known bourgeois feminist, to the Metropolitan Museum of Art in New York in 1917 (See Distel, 1990: 237ff; Weitzenhoffer, 1986).

However, Manet represents the type of ambitious artists who was forcefully striving for a position in the history of art and for whom the crucial issue was not acceptance by private collectors – then as now usually upwardly mobile people, having become rich or super rich, aiming at enhancing their insecure social status. The struggle for recognition as an artist, inclusion in art history, is not decided in the private but in the public realm. White did not take placement in the museum, either in France or in the USA, into consideration. Within the theoretical frame of reference it is also ignored as a decisive aspect of consecrating artists. White disregards that art distinguishes itself from other luxury goods not least by the fact that it ultimately finds its place in a public collection. Nor did he adequately consider the strategies of the producers themselves. He neither took into account the role of Mary Cassatt, nor Monet's initiative of 1890. In that year Monet bought Manet's *Olympia* for about 90 thousand dollars in today's currency from Manet's widow with the help of money he had raised. His intention was to offer this work to the state for placement in the Louvre. Thus he tried to force official recognition not only for the most charismatic figure of the movement, but also for Impressionism in general.

Nor did White consider the even more efficient strategy of another artist. Gustave Caillebotte, who belonged like Mary Cassatt to the aforementioned dozen canonized Impressionist artists, was one of the most important collectors and financial supporters of the Impressionists. His introduction to the group also had nothing to do with Durand-Ruel. Like Manet, Morisot, Degas and Cassatt, Caillebotte came from an upper class background, in his case not in terms of symbolic capital, but in terms of economic capital, being the heir of a wealthy textile industrialist.

Caillebotte had built up a collection of sixty important works by Degas, Manet, Cézanne, Degas, Pissarro and others. As early as 1878 he donated his collection to a hostile state, under the condition, that it would not disappear into a provincial museum, but would be presented in the two most important houses of that time, the Louvre and the Musée du Luxembourg.

> I give to the state the pictures I own; only as I want this gift to be accepted, and accepted in such a way that the pictures go neither into an attic nor to a provincial museum but right to the Luxembourg and later to the Louvre, it is necessary that a certain time go by before the execution of this clause, until the public may, I don't say understand, but accept this painting. This time could be twenty years or more. (Caillebotte, 1883: 197)

It was the Caillebotte's bequest of 1883 that finally opened the door for the Impressionists into a museum in France in 1896, when at least a part of this collection was accepted by a mostly hostile art administration. Here again, Durand-Ruel was not involved in

Caillebotte's highly sophisticated strategy which, according to Denvir, led to the 'decisive official recognition of the impressionists in France' (Denvir, 1993).

Durand-Ruel deserves credit for being the first dealer to recognize the importance of the Impressionists. Contrary to White's portrayal, however, neither he nor other dealers of that time were leaders in the development of modern art and the development of its markets in the nineteenth century. They played their roles in art world networks, but these roles were far from being the decisive ones. Even the role of the 'ideological dealer' (Wijnberg and Gemser, 2000), who developed new business approaches was not invented by Durant-Ruel. In a recent study on the art field of Brussels Jan Dirk Baetens tries to show that the business model of the impressionist dealers in Paris was already fully operational in Belgium in the 1840s. For this reason it cannot not be associated with avant-garde art on an exclusive basis. The conclusions based on a case study of the Belgian art dealer Gustave Coûteaux (1815-1873) read as follows:

> There was nothing in the business approach of Durand-Ruel, the champion of avant-garde artists, that was not already there in the strategies of Coûteaux. The myth that the 'heroic' dealers of the 1870s were equally innovative as the artists they represented should be exposed as exactly that: an artistic myth belonging to the lofty heights of Mount Parnassus – that former realm of absolute and pure beauty, now tainted by a touch of commerce – rather than a historical fact. (Baetens, 2010: 41)

Paul Durand-Ruel seems not to have been a person one would easily credit as a 'genius', which from a sociological point of view seems to be a dubious term anyway. Even psychologists meanwhile have stopped to ascribe creativity to single individuals.

> Creativity does not happen inside people's heads, but in the interaction between a person's thoughts and a socio-cultural context. It is a systemic rather an individual phenomenon. (Csíkszentmihályi, 1996: 400; see also Gardner, 1993)

The limits of Durand-Ruel's strategies are evident as well in some of Anne Distel's remarks, who basically tends to divide the world into geniuses and normal people:

Durand Ruel seems to have bought works by Cezanne only at the express request of certain faithful customers. He did not care for Seurat or Gauguin, though Gauguin's first exhibition in 1893 was held in his gallery. He went so far as to refuse to organize a posthumous exhibition for Van Gogh. (Distel, 1990: 31)

In view of all the evidence on the dealer Durand-Ruel, it seems likely that Harrison C. White credits the wrong person and profession with being responsible for the flexible reception of the Impressionist revolution, for changing the art world in the nineteenth century, and for paving the way for the modern art market dealer-critic system. His apotheosis of the dealer seems to be due to an ideological bias, which is characteristic for a style of thought and a social current that also developed the 'creative industries' hype. It not only celebrates individualism, but also emphasises the role of economic actors in fields of cultural production. Meanwhile even art history has become a target for reinterpretations in the light of this wave of economist thinking.

As already indicated, a more adequate sociological explanation of aspects of the Impressionist revolution will have to place a stronger focus on the strategies of the producers themselves. From an externalist sociological point of view, Impressionism is characterized by the fact that as good as none of its main proponents came from artist's families, as opposed to the academic masters of the state controlled Parisian art world. Hence, they were not exposed in a comparable manner to the influence of academic tradition conveyed by family members or relatives. In response to Arnold Hauser, who writes that the Impressionists 'come very largely from the lower and middle sections of the bourgeoisie' (Hauser, 1989: 166), the part of column b. of table 1, which refers to social origin, demonstrates the privileged descent of both the Degas circle (with Mary Cassatt, Caillebotte and Degas himself) and other canonized representatives of Impressionism, especially Berthe Morisot and Bazille as well as Manet as the movement's forerunner and point of reference. This fact eluded Hauser and was later only insufficiently taken into consideration by Heinich (2005: 229) in French art sociology, mainly regarding Manet and Degas[4] and in the case of Bourdieu also Renoir, whose work is not interpreted in a formalist way. Renoir from his point of view is representing a 'simultaneously lyrical and naturalistic adherence to natural or human nature' in contrast 'both with realist or critical representation of the social world [...] and with all forms of abstraction' (Bourdieu, 1984: 20).

In the resources that Manet had at his disposal due to his upper-class background, including the self-confidence associated with this, Bourdieu sees a basis for the willingness and ability to transcend artistic conventions. Nathalie Heinich extended this argument to include Degas. Yet such an argument soon comes upon its limits when one considers that Monet and Renoir were capable of relevant innovations as well without having such background-related resources at their disposal.

Table 1 includes indicators of the symbolic capital of the impressionists as well as of their posthumous economic success. The measures of symbolic capital are based on the Artfacts.Net ranking of about 60 thousand historical and living artists. Economic success is indicated by the highest auction prize a work of the ten artists considered yielded until the end of 2010 as well as by the number of works above an auction price of 16.5 million USD at this time, which means being among the 130 most expensive art works up to this time. Column e. in table 1 indicates that the overall symbolic capital of Monet and Renoir, artists with a lower middle class and provincial background, in the artistic field seems to be higher than that of Manet. The same goes for the economic value of their works (See table 1, columns f. and g.).

Even according to Bourdieu in the long run economic value is converging with aesthetic value:

> The dominant fractions are what they are if and only if the economic principle of stratification asserts its real dominance, which it does, in the long run, even in the relatively autonomous field of cultural production, where the divergence between specific value and market value tends to disappear in the course of time. (Bourdieu 1984: 583, fn. 41)

Hence, there are two problems for the resources-based argument with regard to the innovative force of Manet. First, only a partial explanation is given, and second, this explanation appears to be too individualistic. The capital directly related to the social background of a wealthy bourgeoisie comes into play in the case of the Impressionist revolution in a different way as well.

Table 1: Impressionists (I): Artistic circles, shows (Salons, I-exhibitions), social positions, long-term symbolic capital and economic success.[5]

Name	a. sex	b. origin[1] geo-graphic	social	c. Salons in-/exclusion	d. I-shows 1874-86	c. symbolic rank 02/2011	auction prices mill. USD (2010) f. max.	g. n>16.5
I. Precursor, reference artist (with impressionist working period)								
Manet	m	Paris	U	15 : 4	0	227	29.6	5
II. Monet circle								
Monet	m	province	LM	4 : 3	4	69	71.8	11
Renoir	m	province	LM	11 : 4	4	155	71	5
Bazille	m	province	UM	4 : 1	0	n.a.	4.7	0
Sisley	m	Paris	MM	3 : 3	4	929	5.1	0
III. Bridges between Monet and Degas circles								
Pissarro	m	Antilles	MM	8 : 3	8	360	13	0
Morisot	f	Paris	U	7 : 0	7	2379	4.6	0
IV. Degas circle								
Degas	m	Paris	U	6 : 0	7	103	33	5
Caillebotte	m	Paris	U	0 : 1	5	2629	13	0
Cassatt	f	USA	U	2 : 3	4	717	5.5	0
V. Postimpressionist 'dissident' (with impressionist working period)								
Cézanne	m	province	UM	1 : 14	2	67	55	8

It is true that it does not suffice to draw attention solely to artistic innovations. Mary Cassatt and Gustave Caillebotte who were part of the upper class Degas circle utilized not only their cultural but also their social and economic capital. They succeeded in gaining the interest of serious collectors and in securing the institutional acknowledgement of Impressionism in the world of leading museums and thus for the 'Jupiter history' of art (Foucault, 1997: 60).

One can hardly deny that there were examples of essential artistic innovations e.g. in the case of Monet independent of the artists' individual social background. For the assertion and institutional recognition of Impressionism in the field, however, the social and economic capital at the disposal of the Impressionist network as a whole was of prime importance. The steps toward the increase in the relative autonomy of the field and the detachment from state patronization could therefore not only find support in the motivations of the artists. A sufficiently large fraction of the artists also had those resources at their disposal, without which such motivations usually don't make much headway. They used this social and economic capital for the 'flexible reception' among private individuals, which White mainly has in mind, but also for placing the works in public collections. Whether one ultimately celebrates the Impressionists for their contribution to breaking the *nomos* of the state, to marginalizing academism, to establishing anomie or plurality, and to increasing the relative autonomy of the art field with regard to the field of power as heroic revolutionaries, or as radical innovators from the bourgeoisie who paved the way to the breakthrough of the art market which is characteristic for modern capitalism is another question.

Notes

1   This text is an expanded and updated version of '"Kreativität und Innovation" im 19. Jahrhundert. Harrison C. White und die impressionistische Revolution – erneut betrachtet', in Raunig and Wuggenig, 2007.

2   The extraordinarily high numbers of visitors of the several Salons – between 300,000 and 1.2 million – are documented in Sfeir-Semler, 1992: 51. This author was part of a movement in art historiography attacked by Bourdieu (1987, 1993) that – in the end with limited success – attempted to rehabilitate nineteenth-century academic painting and a traditional model of

'homo academicus' in general. The main contribution of this revisionist tradition in France is Vaisse (1993), which had an influence on French art history. For competing positions regarding academism and Impressionism, see Nord, 2000.

3   1880 was the last year of the Salon de Paris under dominance of the state. The stronger fluctuations of the empirical curve of applications are either due to the World' Fairs in Paris (1855, 1867), to revolutionary events (1848) or to war (1870/71). Cf. Sfeir-Semler, 1992: 46.

4   In sociological works on the Impressionists, these artists are either viewed as a unity, as in Hauser (1989) or White (1993), or individual proponents are treated as representing the entire group. White not only neglects artistic innovation on the symbolic level as such or deems it less important because he already finds the Impressionist painting technique in the Barbizon School with Daubigny, he also dispenses with discussing the individual artistic actors. Hence, the specific strategies to secure recognition, win over collectors and place works in museums are disregarded as well. In response to White (1993), one must therefore stress that worlds lie between the symbolic innovations of a Daubigny and a Manet, and that one must take into consideration considerable differences on the level of symbolic production between the Impressionists:

> The biggest break going through the group was the division between landscape and figure painters, or between colourists and draughtsmen. Monet clearly belonged to the former, Degas to the latter faction. And while Monet claimed to have no studio and always paint his pictures on location in response to motifs, Degas stresses that no art is less spontaneous than his, the result of reflecting on and studying the old masters. (Dippel, 2002: 12)

5   U = upper class, UM = upper middle class, MM = middle middle class, LM = lower middle class, L = lower class.

Sources of data columns a.-d.: Denvir (1993); Herbert (1998); Rewald (1961); Thomson (2000); White and White (1993); e.: Artfacts.Net (www.artfacts.net); f.: artprice.com (www.artprice.com); g.: MY Arts Inc. (www.productionmyarts.com/arts-et-marche/100-oeuvres-fr.htm)

PART TWO: PRECARIZATION

5

Virtuosos of Freedom: On the Implosion of Political Virtuosity and Productive Labour

Isabell Lorey
translated by Mary O'Neill

In his book, *A Grammar of the Multitude: For an Analysis of Contemporary Forms of Life*, published in German in 2005 as *Grammatik der Multitude: Öffentlichkeit, Intellekt und Arbeit*,[1] Paolo Virno, the Italian philosopher, formulates the following thesis:

> I believe that in today's forms of life[2] one has a direct perception of the fact that the coupling of the terms public-private, as well as the coupling of the terms collective-individual, can no longer stand up on their own, that they are gasping for air, burning themselves out. (Virno, 2004: 24)

The phenomenon, in which Virno examines the indistinguishability between both collective and individual, and public and private experience, is what we know as current 'post-Fordist' forms of production. By this he means more than labor in the traditional sense, that is as a productive activity; it is rather, as he says: 'a composite unity of forms of life' (2004: 49). He concerns himself with the hegemonizing of forms of production based on communicative and cognitive competences, on greater flexibility in the deployment of labor power – on the permanent reaction, therefore, to the unforeseen. Under such forms of production, the person as a whole becomes better: his/her personality, intellect, thinking, linguistic competence and emotions are stretched. According to Virno, that leads to the end of labor divisions (in the sense of the division of labor) and to considerable personal dependencies; not so much on rules and regulations, it is true, but on individual people both in the labor relationship but also in the context of networks, in order to move on to the next job as the need arises. We may refer to these living and working conditions as 'precarization'. However, in this chapter – and in contrast to Virno – the concept of 'virtuosos' does not apply to all the very diverse precarious conditions, but is restricted to cultural producers, whose function is neither avant-garde nor a paradigm for all precarious workers.[3]

Virno describes the implosion of the socio-economic spheres of private and public, of the individual and the collective in relation to the Aristotelian tripartite division of human experience into Labor (*poiesis*), Intellect (the life of the mind) and Political Action (*praxis*) (Arendt, 1998). Despite occasional possibilities for overlap, he maintains, the three areas have until now been presented mostly as being separate from one another: in this schema, labor means the production of new objects in a repetitive, foreseeable process. Set against this is the second area, that of the intellect, isolated and invisible by its very nature, since the thinker's meditation eludes the gaze of others. Finally, the third area of human experience, the area of political action, affects social relations, thereby differing from the sphere of labor, which affects natural materials through repetitive processes. What is remarkable here is that political action, in this sense, has to do with the possible and the unforeseen: it produces no objects but it changes through communication (Virno, 2004: 50ff.). Only political action is considered public in this partitioning since, to borrow Hannah Arendt's phrase, it means 'being exposed to the presence of others' (Arendt, 1998: 132).

Despite frequent criticism of the inappropriateness of this Aristotelian model for the present, this tripartite division of labor, intellect and political action is still very much in circulation. This, according to Virno, stems not least from Arendt's considerable influence. Yet she too speaks of the indistinguishability of the three spheres – rather like Virno, interestingly, in relation to virtuosity, to a particular sense of creativity. In her book, *Between Past and Future* (1977), she compares the leading artists, the virtuosos, with those who are politically active, those who in her view act politically, who are exposed to the presence of others. For with these performing artists, Arendt writes,

> the accomplishment lies in the performance itself and not in an end product which outlasts the activity that brought it into existence and becomes independent of it. [....] The performing arts [...] have indeed a strong affinity with politics. Performing artists-dancers, play-actors, musicians and the like – need an audience to show their virtuosity, just as acting men [and women] need the presence of others before whom they can appear; both need a publicly organized space for their 'work', and both depend upon others for the performance itself. (Arendt, 1977: 153-4)

For Arendt, politics is therefore an art of performance, a performative art. Because of the need for an audience, for the 'exposure to the presence of others', both politics and virtuosity need a 'a space of appearances'. And, as Arendt writes, 'whatever occurs in this space of appearances is political by definition, even when it is not a direct product of action' (1977: 155). With the added qualification, 'even when it is not a direct product of action', one may conclude that 'all virtuosity is intrinsically political'.[4]

In the same text, immediately after stressing how interwoven virtuosity and politics are, Arendt writes emphatically about freedom. Virno, however, makes no reference to it. And yet this nexus linking virtuosity and politics with freedom seems to me to be a central point.

The space of appearances, in other words, the political-public realm – and Arendt always sees the Greek *polis* in her mind's eye – is the place 'in which freedom can manifest itself'. 'Without such a space, established and equipped especially for it, freedom cannot be realized. There is no such thing as freedom without politics because it could not last' (Arendt, 1977: 153, 154). Arendt differentiates this concept of freedom from the freedom of thought and will. She sees the latter in particular as an egocentric burden from Christianity. For her, on the other hand, it is about a political freedom, which has broken away and differentiated itself from the private, from the 'concern about one's life' (1977: 153): it is about a freedom in the public sphere, a freedom of action, not of will or thought. In her view, freedom of will is an apolitical freedom because it is 'capable of being experienced alone' and is 'independent of the multitude' (1977: 157).

Let us return now to Virno, who refers to Marx as well as Arendt to explain the current precarious forms of production and life. However, from his perspective, Marx recognizes the activity of performing artists (among whom he includes teachers, doctors, actors, orators and preachers) as 'labor without work' only, and draws an analogy between it and the activities of servants. Consequently, in Marx' terms, neither virtuosos nor servants produce a surplus value. For him, they both belong to the 'realm of non-productive activity' (Virno, 2004: 54). However, Marx should not be accused of banishing cultural producers in general to the realm of unproductive labor since he does not tie the distinction between productive and unproductive labor to the content of that labor. On the contrary,

> productive labor is to be a definition of labor that has absolutely nothing to do with the specific content of labor, its particular usefulness or the peculiar utility value in which it appears. (Marx, 1988: 113)[5]

Marx defines productive labor, rather, through a relationship: though not a relationship with money in general and with the question of whether an activity is performed for financial reward or for free. The only relationship that constitutes productive labor, for Marx, is the one with capital. 'Productive labor is exchanged directly for money as capital' and is therefore labor that 'sets the values it has created against the worker himself as capital' (Marx, 1988: 112). The service of a doctor as well as that of a cook signifies, on the other hand, an exchange of 'labor for money as money' and is therefore not considered productive (Marx, 1988: 116). Marx also clarifies the distinction between the two exchange relationships of labor, taking the example of a virtuoso performer:

> A singer, who can sing like a bird, is an unproductive worker. To the extent that she sells her song for money, she is a wage laborer or tradeswoman. But this same singer, engaged by an entrepreneur who has her sing in order to make money, is a productive worker since she directly produces capital. (Marx, 1988: 113)

But what happens when the singer becomes her own entrepreneur? Does the relationship between labor and capital implode in her? Should she, by Marx's reasoning, be described as 'unproductive' when she, in her artistic independence and with projects subject to time limits, takes not just her voice to market, but constantly sells her whole personality; when singing 'like a bird' serves to get her the next job? Acting simultaneously as service providers, producers and entrepreneurs of themselves, don't today's cultural producers stand directly opposed to themselves as capitalized life forms in the values they have created, in a manner that resembles and yet is totally different from, the relationship that Marx defined as 'productive labor'?

Virno too concludes that, in post-Fordism, in the era of cognitive capitalism,[6] Arendt's classifications no longer apply and Marx's apparatus clearly does not seem adequate as a means of understanding contemporary forms of production and their related life forms. For these become intensified in new relationships, where

> productive labor as a whole has adopted the particular characteristics of the artistic performing activity. Whoever produces surplus value in post-Fordism behaves – seen from a structuralist standpoint, of course – like a pianist, a dancer, etc. (Virno, 2004: 154-5)

Thus, virtuosity structures, in a way that differs from Arendt's formulation, not just political action but, increasingly, new immaterial labor relations based on a broad concept of creativity, which can by no means be considered 'unproductive'. Against the background of Aristotle's and Arendt's tripartite model, the increasing indistinguishability between productive labor and immaterial, creative activity means that such a virtuoso behaves 'like a political being as a result of this' (Virno, 2004: 55, translation modified). It means, clearly, that the separation into *poiesis*, intellect and political *praxis*, and Marx's distinction between productive and unproductive labor can no longer be sustained. Such a declaration of 'indistinguishability' ought to be understood less as a catastrophic scenario, in Giorgio Agamben's sense of the term, than as the need to develop more appropriate analytical and political conceptualizations.

Let us continue with Virno's thesis that the creative workers who are, in the classical sense, political beings since their labor has 'absorbed into itself many of the typical characteristics of political action' (Virno, 2004: 51, translation modified). This does not mean, however, that increasing virtuosic living and working conditions have resulted in increased politicization. On the contrary, the present day has revealed instead a 'crisis of politics' (Virno, 2004: 51). What is inherently attractive in politics has long been present in post-Fordist labor conditions and, as a result, the subjects within them are not over-politicized; they are instead 'de-politicized' (Virno, 2004: 51). In turn, to the extent that the subjects become depoliticized, 'contemporary production [becomes] "virtuosic" (and thus political)' (Virno, 2004: 51, translation modified). Thus too, when labor often transforms both into intellectual and service labor, and simultaneously into a means towards self-enterprise, intellect coincides to a greater extent with the sphere of labor, which is in turn no longer distinguishable from the classical political praxis. But when labor becomes political in this way, the classical sphere of political action – the public space – also changes. This latter is then constantly created as virtuoso. To put it another way, a permanent re-creation of the public space occurs: because 'exposure to the presence of others', fundamental to Arendt's concept of the public, has evolved into one of the most crucial features of virtuoso working and living conditions. The 'presence of the others' has become both an instrument and an object of labor. Moreover, according to Virno, current modes of production and living are based, in their political virtuosity, on the art of the possible and the experience of handling the unexpected.[7]

What this then means for the increasingly impossible demarcations between public and private as well as between production and reproduction, I would like to develop in the following discussion, by taking the example of specific cultural producers, meaning those on whom precarious living and working conditions are not only imposed but who actively desire them and above all understand them as a free and autonomous decision.[8]

The virtuosos I refer to in what follows are by no means restricted to the artistic field. They can include academics or media representatives, for example. They are engaged in extremely diverse, unequally paid project activities and fee-paying jobs, and consider themselves entirely critical of society. Sometimes they do not want a steady job at all; sometimes they know it is something they can only dream about. Yet such cultural producers start from the assumption that they have chosen their living and working conditions themselves, precisely to ensure that they develop the essence of their being to the maximum in a relatively free and autonomous manner. In the case of such virtuosos, I refer to self-precarization.

The interpellation to self-precarization belongs to an elementary governing technique of modern societies and is not an entirely new neoliberal or post-Fordist phenomenon. Already, with the demand to orient oneself towards the normal as part of the modern trend, everyone had to develop a relationship with the self, to control one's own body, one's own life by regulating and thus controlling oneself. Inseparable from this self-conduct are ideas of actuality. Thus, for example, we still believe that the effect of power relations is the very essence of ourselves, our truth, our own actual core. This normalizing self-regulation is based on an imagined coherence, unity and wholeness, which can be traced back to the construction of a male, white, bourgeois subject. Coherence, once again, is one of the prerequisites for the modern, sovereign subject. These imagined, inner, natural 'truths', these constructions of actuality still foster ideas of being able or having to shape one's life freely and autonomously, and according to one's own decisions. These types of power relations are therefore not easy to discern since they often appear as a free decision of one's own, as a personal insight and then trigger the desire to ask: 'Who am I?' or 'How can I fulfill myself?' The concept of 'personal responsibility', so commonly used in the course of neoliberal restructuring, only operates above this old liberal technique of self-regulation.

Basically, governmental self-regulation, this sovereignty at the subject level, takes place in an apparent paradox since this modern self-regulation means both subjugation and empowerment. Only in this ambivalent structure of subjectivation that – in all its diversity in the individual – was fundamental both in private as well as in the public sphere, both in the family and in the factory or in politics, only in this paradoxical subjectivation does the governability of the modern subject occur. The freedom to shape one's own life, however, was an essential constitutive element of this supposed paradox between regulation and empowerment.

In liberalism, this normalized sovereign male-white subjectivation needed the construction of the abnormal and deviant Other, in this case the marginalized precarious worker. In neoliberalism, the function of the precarious worker now shifts towards the centre of society and becomes normalized. Thus the function of bourgeois freedom can also be transformed: away from the separation of precarious others and towards the subjectivizing function in normalized precarization.

Current living and working conditions refer not least to a genealogy of the social movements since the sixties. The thoroughly dissident practices of alternative ways of life, the desires for different bodies and self-relations (in feminist, ecological, radical-left contexts) constantly sought to distinguish themselves from normal working conditions and their associated constraints, disciplinary measures and controls. The conscious, voluntary acceptance of precarious employment conditions was also generally the expression of a need to overcome the modern, patriarchal division in reproduction and wage labor.

In recent years, however, it is precisely these alternative living and working conditions that have become increasingly economically utilizable because they favor the flexibilization demanded by the labor market. Thus the practices and discourses of social movements in the past thirty or forty years were not only dissident and directed against normalization, but were also simultaneously part of the transformation towards a neoliberal form of governmentality.

On the level of subjectivation, it is increasingly clear that at present alternative living and working conditions have by and large not freed themselves from the structure of a traditional, bourgeois-white-male mode of subjectivation. The ambivalence between a specific bourgeois idea of freedom on the one hand, and (self-)regulation and subjugation on the other is far from removed.

The present virtuosos of this ambivalence may be further described within a few parameters: they pursue temporary jobs, make their living on projects and from contract work from several clients simultaneously and from consecutive clients, mostly without any sick pay, paid holiday leave or unemployment compensation, without protection against wrongful dismissal – basically with minimal social protection or none whatsoever. Most do not have children. There is no longer any dividing line between leisure time and work. There is an accumulation of knowledge during the unpaid hours that is not remunerated separately, but which is naturally called on and used in the context of paid work. Constant communication via networks is vital for survival. Quite a few of them regard themselves as left wing and critical of capitalism.

But the practices we are concerned with here are linked with desire as well as conformity. For, again and again, these modes of existence are constantly foreseen and co-produced in anticipatory obedience. The unpaid or low-paid jobs, in the cultural or academic industries for instance, are all too often accepted as an unalterable fact; nothing else is even demanded. Conditions of inequality often go un-remarked. The need to pursue other, less creative, precarious jobs to finance one's own cultural production is something one puts up with. This financing of one's own creative output, enforced and yet opted for at the same time, constantly supports and reproduces the very conditions in which one suffers and which one at the same time wants to be part of. It is perhaps because of this that creative workers, these voluntarily precarized virtuosos, are subjects so easily exploited; they seem able to tolerate their living and working conditions with infinite patience because of the belief in their own freedoms and autonomies, and because of the fantasies of self-realization. In a neoliberal context, they are so exploitable that, now, it is no longer just the state that presents them as role models for new modes of living and working.

Experiences of anxiety and loss of control, feelings of insecurity as well as the fear and the actual experience of failure, a drop in social status and poverty are linked with this state of self-precarization. It is for this reason too that 'letting go' or other forms of dropping out of or shedding the hegemonic paradigm are difficult. You have to stay 'on speed' or else you could be eliminated. You always feel threatened. There is no clear time for relaxation and recuperation. Then the desire to relax and 'find oneself' becomes insatiable. Such reproductive practices usually have to be learned all over again. They are no longer the most natural thing in the world and have to be fought for, bitterly, in a struggle with oneself and others. This in turn is what makes the longing for reproduction, for regeneration, so hugely marketable.

In the current context of precarious, largely immaterial and mostly individualized labor and a 'life' that mirrors it, the function of reproduction also changes as a consequence. It is no longer externalized with others, primarily women. Individual reproduction and sexual reproduction, the production of life, now become individualized and are shifted in part 'into' the subjects themselves. It is about regeneration beyond work, also through work, but still very often beyond adequately remunerated wage labor. It is about (self-) renewal, creating from oneself, recreating oneself through one's own power: of one's own accord. Self-realization becomes a reproductive task for the self. Work is meant to ensure the reproduction of the self.

Following Virno, one may conclude that the separation between public and private is imploding not alone in a newly depoliticized public sphere, a 'publicness without a public sphere' (Virno, 2004: 40). A further separation reinforces this implosion: the one between production and reproduction in the modes of subjectivation described.

At the same time, and in parallel, the traditional social and economic spheres continue to exist, together with gender-specific segmentation.

This subjectivation, which one cannot really differentiate structurally according to gender,[9] is evidently contradictory because of the implosions: in the simultaneity of precarization on the one hand – linked with fear, with the feeling of vulnerability and fragmentation – and with the continuity of sovereignty, on the other. This continuity of modern sovereign subjectivation takes place through the stylizing of self-realization, autonomy and freedom, through the shaping of the self, personal responsibility and the repetition of the idea of actuality. In general, this sovereignty appears to be based, in the first instance, on the 'free' decision for self-precarization.

However, that could be a key reason why it is so difficult to see structural precarization as a neoliberal, governmental phenomenon that affects society as a whole, and which is really not based on any free decision; why critique of it is still rare; and why a counter-behaviour is still largely absent. In this case, the new public sphere is a space for opportunism and conformity.

Even with Hannah Arendt, whose analyses clearly do not seem relevant for the current economic and social processes of transformation, the fantasies of self-chosen freedom and autonomy presented here are open to criticism. For they come very close to Arendt's concept of 'freedom of will' and its opposite of 'political freedom'. If 'the ideal of freedom (…) has shifted from the power to act to the desire to act', then it can 'no longer be the virtuosity of common action, the ideal was rather sovereignty, independence from everyone else and, if necessary, self-assertion against them' (Arendt, 1977: 153). Political freedom functions, however, only 'in the condition of non-sovereignty' (Arendt, 1977: 154).

Instead of reflecting on their own involvement in the context of precarization, discussions frequently take place in left-wing circles about who still belongs and who no longer does, who is the subject of precarious poverty as opposed to precarious luxury. It still seems indispensable, first and foremost, to specify the collective to be politicized, which is invariably other people. Indeed I think that, as long as one's own self-precarization and the fantasies around it, operate beyond the mainstream, the bourgeoisie or wherever else, precisely because their own ideas of freedom and autonomy are valid in that particular niche, it will be impossible, both theoretically and politically, to understand how a subjectivation that is optimally governable in structural terms evolves through self-chosen living and working conditions – which is none other than a voluntary submission to neoliberal, governmental forms of regulation.

If one follows Virno's thesis about the implosion of the Aristotle-Arendt tripartite division, then one must also thematize a crisis in leftist politics. Should we not then be asking the following questions: are new public spheres constantly evolving through unreflective self-precarization; are the separations between private and public, between labor and production in one's own subjectivation being dissolved; yet is it not in this very same process, as Virno maintains, that depoliticized subjects emerge?

Notes

1   This is the subtitle ('Public Space, Intellect and Labour') of Klaus Neundlinger's translation (Virno, 2005a), which is the source for citations in this chapter. A second German version, translated by Thomas Atzert (Virno 2005b) renders the subtitle *Untersuchungen zu gegenwärtigen Lebensformen*, a formulation closer to the English translation (Virno, 2004).

2   Translator's note: This is to be understood as a reference to 'today's forms of production'.

3   The term 'cultural producers' is used as a paradox here. It refers to an imagined version of the designated subjects: that of their own autonomous production and of the shaping of their selves. At the same time, however, it deals with the fact that these modes of subjectivation are instruments of governing and thus functional effects of western modernity's biopolitically governmental societies. Consequently, the meaning of the term 'cultural producers' is contradictory, lacking in coherence. The term does not primarily denote artists. For a more detailed discussion, see Lorey, 2009.

4   Arendt, as cited by Virno, 2004: 53. In order to depoliticize the performing art activity as a virtuoso, one must therefore create lasting, durable products. This is the sense in which Virno's Glenn Gould example should be read.

5   I wish to thank Karl Reitter for this reference.

6   See Corsani, 2004.

7   See also Virno, 2003.

8   For a more detailed discussion on this, see Lorey, 2007: 121-36.

9 This is certainly due in no small part to the fact that the virtuosos discussed here do not have children. One reason for this is their precarization despite self-exploitation and imagined self-realization. The socially structuring lines of separation do not significantly follow gender lines here. For a discussion of how this changes with the 'additional condition of motherhood' or 'duties of care that are still linked with femininity', see Voß and Weiß, 2005: 65-91. On the neoliberal restructuring of gender relations between 're-traditionalization trends' and 'flexibilized gender image(s)', see Pühl and Sauer, 2004: 165-79.

6

Experiences without Me, or, the Uncanny Grin of Precarity

Brigitta Kuster and Vassilis Tsianos
translated by Aileen Derieg

I.

We will start with a story that many probably have experienced already in much the same way.[1] It relates to the production of social meaning through forms of address.[2] A person applies as a freelancer for a job as proofreader for a publication. The person does not know those offering the contract, but the job has been passed on through networks of various personal contacts, so this person makes a phone call and speaks with a representative of the editorial team for a publication on an academic conference, of whom it may be assumed that this is not the person to make the final decision, and offers her work. She introduces herself and addresses this representative informally. The response from the other side is a moment of hesitation, after which the respondent takes a breath and answers with a formal mode of address. The moment of a brief communication crisis arises, but our applicant quickly assesses the situation and switches – naturally without making an issue of it – to formal address. She thus subordinates herself to her conversation partner, who has taken a position of distance through the mode of address. With the informal mode of address, the freelancer's offer anticipated, one could say, the resource of trust, the portion of the informality of the work she was applying for, which in her experience represents a conventional requirement of these kinds of jobs. What she was to supply is a non-standardizable final product, because no one will be able to check whether she has done the editing well. What distinguishes her as a 'good worker', in comparison, although this will be evident, at most, in a future, reactivated working relationship, is that she does the job in a way that could be described from the perspective of her employer as trustworthy and skillful self-responsibility. The aspiration to equality with a potential contract employer, which this contractor activates through the mode of address, represents an almost essential precondition for the manner in which the work of single persons within the project framework, in which mostly knowledge and cultural workers are active, becomes productive. In fact, the working conditions in these areas presuppose a more casual relationship between non-designated production and standardized forms of utilization as 'normal': individuals are knowledgeable and active in the areas in which their labor is utilized at certain times.

The crucial negotiation between the informal and the formal modes of address is what struck us as interesting in this story. It indicates the instability, the flexibility, the mutability, but also the risk of a 'false', inappropriate or possibly ineffective mode of address, from which there seems to be no escape. This is specifically because it also always simultaneously indicates both the intactness of the social places and relations offered by this mode of address and that it is no longer possible to operate solely with these social places and relations with these work requirements: an informal mode of address among equals or an informal mode of address directed upward and marking a challenge – and opposite to this a formal mode of address in a certain or indeterminate social situation enabling a radical difference among equals. Someone can address me formally and indicate specifically in this way that they are indeed the boss.

The rejection of being addressed formally by a boss and in its place the attempt to generalize an informal mode of address as an addressability among equals, which characterizes our freelancer, could be taken in an expanded narrative context of the story of modes of address in work situations as a criticism of the rigid hierarchies of Fordism and the places they offered in institutions of so-called normal working and living conditions. The informal mode of address as a type of behavior relating to the production conditions has meanwhile largely become established in cultural or knowledge production. The institutions in this field themselves, however, appear to be oddly unaffected by this. In terms of her authority, for instance to sign a work or fee contract, the formality of the response of the representative of the editorial team on the telephone, speaking with the voice of an institutional place, did not, in fact, occupy this place at all. The informal mode of address, according to our thesis, characterizes a new paradigm of productivity, but one which, on the other hand, does not have an external relationship to the institutions: the demands on the skills and abilities of the subjects are immediate and equal; they are the person addressed informally and hence also represent 'more' than what is expected from a person addressed formally.

In a sense, the performative 'informal address' of our freelancer holds aspects of what could be called an instituent practice, where the level of recognition does not consist of the prospect of a place (in an institution), but rather a recognition 'as an equal' through an increase in productivity and the activation of the abilities employed – as the freelancer is contacted again, for instance, or recommended somewhere else, thus circulating in the network of contracts as a potentiality that can be actualized at any time. It is at the point of this potentiality where the implicit threat also starts, which resonates in the communication crisis between the informal and the formal mode of address or in the distancing formal mode: it already articulates the possibility of exclusion – specifically at the level of no longer appearing as one informally addressed – from a future past that defines the present. Inherent to the instituent practice of our freelancer are thus not only traits of productivity, assets and promise, but also the creased brow of a fear that stems from the search for a protective closeness in being informally addressed.

So if we develop the thesis with this story that a kind of formula of the crisis of subjectivation in precarity is evident within the intact and simultaneous appellations as one informally addressed and/or formally addressed, then the question of the location of instituent practices cannot choose between self-precarization or self-exploitation on the one side and possible resistive or even affirmative forms of self-institution on the other, but must instead address exactly the arrangement that covers the informal appellation and the formal appellation equally and enables a compulsively desiring subjectivation in precarization.

II.

Spinoza could be suspected of anticipating precarity when he thinks of the addressability of the subject as an attributability, which can prove to be a pleasure as well as a pain; they are emotions that are both equally indeterminate on the one hand and tied on the other to the project that the subject adheres to. With Spinoza we can imagine the same origins of hope and fear in precarity as a social pulsing of the relationship between pleasure and pain:

> Hope is an inconstant pleasure, arising from the idea of something past or future, whereof we to a certain extent doubt the issue. Fear is an inconstant pain, arising from the idea of something past or future, whereof we to a certain extent doubt the issue. (Spinoza, 1883)

Our idea here is to grasp precarity as an outrageous indeterminacy, in other words as the wavering of the affection between the familiar, informal addressee of a possible pleasure in the future and/or past of equals, and a pain, always brought about through this same past or anticipated future, over the formal mode of address as a moment of fear that grips the one informally addressed. The latter's pleasure, however, has long since been inscribed in the production paradigm of post-Fordism. Less attention, though, has been given to her pain and its productive inscription. It may be observed that this pain is immediately coded out or recoded as a pleasure. Pain is the compulsion to make pleasure capable of being articulated, being utilized and distinguished, and even to increase it. It is something like being overcome with doubt about the good issue of something that I can nevertheless not avoid pursuing. It is as when something that I do with pleasure is not commensurately honored, and I do it despite that as though it were being commensurately honored, because I do not have the nerve to articulate the conflict. In some mysterious way, it seems that the pain irritatingly accompanies production processes of subjective labor. What is vacillating, indeterminate about precarity is, in our opinion, linked with a politics of pain, even fear, which reveals itself as the debate about security: what is scandalous about precarization, according to most critical discourses, is found in the absence of guarantees for places. This form of criticism is a disambiguation – informal or formal mode of address – because it reduces the indeterminacy. We also argue in favor of a determination, a disambiguation, but in the exactly opposite direction of scandalization. It relates less to the pain, in other words the anxious concern for security, but more to the pleasure that paves an insecure path with fear. Because we think that fear, seen in the context of security, generates more fear.

Back to Spinoza, who was no melancholic and thought of the indeterminacy of the emotion, of pleasure and pain, in modalities of time:

> However, as it generally happens that those, who have had many experiences, vacillate, so long as they regard a thing as future or past, and are usually in doubt about its issue [who are in other words exactly there, where our experience with precarization currently is] it follows that the emotions which arise from similar images of things are not so constant, but are generally disturbed by the images of other things [perhaps the images of furnishings that would make the indeterminate space of precarization more inhabitable], until men become assured of the issue. (Spinoza, 1883)

III.

Taking recourse to the distinctions between fear and anguish in Kant and Heidegger's works, Paolo Virno develops the thesis that the difference proposed by these authors between a specific, socially immanent fear of something and an absolute anguish that accompanies being-in-the-world is currently vanishing, because experience in post-Fordism is coupled with a changed dialectic of fear and security, as Virno says. He identifies indicators of this transformation in the fusion of fear and anguish into a fear that 'is always anguish-ridden' and in a life that assumes 'many of the traits which formerly belonged to the kind of terror one feels outside the walls of the community' (Virno, 2004: 33).

A virtually mythic image of fear is presented in the film *The Village*, by M. Night Shyamalan. The film is about the village of Covington in an indistinct period, which is reminiscent, however, of the early US American colonial period in its atmosphere. In the middle of a forest, cut off from possible other villages or inhabited zones, a community live a simple, autarkic life. On the basis of this film we want to take a closer look at the fusion of fear and anguish, specifically as a differentiation of the way in which fear and anguish reluctantly conjoin in various moments of the transformation of the sociality of this village.

The rules in the village are reproduced through the fear of the inhabitants of the forest surrounding the village, called only 'those we do not speak of'. They are the threatening outside of the community, with which a pact has been made: as long as no villager enters the forest, 'those we do not speak of' will not attack the village. The village recognizes social forms of care, ways of dealing with fear, but also the subjectivation of courage, as when the young men standing with their backs to the edge of the forest open their arms. The first dramatic turn of the film then consists of the emergence of fearlessness, yet it does not grow out of some kind of a violation of the rules, but rather out of their subjective embodiment, which only just misses them.

Lucius Hunt is a member of the village who even goes beyond the mere fulfillment of these rules. He is so much and so seriously preoccupied with them that it leads to his wish to leave the village, to overcome the limitations of the community. The argument for this that he presents to the ruling council of elders is the vulnerability within the community. He states that he wants to obtain medication from the city beyond the forest to heal another member of the village, Noah Percy. His wish qualifies the boundary to the forest as an instable one. Lucius is fearless in this respect, because he believes that by embodying the rules immanent to the community he can counteract the fear, that he can be 'pure' and invulnerable.

The second figure of fearlessness is Noah. The proposed healing is intended for him. However, he is not actually depicted as sick, but rather as someone who is 'different', as someone who, for some undefined reason, embodies and lays bare what is monstrous about the rules. Unlike all the others, he does not fear 'those we do not speak of', but seems instead to await their arrival. The color red is a forbidden code, the color of 'those we do not speak of'. Everything that has to do with this color is carefully avoided in the village, because according to the rule it attracts 'those we do not speak of'; the color yellow, on the other hand, has a protective effect. Noah wanders through the area between the village and the forest collecting red berries, which he enjoys carrying secretly around with him, even in the village. He laughs with delight when the others tremble.

The third figure of fearlessness is Ivy, the daughter of the head of the village. She is blind, but she can feel colors. She has a view of that which remains hidden. She surmises, 'Sometimes we don't do things we would like to do, so that others don't know that we would like to do them'.

The exposé of the film, which follows these different embodiments of fearlessness, shows that the politics of fear do not at all function smoothly. Fearlessness is the intimate tie that binds Lucius, Noah and Ivy. It is restless and timid, yet it creates no fear. All three of these figures are potential violators of the boundary, but they do not attack the matrix of the village. The second dramatic turn comes with an interruption when something happens. It consists of a re-territorialization of the intimacy of the bond between the three figures: three become two with the announcement of the marriage between Lucius and Ivy. It describes the moment when Noah realizes that he will then be alone with his matrix of fearlessness. He tries to kill Lucius with a knife. Due to Lucius' life-threatening injury it is Ivy who sees herself forced to continue his project of leaving the village in a different way. She wants to go away so that Lucius can be healed with medicine. The circumstances of her leaving have nothing to do with either exodus or the wish to evade being inscribed in the community of the village, nor with what is attributed to Noah. Her project is functional and it is formed step by step by the events that have been set in motion. At this point it seems that the dramatic secret of the film and thus of the village community must be revealed. It is none other than Ivy's father, the head of the village, who is supposed to most strongly embody the principle of the isolation of the village, who is confronted with the failure of security – especially that of his daughter – that is ensured by the politics of fear. He sees himself forced to articulate to Ivy the terrible secret about 'those we do not speak of', so that she need not be afraid on her way to the city: 'those we do not speak of' do not even exist, or rather they are red costumes worn by the members of the council of elders to frighten the others and prevent an exodus. Through her father's revelation Ivy becomes a subject of the knowledge of the initiated. And she is given safe directions for the path to the city. Her fearlessness is enlightened.

The third dramatic turn then relates to the appearance of anguish. Ivy finds herself in the forest according to all the rules of the plan – and she is approached by one of 'those we do not speak of', which do not exist, as she knows. She tells herself, this is not real. This is not fear, but anguish. And yet there is no other practice with regard to the non-real than a thoroughly real, haptic action. 'Being truly anguish-ridden', according to Virno, 'is just a certain way of confronting anguish' (2004: 35). She battles with the unspeakable, and falling into a hole it is fatally wounded. While Ivy was being initiated to make her way through the forest, by chance Noah discovered the red costume, with which he connects and becomes one of 'those we do not speak of' himself. He embodies the founding myth of the community, affirms its fear, becomes its fear. With it he has set off into the forest to meet Ivy. The impossibility for Ivy to be afraid at the moment of encountering the unspeakable, is frightening. From this point on, she no longer goes, she flees. Yet her flight is not simply a practice of anguish, but rather this is where fear and anguish fuse together. Although the directions are still valid, she follows them driven by anguish, fleeing. In Virno's terms this is precarity. For the fusion of fear and anguish he proposes the term uncanny.[3] With our film example we can see that this uncanny flight represents a weapon of precarity. Fleeing along the coded path, Ivy encounters a wall, the existence of which she was not informed of – a further limitation, but one that remains unfounded. Since fleeing enables her to break through this wall, she shakes the foundations of the outrageous indeterminacy of precarity, one could say. With this breakthrough the filmic narration of *The Village* disambiguates its indeterminacy and determines it as a temporal, chronological confusion: we find ourselves not in the nineteenth century of the village, but rather in the present day. The terrible truth is that the village is nothing other than a reservation founded for protection against violence and guarded by security personnel. This determination in the narration of the film finishes with a happy end. The thorn of the uncanny that Ivy's story of flight bears is pacified, the village's identity-founding politics of fear are maintained, the rules of the village community are reproduced at a new level. Yet one could also imagine the return to the village being accompanied by an uncanny smile or even grin on Ivy's face, in which the possibility of being something else begins to show.

Judith Butler, at the end of her text on *The Psychic Life of Power* (Butler, 1997), explores the boundaries of subjectivation. Discussing Giorgio Agamben, she raises the question of the lines of flight of desire, which remain at a distance from the determinations of being that entice identity. She is concerned with a willingness not to be, which can assume a form of linguistic survival to assure itself, as she says quoting Agamben:

> In fact there is something that human beings are and have to be, but
> that is not an essence and not a thing in the narrower sense: it is the

simple fact of one's own existence as a possibility or potentiality. (Butler, 1997: 131)

Butler inscribes a desire into this statement from Agamben with her commentary:

Here the assertion can be read into this that this possibility must dissolve into something, yet without being able to overcome its own status as a possibility with this kind of solution. (Butler, 1997: 131)

Notes

1   For inspiring discussion prior to this text, we would like to thank Efthimia Panagiotidis, Frank John and Isabell Lorey.

2   Translator's note: In German, as in other languages, the informal second person pronoun (*du*) is different from the formal second person pronoun (*Sie*). Even though this distinction is obscured by the undifferentiated second person pronoun in English ('you'), the same kind of negotiation still takes place in comparable contexts.

3   'We would need to find a new term here, different from 'fear' or 'anguish', a term which would take the fusion of these two terms into account. What comes to mind for me is the term uncanny. But it would take too much time here to justify the use of this term.' (Virno, 1994: 65-7)

7

Wit and Innovation

Paolo Virno
translated by Arianne Bové

The human animal is capable of changing forms of life and diverting from consolidated habits and rules.[1] We would go as far as to say that the human animal is 'creative', were this term not so equivocal. Put in this way, this is an indubitable observation, but far from a happy conclusion, it prompts all sorts of questions and doubts. Which elements of praxis and discourse give rise to unpredicted outcomes? How is a state of equilibrium broken? And finally, what makes an action innovative?

The tried and tested way of settling the discussion whilst appearing to fully engage with it demands that the term 'creativity' is employed in such broad terms that it becomes coextensive with 'human nature'. Thus we rapidly come to several reassuring tautologies: the human animal is supposedly capable of innovation because it enjoys the gift of verbal language, because it does not inhabit an invariable and delimited environment, or because it is historical; in short, the human animal can innovate because it is… a human animal. Applause and the curtain falls. This tautology eludes the most interesting and awkward issue: that transformative action is intermittent, rare even. To try to explain it by appealing to distinct features of our species is to bark up the wrong tree: these features are equally present when experience is uniform and repetitive.

According to Noam Chomsky, our language is 'constantly innovative' because it is independent from 'external stimuli or inner states' (and for other reasons that 1 won't recount here) (Chomsky, 1991: 6-7, 113-46). So far so good; however, why does this unremitting independence only occasionally give rise to unusual and unexpected verbal performances? It is no surprise that, having attributed it to language in general, that is, to human nature, Chomsky goes on to conclude that creativity is an unfathomable mystery. Another example of this can be found in philosophical anthropology. Arnold Gehlen claims that *homo sapiens* is an instinct forsaken animal continuously faced with an overabundance of stimuli that have no biological direction and whence no univocal behavior can derive: that is why his action, 'unfounded' as it is, can be nothing other than creative (Gehlen, 1985: 60-87). Yet this still fails to answer the crucial question: how is it that such overabundance of purposeless stimuli primarily produces stereotypical performances and only rarely gives rise to sudden innovation?

It is legitimate to deduce the conditions under which conduct can vary from some defining features of our species, but it would be a glaring mistake to identify these conditions of possibility with the particular logical-linguistic abilities used to actually modify a particular behavior. Between one and the other lies a hiatus: the same discrepancy that separates the a priori intuition of space from the inferences through which a geometrical theorem is formulated or understood.

Neither the independence of statements from 'external stimuli or inner states' (Chomsky) nor instinctual forsakenness (Gehlen) can explain why when asked 'How is it going?' by a blind man a lame man replies with a cutting and creative 'As you can see'. Chomsky and Gehlen only point to the reasons why the lame man can react this way to the blind man's involuntary provocation (besides many other less surprising ways: 'well, and you?', 'smashing!', 'could be worse'); they say nothing of the effective procedures that give rise to the unpredicted swerve in the dialogue. The logical and linguistic resources used by innovative action are more circumscribed and less generic than its conditions of possibility. Despite being a natural prerequisite of all human animals, only under certain critical circumstances do these resources get used and gain greater prominence. Such circumstances would be: when a form of life that once seemed incontrovertible begins to seem ill-fitting; when the distinction between 'grammatical' and 'empirical' realms (respectively, the rules of the game and the facts to which those rules should apply) becomes blurred; when, however fleetingly, human praxis runs up against that tight corner known by jurists as a state of exception.

To avoid the danger of tautology I propose a very limited, almost narrow, acceptation of 'creativity': the forms of verbal thought that allow for change in one's behaviour in an emergency situation. A tautological reference to 'human nature' explains neither the state of equilibrium, nor exodus from it. Vice versa an investigation into the logical and linguistic resources that only become prominent in crisis emphasizes the techniques of innovation as well as throwing a different light on repetitive behavior. Rather than the constitutive independence of verbal language from environmental and psychological conditioning, it is the unexpected joke of the lame man that clarifies salient characteristics of stereotypical responses that probability would have had as given. The suspension or change of a rule shows the often unperceived paradoxes and aporias that underlie its most blind and automatic application.

The following pages focus on wit in the belief that it provides an adequate empirical basis to understand how the linguistic animal occasionally imprints an unexpected deviation on its praxis. Moreover, wit seems to be a good example of the narrow acceptation of 'creativity': one that does not tautologically coincide with human nature as a whole, but is rather tried and tested exclusively in critical situations. The main textual reference is to Freud's essay *Der Witz* (1960, first published in 1905); to my knowledge there is no other significant attempt to chart a detailed, botanical, so to speak, taxonomy of different kinds of witticism. The profound commitment of the author to clearly identify the rhetorical devices and patterns of reason behind the occurrence of the scathing joke is notorious. I must warn the reader that my interpretation of the material gathered and reviewed by Freud is rigorously non-Freudian. Rather than focusing on its affinity with the labor of dreams and the functioning of the subconscious, I would like to highlight the tight connection between wit and praxis in the public sphere. It should not come as a surprise that in regard to successful witticism I am going to say nothing about dreams and much about *phronesis*, which is the practical shrewdness and sense of measure that guides an agent in the absence of a network of protection from his fellow beings.

Wit is the diagram of innovative action. Along with Peirce and mathematicians, I intend diagram to be the sign that reproduces a miniature version of the structure and internal proportions of a given phenomenon (like an equation or a geographical map). Wit is the logical and linguistic diagram of enterprises that interrupt the circular flow of experience in situations of historical or biographical crisis. It is the microcosm inside which we can neatly discern changes in the direction of arguments and shifts in meaning, that in the macrocosm of human praxis cause a variation in a form of life. In short: wit is a circumscribed linguistic game with its peculiar techniques and its eminent function is to exhibit the transformability of all linguistic games.

This general premise is articulated in two subordinate hypotheses that we ought to state now. Here is the first. Wit has much to do with one of the most insidious problems of linguistic praxis: how to apply a rule to a particular case. In fact, it has to do with insidiousness, the difficulties and uncertainties that sometimes arise at the moment of its application. Wit constantly demonstrates that there are many different and even contrasting ways to comply with the same norm. But it is the divergences arising through the application of a rule that often provoke a drastic change of the latter.

Far from being situated above or outside of norms, human creativity is even sub-normative: it manifests itself uniquely in the lateral and improper paths that we happen to inaugurate when trying to keep to a determined norm. Paradoxical as it may seem, the state of exception originally resides in the only apparently obvious activity that Wittgenstein names 'rule-following'. This entails that every humble application of a rule always contains in itself a fragment of a 'state of exception'. Wit brings this fragment to light.

The second subordinate hypothesis is that the logical form of wit consists in an argumentative fallacy; that is, an undue inference or an incorrect use of a semantic ambiguity. For instance: the attribution to a grammatical subject of all the properties of its predicate, the swapping of the part for the whole or the whole for the part, the institution of a symmetrical relation between antecedent and consequent, the treatment of a meta-linguistic expression as if it was in language-object. To say it in other words, there is a punctual and meticulous correspondence between the different types of wit catalogued by Freud and the paralogisms studied by Aristotle in his *On Sophistical Refutations*. In the case of wit, argumentative fallacies reveal a productive character; they are useful to something and indispensable mechanisms for verbal action that produces 'bewilderment and illumination', surprise and enlightenment (Freud, 1960: 11-14). Here a delicate question arises:

whilst it is true that wit is the diagram of innovative action, we need to presuppose that its logical form, that is the fallacy, has an important role in so far as it changes one's mode of living. However, isn't it bizarre to ground the creativity of *homo sapiens* on reasoning in vicious circles and error? Of course it is bizarre and worse even. But it would be foolish to believe that someone is so foolish to warmly support such a hypothesis. The really interesting point is to understand the circumstances and conditions where a paralogism ceases to be a paralogism, that is, where it can no longer be considered mistaken or false (in logical terms). It follows that only under these circumstances and in these conditions the 'fallacy' becomes an indispensable source of innovation.

Notes

1   This chapter is a translation of the 'Prologue' to Virno, 2005c.

PART THREE: CREATIVITY INDUSTRIES

8

GovernCreativity, or, Creative Industries Austrian Style

Monika Mokre
translated by Aileen Derieg

As in more or less every country – and especially every big city – between Finland and India, the 'creative industries' (hereafter 'CI') have been a big issue in Austrian cultural and economic policy for the last decade. This new interest in the CI can be seen as a result both of international developments and of national specifics.

Internationally, we could observe the commercialization of culture and the arts since the 1980s when festivals and popular exhibitions became an important part of cultural politics. This development was complemented by debates on the economic impact of creativity in the 1990s.

The specific hype around the CI in Austria, however, was closely related to the change of government in 2000, when the Social-Democratic Party failed to become part of the Austrian government for the first time since 1970. Instead, the conservative People's Party formed a coalition with the radical right-wing Austrian Freedom Party. This change led in turn to broader changes in Austrian politics that can be summarized – rather polemically – as the rise of neoliberal economic concepts in combination with a considerable increase of repression towards critical political forces, not least of all in the arts. The conservative/right wing government was replaced in 2006 by a coalition of the Social-Democrats and the Conservatives. However, the focus on the CI as well as the disregard of contemporary critical art remained part of Austrian cultural politics. And the Social-Democratic municipal government of Vienna has been at least as active in the field of the CI as the national government. Still – and although phrases of the kind 'what would have happened if?' are among the most senseless in historical analyses – I think it plausible that the predominance of the CI in Austrian cultural politics is, to a high degree, caused by the general change of political aims that started in 2000, as this change was both an effect of the international hegemony of neoliberal political concepts and one of the causes for their success in Austria.

The forms of CI hype are well known, since they are more or less the same everywhere:

- Narratives about the CI begin with the trivial assumption that creativity is an important economic factor.
- Afterwards, definitions of the CI are delivered that are too broad to be really classified as definitions.
- On the basis of these definitions statistical data prove that the CI are (1) a crucial economic sector with (2) virtually limitless future possibilities.
- Then we usually find the assumption, shared by more or less all countries and cities focusing their attention on the CI, that the country or city in question has especially favorable conditions for this sector, although specific policy measures are necessary in order to further improve the situation.
- Finally, consequential positive prospects for employment, economic growth and success in international competition are described. And if working conditions in the CI are mentioned at all, profits and work satisfaction for those working in the creative industries are promised.

However, these international developments and assumptions overlap with specific national situations, and it is out of the combination of these two factors that concrete conditions for the CI develop. Let me therefore briefly describe crucial factors of the Austrian 'culture of cultural politics'.

Austrian Cultural Policy

For a long time, it was something like an Austrian truism that culture and the arts are a public responsibility and should therefore be largely publicly funded. The roots of this specific relationship between politics and the arts can be traced back to the eighteenth century and thus to the Austro-Hungarian monarchy. The prosperity of the Habsburg territories was an important reason for the flourishing of the arts as well as for their dependence on state support, but generous public support for culture and the arts has survived the end of the monarchy. It is also a legacy of the Habsburgs that the lion's share of public funds for the arts is centrally distributed, that is by the Republic of Austria. Furthermore, the strong dependence of cultural and artistic institutions as well as individual artists on the state led to an equally strong state influence on cultural activities. In short, it may therefore be stated that, up to the late twentieth century, Austrian cultural policy was marked by the centralist and absolutist power of the Habsburgs. In accordance with this tradition, most public funding for culture and the arts went (and still goes) to the cultural heritage – including historical buildings, museums and the performing arts institutions that developed into high art. And it should also be mentioned that, overall, public financing for culture and the arts in Austria is still very generous in comparison to many other European countries.

However, this longstanding tradition has also been subject to changes. Above all, in the aftermath of the political movement of 1968 (and at the beginning of the government of the Social Democrats without coalition partners) cultural policy began to recognize and also to finance more contemporary art forms and projects. In comparison to the funds for the cultural heritage, public financing for contemporary projects has always been peanuts; still, it was enough to bring about a certain dynamic in the artistic and cultural scene in Austria.

The support for contemporary art by the Social Democrats came out of a certain political sympathy with the respective artists and art forms as well as a need to contest the conservative cultural hegemony in Austria. However, it always remained half-hearted and without a real cultural political program. The programmatic understanding of cultural politics was mainly a by-product of the general welfare orientation of Social Democratic government summarized in the slogan: 'Cultural policy has to be understood as part of social policy.' Most of all, this statement included a mission to open high culture to the lower classes – as audiences, not as producers. In this way, a traditional understanding of the educational impact of high culture was combined with the egalitarian claim of Social Democracy. And it needed only a very slight change of focus to transform this egalitarian claim into the call for commercialization in the 1980s: The claim that the uneducated masses should learn to appreciate the high arts was changed into the claim that the arts should meet the taste of potential consumers of the arts.

It goes without saying that both concepts are highly problematic from the perspective of a democratic understanding of cultural policies – the paternalistic public hand is replaced by the invisible hand of the free market. However, this description also only partly holds true for Austrian cultural policies. Rather surprisingly, commercialization in Austria went hand in hand with increasing public expenditure.

Two examples will make the point: While in the early 1980s the musical *Cats* was performed in all larger European cities, Vienna was probably the only city where these performances were highly subsidized. In an Austrian region, subsidies for the performing arts were calculated as the equivalent of earned income. Thus, those productions with the highest share of earned income also got the highest share of public money.

These contradictory or – to put it more bluntly – rather senseless ways of financing the arts can be understood as the overlapping of different traditions and new developments that is also of crucial impact for the Austrian way of dealing with the Creative Industries. While the international trend towards commercialization was followed, the traditional state dependence of the arts was maintained. While cultural policy popularized the arts, commercialization did not quite work out.

The most important influence of Social Democratic politics, however, is not to be seen in the changes of the cultural field, but in its general orientation towards distributional politics that led in Austria to the development of a strong and very successful welfare state. This welfare state was based on social partnership and resulted in a comparatively high level of social security that has been upheld for a longer time than in many other countries. The Austrian welfare model (like most welfare models of this time) was oriented towards large enterprises (of which, in the Austrian case, quite a few were state owned), fulltime employment and a high degree of job security as well as a substantial social net. However, while social security has indeed been an important feature of the Austrian model, empirical studies have frequently shown that secure fulltime employment has only ever been the dominant model for a part of population – specifically for male

Austrian citizens working in large enterprises. It has more rarely applied to women and never to foreign workers. Nor does the model work in the case of artists – regardless of their sex or nationality – who are not employed in the flagships of the Austrian cultural heritage. (Those who are so employed, however, have been subject to labor laws of a rather absurd rigidity. For example, the prolongation of a performance or rehearsal of the Viennese Burgtheater leads very quickly to exploding costs as overtime has to be paid not only to those actually working but to the whole shifts of light and stage technicians, and so on.) Independent artists have lived precariously for a long time – and are therefore today euphemistically called the avant-garde of the new creative entrepreneurs. Still, the ideal of 'regular employment with regular payments' made it possible to criticize these conditions and, in fact, subsidies for small and independent artistic projects somehow rose simultaneously with the subsidies for cultural heritage – although on a much smaller scale.

In sum, traditional cultural politics in Austria has exhibited the following features: an understanding of culture and the arts as a public task that led to a financial structure based almost exclusively on public subsidies; an understanding of culture and the arts as mainly consisting of the cultural heritage; the non-existence of acknowledgement of popular culture; the lack of programs and formulated aims of cultural policies; and the assumption of a welfare state based on regular employment.

Creative Industries Austrian Style

In fact it is hardly surprising that the first attempts to introduce the CI in this specific national situation were mainly characterized by helplessness. When the then new state secretary for the arts in Austria, Franz Morak, published his first press releases in 2000, one could not avoid the impression that he expected Austrian CI to emerge simply due to his mentioning them. Ten years later we can state that, in a way, this is in fact what happened: political speeches are performative speech acts, if there is enough power behind them. They actually make a difference – however vague their contents may be. And vague they were, indeed. Morak told us that everybody is creative, that creativity is part of nearly every form of activity, that creativity is important for economy. He mentioned the White Paper of the Commission with its impressive figures of economic growth and employment chances (and he did not mention that evidence for where these figures came from was nowhere to be found in this paper), he mentioned the CI programs of the UK, and he mentioned the one and only extremely successful Austrian enterprise that could be regarded as part of CI, Swarovski glass, which produces jewelry and other luxury items out of crystal glass. Then came studies proving the excellent conditions for the CI in Austria and especially in Vienna, citing a lot of numbers (of equally dubious origin as the ones in the White Paper) on the tremendous growth rates to be expected in the CI. And, finally, measures to support the CI were developed by the Republic of Austria and the city of Vienna.

Quartier 21

Let us take a look at these measures. One of the most prominent and also most contested one was the creation of a cluster of Creative Industries in a rather prominent and central space, the MuseumsQuartier Vienna. The history of the MuseumsQuartier would be a subject for another essay (maybe not a very interesting one, but certainly a rather entertaining one), but to make a long story short: The MuseumsQuartier is, basically, a complex of traditional arts museums in a partly historical building near the city centre. It was founded because (1) this historical building had to be utilized somehow, and (2) because some big museums in Vienna needed space to show their collections. As an English colleague of mine put it: it is a housing project for museums. As this is neither a very attractive nor a very trendy way of developing a cultural quarter, the MuseumsQuartier needed a fig leaf to make it more hip. This fig leaf was the 'Quartier 21' offering space for contemporary cultural and artistic production and, above all, the CI. In this way the MuseumsQuartier could be peddled as a place that is not only devoted to the exhibition of creative achievements, but equally to their production, that not only deals with cultural heritage, but also with contemporary cultural activities.

In a way, the Quartier 21 fits perfectly in traditional Austrian cultural politics as described above, since it is a centralized, top-down project (internationally rather unusual for the development of a cultural cluster). On the other hand, it also shows the inability of Austrian cultural policy to deal with the CI.

The (state owned) company administrating the whole MuseumsQuartier wants to make money in the space of the Quartier

114

21. Therefore it asks for rents – which are subsidized because rents in this part of the city are very high, but even with the subsidies, the rents are still too high for most small companies starting something in the field of the CI. Consequently, it was difficult to find tenants. Consequently, quite a few of them had to leave again as they could not afford the rent. Consequently, the only criterion for the selection of tenants has been their ability to pay the rent. Consequently, no synergies between the tenants emerge – similarly to the big museums in the MuseumsQuartier, which do not cooperate because they did not move there in order to cooperate, but in order to have new, more attractive buildings. The tenants of the Quartier 21 do not cooperate for the same reasons.

The location of the Quartier 21 – although it is generally a very attractive site – is particularly poorly suited to small companies needing circulation in order to get attention and to sell their products. While there are many tourists in the courtyards of the MuseumsQuartier, only the most adventurous enter one of the small doors to the Quartier 21.

Public Support for the CI

Let us now come to another way in which Austrian cultural policies deal with the CI, namely public support. The Republic of Austria as well as many Austrian provinces and, most prominently, the city of Vienna have developed programs to support and further the CI. Probably the most important of these programs are the program 'impulse' by the Republic of Austria and 'departure' by the city of Vienna. None of these programs is really adequate to the needs of the CI. Applications for financing are complicated and time consuming, and, thus, in many cases, not manageable for the many self-employed or companies with one or two part-time employees, which make up most of the CI in Austria. Consequently, many of the supported projects come from relatively successful CI companies that would probably have been able to develop their products without this support. Although nobody would announce this officially, this bias towards the larger and more successful CI enterprises seems to be intended. Every study on the CI in Austria has shown that most enterprises in the CI have an under-critical size. Obviously, the solution for this problem chosen by the city of Vienna is not to help these enterprises to enlarge, but to let them die while focusing their support on the fitter ones. This strategy is at odds with the proclaimed aim to foster the CI as a economic sector, because in this way not many CI companies will, in fact, survive.

Both programs mainly finance projects. Thus, even those lucky enough to be supported for some time are not able to plan beyond the time span of their current project. This again can be seen as an older feature of Austrian cultural policy implemented in the field of the CI: while it seems probable that none of us will live to see the day on which public financing for the large Austrian cultural institutions will end, independent artists have always had to live from one project to the next. And we all know what this means for individual planning, for the possibility of having children and so forth.

From a different perspective again, the program does not fit its self-defined aims. The internationally unavoidable Richard Florida, who is also the godfather of Viennese CI, does not actually make many points in his bestsellers, but one of the most prominent ones is that cities need a specific infrastructure in order to be attractive to CI people. And infrastructure does not develop through project support, but through investment in infrastructure.

GovernCreativity

If we summarize the points I have made so far, we can state with some confidence that Austrian policy on the CI is a failure. Therefore, we could expect that the CI in Austria – which were more or less invented by cultural politics, after all – do not exist. However, this is not true. On a small scale, CI clusters have actually developed in Vienna – one of them around the MuseumsQuartier, not in the Quartier 21 but in the surrounding streets, in cheaper buildings. Others can be found in former industrial buildings, not financed by the public hand but developed by the initiative of those working there. People in these clusters frequently do not earn enough to plan for longer than a year, they almost never earn enough to be able to re-invest in their companies; they are usually young and childless, not because the CI are so hip but because you have to find something more secure if you become older or want to raise children.

And many of them like their working and living conditions, at least for the most part. They feel that they are, in fact, a kind of avant-garde, and they pride themselves on not holding a 9-to-5 job (but probably 9-to-9 self-employment).

I presume that, here again, international trends as well as specific national situations are the reason for this attitude. For one, it is simply the dogma of neoliberal times that is successfully implemented as a form of governmentality in Foucault's sense. 'Bear the risk for your own life and be proud of it!' Secondly, the paternalistic form of Austrian cultural policy has frequently led to a strong and strongly felt dependence, not only on public funding or on an entity as abstract as the state, but on concrete politicians and their fancies. It is hardly surprising that this is no attractive alternative.

And the concept of the creative entrepreneur trickles down (or sideways) into other parts of society, not least of all into the artistic field in a narrower sense. While it is officially maintained that the CI do not impact classical arts subsidies, parallel to the development of public support for the CI, subsidies for smaller cultural and artistic initiatives have continuously been reduced. And more and more often, I have the opportunity to listen to artists evaluating their own work in terms of its commercial success – something rather unheard of in Austria where the arts were frequently defined precisely by their need for public support.

Contrary to what I said before about the failure of Austrian CI policy, one could also – and probably more plausibly – claim its tremendous success. After all, it is the main aim of neoliberal policies to reduce public support in order for the free market to flourish.

And Now?

What does this mean for a critique of cultural industries? In which ways does it make sense to criticize what is currently happening in Austrian CI? If I were still the Marxist of my earlier years, I would introduce here the notion of 'false consciousness'. Alas, from the perspective of my older, post-Marxist days, this notion does not really seem helpful. Still, I think a general critique of CI as aimed at within this seminar of eminent importance: to show (1) in which ways the hype of the CI is deeply embedded in a certain political and economic paradigm, and (2) which consequences this hype has for the cultural field as well as for society as a whole. At the same time, however, I think we cannot simply ignore the fact that an increasing number of people work in the CI and want to work there. For this reason, I find it equally important to think about new ways of political organization and of social security adapted to the working and living conditions as well as the wishes of these people. Given the strong and one-dimensional tradition of the Austrian welfare state, this is not an easy task. We do not have much experience with political organization outside of political parties and traditional trade unions. But maybe, at least in this way, it might be useful that the CI are an international hype – hopefully, not only neoliberals but also critics of neoliberalism will be able to successfully copy models from other countries.

9

The Los Angelesation of London: Three Short Waves of Young People's Micro-Economies of Culture and Creativity in the UK

Angela McRobbie

This chapter suggests that the recent development of the creative economy in the UK in terms of small-scale entrepreneurial activities can now be understood as three consecutive short waves. This is activity undertaken not at company or organization level, but more independently by (and here I apply a kind of Bourdieusian frame), both (upper) working class and (lower) middle class young people in the UK, who have, for a variety of both historical and social structural reasons gravitated to the spheres of culture and creativity and have also in effect become individualized and disembedded from employment in large-scale social institutions, thus corresponding with an updated version of Bourdieu's category of cultural intermediaries (Bourdieu, 1984). Of course we could put this another way round and see the regulative dynamics of the post-Fordist employment environment exerting its effect by addressing a certain class strata of young people as now more fully agents of their own employment destiny, where in the past they would have been interpellated more surely as subjects of state or institutional employment, or else (*pace* Bourdieu or indeed Ulrich Beck) they would be a better educated strata of unemployed young people.

In fact I am assuming for the sake of this short intervention that readers are familiar with the value of the Bourdieusian, and Foucauldian dynamics in this debate. Here I aim instead to emphasize what is indeed entailed when such subjects are called into action, and what comprises their activities. This is followed by a parallel analysis of how the New

Labour government has developed a rapid response strategy to the idea of a cultural economy. New Labour's cultural policy agenda has been both radical and pervasive and is predicated on an outcome which is certainly nebulous or intangible in regard to the actual occupations and livelihoods which will emerge, but lucid in regard to the logic of unburdening both state and employers from fulfilling statutory obligations to employees.

Indeed let me start by saying that twenty years ago it was possible to talk about high culture and the high arts, opera, ballet, fine art, classical music, great literature and so on, as very separate from low culture, meaning popular music, sub-cultural activity like graffiti, style, black expressive cultures like rap and hip hop, and also of course popular entertainment, including film and television. And of course this distinction and the ensuing patterns of consumption also told us quite a good deal about how social hierarchies of class, race and sexuality and gender functioned in the UK. I am not claiming that there is no longer a division of this type between high and low culture, indeed at some point we may wish to have a discussion about how new micro-distinctions are produced in regard to hierarchies of art and culture in response to the creation of new more fluid and unstable positions in cultural labor markets, but for the moment such a process can only be alluded to.

I will be suggesting that when the arts and culture per se, become the focal point for capitalization (the logic of late capitalism as Fredric Jameson famously put it), when culture broadly becomes absolutely imperative to economic policy and urban planning, when art is instrumentalized so that it begins to provide a model for working lives, and labor processes, and when government opens a Green Paper document as it did in 2001 with the words 'Everyone is creative', then it becomes apparent that what in the past was considered the icing on the cake, has now become a main ingredient of the cake (DCMS, 2001). And what had been in the past left to its own devices (subculture and style, or black expressive culture or the punk avant-garde) has been plucked, over the years, from obscurity, and is now promoted with tedious regularity under the prevailing logic of revival in the window spaces of Selfridges and Harrods almost every season, as a leading edge feature of the UK's contribution to the new global cultural economy. Our imagined community and branded national identity now comes to be constituted through practices that are understood to be creative. This appellation is then deployed in policies which introduce such things as

Creative Partnerships[1] into schools across the country to incorporate a kind of third sector of education and training which is neither technical nor strictly academic and into which are slotted substantial numbers of young people. We still have no real idea of how this will work out on the longer term and what kinds of careers will develop, but this notion of creative education emerges as a modernizing and mobilizing strategy that will tap into young people's existing attachment to arts, popular culture and contemporary media. This then is where the investment is being made, in a perceived immersion in and connection with the field of media and culture.

What follows is to begin with a narrative account of this development, with particular reference not to the big media industries and communications corporations, and not to the role of government and the subsidies which have always gone to national theatre, the large orchestras, opera and ballet, but instead to the innovative youth subcultures which have largely comprised of young people who occupy precarious positions in regard to educational and cultural capital.

I undertook an investigation of small-scale UK fashion designers in the 1990s in the UK. I focused on fashion because it was female-dominated and a sector which had no back-up from fashion equivalents of the music industry, as was the case for young people in bands, nor did it have the prestige and cultural capital associated with the fine arts, even if that meant earning a pittance and remaining totally unknown as a struggling sculptor or visual artist, it still carried more (usually masculine) gravitas than being a fashion designer (McRobbie, 1998). So I was interested in the popular, feminine and sub-cultural aspects of fashion design, but less on the consumption and more on production. This research was actually precipitated from my earlier youth culture research, I was fascinated by the way in which, as these forms matured in the context of post-war UK society, into the mid to late 1980s they seemed to create their own informal labor markets. In one short article I examined the work of sub-cultural entrepreneurs, the young people who were influenced by the post punk do-it-yourself ethos and who sought to create not an 'alternative cultural economy' in the late 1960s sense but instead an 'indie' or independent economy (McRobbie, 1989/1994). And then Sarah Thornton coined the term sub-cultural capital, which showed how these forms were able to generate their own micro-economies and micro-media (Thornton, 1995). Indeed it was within the world of rag markets and second hand dresses that what was

121

later to become the absolute distinctiveness of British fashion design emerged, there was it seemed a fruitful and fortuitous overlap between the stylish pursuits of young women on the edge of subcultures and the wide range of fashion design courses available in every art school and small art college across the country thanks to the work of the great nineteenth century Victorian administrators, the social reformers as well as the advocates of arts and crafts, and then later in the twentieth century the pioneers of art and design. There was in effect wide provision of education, training and skills for a wide sector of the female population from the respectable working class and from the lower middle class especially in the big industrial cities like London, Manchester, Birmingham and Glasgow. By the 1980s and early 1990s, this provision in the UK art schools and universities had become greatly expanded (more than 5000 fashion and fashion-related graduates per annum) but still directed towards the less-privileged school leavers, including young women from immigrant families, or girls whose parents, mostly mothers, wanted to see them doing a job they enjoyed in a white collar or semi-professional/professional environment.

The first wave of self-generated sub-cultural entrepreneurs who were to be found busily inventing styles, sewing in their own kitchens and then selling what they made at weekend street-markets provided what we would now call incubators for experimenting in creative self-employment. This 'first wave' in my own analysis made an impact as young female pioneers of the small scale enterprises during the years 1985-1995, through close connections with the new magazines also spawned from youth culture like the influential Face and iD (by the way all who worked on these were unpaid) they gained all the publicity they needed to launch hundreds of 'small labels' on a cottage-industry basis summed up in the phrase 'I was knitting away night and day'.

However this burst of colorful activity had success at the level of press and media attention but was financially unsustainable leading to bankruptcy and debt. These were always under-capitalized, and received very little support from government, for example they were not eligible for fine art awards. They in fact emerged out of the shadow of unemployment during the Thatcher years and the most the young designers could expect was a small bank loan scheduled to be paid back with low interest rates. Working literally from the kitchen table to the small shop or outlet they were not able to manage sales abroad, many of them had their work bought from the shop rails but only to be copied by high street retailers and also by bigger name designers in Europe and in the US.

But there was this incredible bubble of creativity and huge amounts of energy and also impact between the worlds of fashion and popular music at that time. This was also a feminized sector and the young women I interviewed also benefited from the impact of feminism in schools and in college, in terms of following an independent career and equally important they had parents or mothers who encouraged the idea of meaningful or rewarding work. Mostly from lower middle class backgrounds and upper working class this was the sector of the population for whom the idea passed on by parents of 'refusal of mundane work' was most visible. In his contribution to this volume, Maurizio Lazzarato describes this refusal of tedious, repetitive, exploitative and mundane work as part of the workers struggle of the 1970s now extended inter-generationally. We can add to his argument a double-inflection, at least in the UK, first a feminist dynamic that permits the refusal of under-paid women's work and its replacement by more independently defined work which also becomes a source of self-realization. Here there is also a hope for a better working life for daughters on the part of mothers. For these young women we could say new forms of work (what Lazzarato calls 'immaterial labor') become sites of 'passionate attachment'. Creative work is a space of romantic idealization perhaps more rewarding than personal relationships. And second we could develop a very interesting argument here which connected Lazzarato's account of mundane job refusal as a vector of class struggle with the Birmingham CCCS analysis of working class youth cultures as in effect also playing out at symbolic level the sublimated class struggle which the parent culture both buried and also transmitted to their children (Hall and Jefferson, 1976). If the latter analysis provided (*pace* Althusser) an account of sub-cultural style in its spectacular modalities, then the former helpfully elucidates the productive features of these micro-economies. This adds to existing analysis a logic of inter-generational class struggle in my own case of course inextricably intersecting with gender.

This moment of the first wave did not last, but the ethos has subsequently been extended across a much wider section of the young population. It failed really because government wanted the sector to understand free market forces and competition. They had to learn lessons the hard way, despite advocates who pushed for better support and investment. However this championing by a few people like myself was at the time also rather lonely because the old left and the trade unionists were not interested in such small-scale activities, they had doubts about any progressive politics emerging from these forms of self-employment, and indeed they saw such work as self-exploitation, based on deluded fantasies of success, or else as small petty bourgeois businesses with no politics of solidarity and also unrealistically positioned in relation to the predatory high street and the big fashion retailers. Nor were academic feminists specializing in work and employment particularly interested since their attention was invariably drawn to the conditions of working class women in more traditional workplaces. So these incubators had little support and by the mid to late 1990s they were disintegrating and being replaced by 'second wave' multi-taskers.

In the 2002 article Club to Company I chart the characteristics of the second wave young creatives in the more 'speeded up' cultural economy in the UK which benefits more directly from the growth of new media and the hovering presence of venture capitalists which converge in the clubbing spaces of network sociality (McRobbie, 2002; Wittel 2001).[2] These include a) de-specialization b) hybrid job designations e.g. events organizer, arts advisor c) internships, work for nothing and job creation from unpaid work d) the night economy creating day-time livelihoods with the growth of leisure culture, clubbing and party economy, e) the expansion of network and freelance culture in the light of big institutions undertaking organizational change, shedding the workforce and then taking them back on as self-employed f) the growth of London and other global cities as creative centers for arts and culture as attractions for the finance sector and for tourism and consequently the increase in the labor markets for multi-skilled and adaptable young people, g) decline in possibilities for association and collectivity in the light of the speeded-up new media and internet economy, replacement by network sociality, such as the informal grapevine for job search, in the club, or bar, in culture sector districts. I argued this is a more thoroughly neoliberalized model. There is hardly any need to deal with bureaucracy, and without any of the anti-discrimination legislation in place what happens is that old and more elite and socially exclusive patterns re-emerge and come to distinguish the world of second wave small-scale creative economies. Issues of race and ethnicity, of gender and sexuality have no space for expression because either it is assumed in this cultural field that such issues have now been dealt with and that equality is taken for granted, or else there is such competitive individualization that there is no forum, no space or time for such concerns to be aired in a public milieu. Hence there is re-internalization of anxiety, privatized modes of anger or disappointment, the must-try-harder ethos, patterns of self-blame in such a hyper-individualized environment (as Bauman explains) and in addition the non-existence of protection, means that new forms of self reliance must also be invented. (Where it is normal to be holding down let us say four projects at one time, if at least one of them is a contract with a public sector organization or agency of the state, then at least there will be some minimal workplace entitlement, for example pay for sickness, or holiday.) Thus notions of security become not fixated on full time employment but sought out in partial or fractional employment.

The third wave springs into life in the last five years. It bears all the hallmarks of the Blair period. It is characterized not by the post-punk ethos of the first wave or the party or night-time entrepreneurialism of the second wave, but by the Hollywood effect, the winner takes all, indeed if the UK has taken the lead from the US in matters of war and on the battlefield, so also, in the field of culture and creativity are we looking to the US and to the global entertainment industry as the source for shaping working lives, the Los Angelesation of London and the impact this has for the rest of the UK and for UK isolationism in the context of European cultural policy. More significantly the US is also looked to for rationalizations regarding the shift towards the concept of creativity and its role in the economy.[3] Blair's go it alone agenda is also mirrored in the new creative economy. This third wave is more nebulous and hard to define, partly because it is so bound up with deeper social transformations that involve re-defining notions of selfhood and which encourage more expansive forms of self reliance. These new more flexible forms of selfhood are institutionally grounded in education through pedagogical styles as well as the transformation of the curriculum. In the arts, media and culture self-reliance corresponds with styles of working on a project-by-project basis.

The third wave I am attempting to describe typically entails having a single project which is one's own work, a kind of magic card which it is hoped will one day come to fruition, but which in the meantime is propped up by three or four more mundane and income-generating projects. The underlying logic of the third wave is the idea of the one big hit. If the typical arts or humanities graduate leaving university needs to learn to navigate her or his way around the world of funded projects in order to put together a living (for example, two days editing an on-line fashion magazine, two days working as a stylist for a fashion agency, one day a week in reception at a gallery) then she will be spending also a lot of time networking, keeping doors open for when projects finish, and new ones begin. But what she really wants is in fact a big hit of her own, something that allows her to position herself more strongly and emphatically in this competitive creative labor market. This is usually something related to her own work that she will nurture at weekends and in the evening. A single big hit is what almost everyone inside the creative economy is hoping for, because it can have a transformative effect, it can lift the individual out of the pressure of multi-tasking and all the exhausting networking this entails. The one big hit also provides a facilitating connection between the small-scale activities that can be carried out without major investment by the independent producer, and the large company sector which are able to provide the capital to turn the small original into a global product. This projected passage from micro-activity carried out at home or round the kitchen table to macro-activity involving key players from the global culture industry also functions as another mode of self-disciplining. This is most evident in the encouragement on the part of government to uncover one's own potential, to search out the special qualities of creativity that we all surely possess. This ethos is a key feature of the so-called talent-led economy. This shift into third wave cultural working relies on a total mobilization of self, so that every ounce of potential can be put to good economic use. It requires an inflated degree of self-belief that is surely unsustainable.

The one big hit can mean a variety of things, but in essence it produces a ripple effect in terms of widening options and possibilities and it also enhances the status and power of the 'award-winner' in the cultural economy. For the final year student of fashion it will mean a big hit with the degree show that lands a short contract job offer with a French, American or Italian fashion house, in television it typically means one big idea which establishes a niche or a genre, in music it means a single track which doesn't need to make it to the top of the charts but will succeed if it crosses over from the dance floor right onto the soundtrack for an advert on television (Shake Your Ass by Groove

Armada), or indeed as background for any number of gardening or make over TV programs (for example, the ubiquitous Gotan Project).

While the dream of the big hit has always existed (as Adorno pointed out in his famous Culture Industry essay) it has in the last few years become normalized and located right in the heart of culture industry discourse. As London seems to become a 'one-company town' and as other cities in the UK each set up their own cultural strategy, the big hit in the creative sector is conflated with the star system as a means of branding a national and international image of cities across the UK (for example, Edinburgh is promoted through its association with JK Rowling and Harry Potter, Irvine Welsh and *Trainspotting*, Ian Rankin and his detective hero Rebus). The most sought after big hit is frequently a novel or diary (following the lead from *Bridget Jones's Diary* or the more recent *The Devil Wears Prada*) that will be published and then made into a film. There are some examples, which have been so unexpected that the author is catapulted into a very different working environment from what she has been used to as Lionel Shriver, the author of the novel *We Need To Talk About Kevin* has recently described.[4]

Let me move to a conclusion of this discussion of the normalization of the exceptional big hit, and the way in which being in search of one's own talent is now the key element of what used to be called labor discipline. In the UK at least, this seeking out of ones own creativity, as a kind of inner self, is a dominant feature of contemporary governmentality. Within a framework of subjects relevant to this practice of cultural governance the new self is defined as primarily productive and creative, the two become inseparable with the latter compensating for the exhaustive dynamics of the former.

The third wave of creative economy pushes for change also in more bureaucratic, rigid or seemingly inflexible and professional institutions such as the university. And although more directly experienced by people under the age of 45, it increasingly has an impact across all ages of working people. The one big hit model is also supremely exportable, in projects across diverse institutions it can mean a windfall, the guarantee of an extended lifetime of a range of activities in private and public micro- and macro-organizations. The competitive ethos that underlies the rationale for the one big hit comes to be applied across the various sectors as part of a changing regime of accountability and auditing. In the context of small independent projects even those funded ultimately by the state, this model normalizes precariousness and uncertainty and makes irrelevant formal social relations of working life including statutory obligations, it thus permits the by-passing of the old order and of protective and anti-discriminatory legislation associated with the previous regime of Social Democratic and welfarist provision. By-passing is then an instrument of neoliberal reform which under the rubric of what Blair calls modernization in effect de-commissions (or at least makes marginal, puts into cold storage) the field of statutory obligations in working lives.[5] This strategy can be seen in operation across a wide range of sectors in which government has a role to play. The impact of American thinking in regard to the place of creativity in the contemporary economy is highly visible and this work emerges from business schools where there is a focus on psychology and cognitive sciences rather than sociology. However it is the mark of New Labour's highly innovative approach that these ideas are made to converge with more conventionally social policies designed to alleviate disadvantage. For example the Chancellor's award of £30 per week to 16 year olds from poor homes as a way of ensuring that they stay on at school until 18 and gain qualifications to take them into university or college, intersects with initiatives being undertaken elsewhere in the education system to make arts and creative education a much more significant and mainstream element of the curriculum, in effect a good reason to stay on at school.[6] Other activities and proposals also contribute to the combination of arts, enterprise and upskilling within the educational field, for example Scottish Enterprise, the possible raising of the school leaving age to 18, the role of Creative Partnerships in secondary schools, and the introduction of new media and arts qualifications.

These diverse programs and proposals constitute intense activity on the part of government, and from then we can begin to discern a kind of theatrical effect. Young people are being trained as though for the stage, even when working lives will be far removed from the 'greasepaint'. But even David Brent, the lead character in Ricky Gervais's *The Office*, also a global success for BBC TV, sets his aspiration well beyond the tedium of the Slough paper company that he manages. It is his nighttime career (not so far successful) as a stand-up comedian that lifts him out of the limited horizons of office work. The upskilling curve also transforms traditionally low paid or routine jobs into something more spectacular.

The most recent papers and policy documents by the UK government on matters of culture and economy envisage remarkable growth in the creative sector and also make a strong case for the production of complex culture against the dangers of 'dumbed-down' entertainment (DCMS, 2004). Taken alongside the cultural (rather than social) engineering undertaken in the education system to upskill young people who might otherwise fail, this strategy also has the intention of expanding the middle classes and making them more self-sufficient, indeed it may be that this is, at the present moment in time, a sufficient outcome, from the point of view of New Labour. This would also entail some kind of coming to terms with long term permanently transitional work, it would also require higher degrees of self responsibility and the internalization and individualization of failure, it would sideline past work ethics which as Sennett (2005) has shown value process, craft, solidarity and the patterns of the ordinary working day. It would make of us all, if not singers, dancers and Spice Girls, then at least individuals or subjects for whom unprecedented degrees of self-belief will be needed to sustain a life in the new world of precarious creative labor. This theatricalization effect is characterized by a nebulous or even opaque sense of outcome. Government reports are almost evangelical when it comes to indicating the benefits of the new creative ethos in education and employment, but there is silence in regard to the actual kinds of work that will be created by all of this effort at the level of policy. In addition the discourse of creativity is marked in its preference for the language of US psychology and its evasion of research and the critical vocabularies associated with European including UK sociology and of course cultural studies.

While the neo-liberal effect is not hard to pinpoint in terms of the by-passing mechanism referred to above, I would say that there is a good deal more to this revolution in the category of work and productive activity than the obviously pejorative label neo-liberal suggests. Earlier in this article I alluded to the proposal from Lazzarato that the desire for meaningful work emerges from a context of previous generations of class struggle. We could attach onto this a more Foucauldian sense of the desire for new more rewarding work as a variant on self-aestheticization, a body politics rendered at the level of re-orchestrating the available technologies of self inscribed in current practices of governmentality.

To focus on such a terrain would be to understand these sites of creativity and productive activity in regard to self-employment as micrological sites of conflict and tension. What remains of class struggle is now deflected onto this field of precariousness. The most apparent sign of success on the part of New Labour in the UK, is the by-passing of 'old labour' and its terrain of entitlement and protection, and in addition the newly configured landscape of mental labor as the site for the extraction of surplus value on a scale undreamt of by previous theorists of labor process, with the added advantage that this now entails the suspension of critique in favor of the hope, indeed expectation that there will be some tangible reward in such a form that will promise both status and security.[7] What is also by-passed in the new discourse of creative self-realization is the intellectual landscape of critical aesthetics certainly associated with the Marxist philosophical tradition which of course disputed the myth of genius, which undermined the ideology of individual creativity, and indeed which in subsequent writing from Bourdieu to Barthes and from Foucault to Derrida, drew attention to the inflated place of the author or artist as a field of secular belief which among other things devalued an ethics of collaboration and a politics of critique. Thus what appears to be at stake in the new field of mental labor is the role and meaning of intellectual labor, currently being seen as outmoded in contrast to the creative energies of the new cultural producer. In such a context this process of championing new forms of creative education (for example, the live project, the links with industry, internships, the role of creative partnerships) also occludes the place of theory, and the space of critical pedagogy.

Notes

1   See http://www.creative-partnerships.com/.

2   See http://www.nelp.de/beitraege/02_farbeit/mcrobbie_e.htm.

3   Kim Allen is currently researching New Labour implementation of US theories of creativity in the school, training and the workplace.

4   See various interviews with Lionel Shriver in the UK *Guardian* and *Independent*.

5 This is a polemical point on my own part, in need of further elaboration regarding legislation to cover part time working, and the role of the industrial tribunal system.

6 See the PhD by Kim Allen (2005), in particular the growth of Arts Academies, performing arts education and media arts provision across all sectors of the UK education system.

7 An example from the academy: write a PhD thesis, then use all the research to write a novel. If it succeeds, as was the case for author Sarah Waters, the author of among other novels *Fingersmith*, and *Tipping the Velvet*, then the rewards in terms of BBC TV adaptations can be tremendous.

10

Unpredictable Outcomes / Unpredictable Outcasts: On Recent Debates over Creativity and the Creative Industries

Marion von Osten

Let me begin with a question: how does the currently hegemonic discourse of creativity, the creative industries and the artist as a role model for the new economy correspond to or conflict with the field of cultural producers and cultural activists? To bring out the problem even more sharply, I would first of all put in question the assumption that the 'creative industries', about which we are talking and against which we are struggling, are already in existence. Are they really there before us? Or do we perhaps face a field of political visions that aim to privatize the cultural sector in general but have not yet been realized in anything like an 'industry'? I don't think we can speak yet of an industry as such, either in the UK, where the discourse of 'creative industries' is established and the where cultural production was reorganized and repositioned (Davies, 2001), or in Germany, where the Social-Democratic Schröder government set in motion, with different results, a transformative shift toward a culturalization of the economy and a corresponding economization of culture (Pühl, 2003). Have we really reached a moment in which social interactions and forms of autonomous labor open possibilities for making a living in self-organized ways, ways that at the same time are exploitable by capital as immaterial resources? Or do we find ourselves within a transformation process in which outcomes are produced by diverse interactions, some of which can be said to be industrial, within a cultural field increasingly dominated by the interests of capital? Or is there, as many critics since Adorno have held, an unbridgeable contradiction in any industrialization of cultural production, insofar as 'creativity' has nothing at all to do with the sphere of economy?

In the midst of all of this, I propose that we reflect on our discourse. Being in the midst means that there is still space to influence and change the discourse, even our own. I would therefore like to discuss creativity as a discursive term, in the genealogy of which we can see both a process of secularization and the reflected constitution of the modern form of subjectivity that plays such a central role in capitalist societies. The suggestion that the mass production of cultural goods directly contributes to a blunting or loss of capacity is not part of my argument. What interests me instead is the symbolic function of the debates about creativity and creative industries for the cultural representation of political, economic and social processes. In this light, I doubt that the so-called creative industries are already here. What there is, at least, is a discourse about them and the international will to make them a reality as soon as possible. We participate critically in this discourse and shape it too.

With regard to the term 'industry', it has been observable in recent years – even in this book, in our use of language – that a qualitative shift is taking place, that the social and cultural could be transformed by processes of partial industrialization and by technology undergoing partial industrialization processes and technologies – at least if we do not intervene to stop it. Examples of this include the current debates about cognitive skills or abilities in general, which the new subject of labor in post-Fordist societies should learn or already possesses. In these debates, social competence, creativity and intelligence are now increasingly presented and discussed as separate, abstract entities. The question, what and why and for whom something can be done with these abilities, thus appears to be of no relevance. Social and cognitive abilities are treated as values and as self-standing resources, resources that can be produced and improved by training methods, or exploited by capital. But this can only happen if these abilities are conceptualized as non-relational and segregated from each other and if they are highlighted and represented as entities within scientific and popular perspectives. Another example here is the requirement of 'lifelong learning' that is isolated as a process and emphasized as a value in itself. The concept 'lifelong learning' no longer asks what should be learned and why; instead the process of learning itself, whatever that should be, is simply assigned a positive value. So it is not about learning for something, but rather the learning of a readiness to learn, according to which the subject is thought of as oriented toward the market and increasingly accommodated to changes in conditions. The subject conceptualized in this way holds itself in ready dependency to every situation and is 'trained' in the sense of having its abilities rationalized in strict conformity to the moment. It is contingent and dependent on the context, and at the same time, however, it is expected to perform and make choices autonomously.

This new conception of the subject of labor, then, is made up of fragmented and abstracted cognitive processes that can be treated industrially in the future. This process of abstraction and the establishment of technologies to improve and optimize cognitive capacities can be linked to the key processes and technologies of industrialization developed in earlier periods of the industrial age. Then, the movements of laboring bodies were abstracted and fragmented, in order to synchronize the body of the worker with the actions of machines. With Taylorism, abstracted movements became the object of research and training, and the rationalization of body-machine-management relations was fully realized. This newly composed relation between body, machine, management and sciences became the international standard, opening the way to the full development of the Industrial Age and mass production. In this new era, the struggles of labor also began to be more successful. The Marxist analysis of capital and its relation to labor-power, reflected in the experiences of the workplace and in organizations and parties, became an aspect of everyday life.

Against this background, it makes sense to think about the discourse of 'creative industries' as a technology that aims not so much at the capitalization and mobilization of the cultural sectors in particular as at the restructuring of relations between the subject of labor and processes of valorization, optimization and acceleration. For what is usually forgotten in the debates about creative industries is that this discussion about creativity and cultural labor has an impact on the understanding and conceptualizing of labor, subjectivity and society as a whole. Through the vocabulary of creativity and the references to bohemian life and work biographies, society is transformed in ways that affect policymaking as well as the general political field – and not excluding our own discourse.

Creator of New Ideas

Artist-subjects, intellectuals and bohemians are specifically European constructs. Since the sixteenth century the creative, world-making ability has been regarded not as an exclusively divine power, but a human one as well. A mode of production based on a new relation between intellectual and manual abilities emerged in distinction from activities that are purely a matter of craft. In this sense, the term 'creativity' included reflexivity, technical knowledge and an awareness of the contingency of the creative process. In the eighteenth century, creativity was defined as the central characteristic of the artist, now thought of as an autonomous 'creator' who brings forth the world all over again. In the emerging capitalist form of society, the concepts of 'aptitude' and 'property' were combined with the traditionally male notion of genius to produce the idea of the artist as an 'exceptional subject' – the owner of an ingenious and exceptional artistic mind. From then on, notions about 'creative talent' and what it means to 'be creative' have served bourgeois individualism as a more general description of activity meant to transcend or elude economic determinants. The culturalization of labor and production has been based as well on forms of image production. These forms, which organize a specific regime of the gaze through institutional frameworks such as museums, galleries and their related cultural discourses, have been central to the constitution of national ideologies in the nineteenth century.

The figure of the artist as exceptional creator of innovations in modes of production, notions of authorship and forms of living circulates today in various discourses of social transformation. Moreover, the classical exceptional subjects of modernity – artists, musicians, non-conformists and bohemians – also function as role models in European Union debates on labor and social politics. This can be seen clearly in Germany and Switzerland – and in the UK, the frontline. As Angela McRobbie argues in her influential text 'Everyone is Creative':

> One way to clarify the issue is to examine the arguments presented by this self-consciously 'modern' government, which since 1997 has attempted to champion the new ways of working as embodying the rise of a progressive and even liberating cultural economy of autonomous individuals – the perfect social correlative of post-socialist 'third way' politics. (McRobbie, 2004)

In political debates, the figure of the artist – or 'cultural-preneur' as Anthony Davies once named it – seems to embody that successful combination of an unlimited diversity of ideas, creativity-on-call and smart self-marketing that today is demanded of everyone. Subject positions outside the mainstream labor force are presented as self-motivated sources of productivity, and those who occupy these positions are celebrated as passionately committed 'creators of new, subversive ideas', innovative lifestyles and ways of working. Among the reasons for this change in values is the fact that, as formerly stable institutional and organizational arrangements have been loosened by deregulation, the typical, masculine, long-term job biography has been eroded. From the perspective of groups oriented toward long-term labor biographies, such as bourgeois or labor parties – it now becomes difficult to determine how and when to differentiate between 'work' and 'non-work' – or even why one should need to do so. The figure of the artist seems to be the point of reference for this new understanding of the relation between life and work, and for mediating it to broader audience.

In the general political debate in the UK and Germany, support for the employed or unemployed depends now on their willingness to align working time and lived time 'productively', as required. Activities once experienced as private now take on economic functions. The 'labor-entrepreneur' must simultaneously be the artist of her/his own life. It is precisely this mystification of the subject of exception, the 'artist' whose way of working is based on self-responsibility, creativity and spontaneity, which grounds the slogans of today's discourse on labor. This can be seen in the rhetoric of the Hartz Commission tasked with drawing up plans for the structural adjustment of the German labor market; in this terminology, the unemployed emerge as self-motivated 'freelancers' and artists, journalists and other self-employed or freelance professionals are revalorized as 'the professionals of the Nation'.

The classical subject of exception, with its precarious employment situation, has thus been discursively transformed into a model economic actor. In current managerial and consulting discourses, creative action and thought are no longer expected only of artists, curators and designers. The new flexible, time-based employees are the customers of the booming creativity-promotion market, provided with the appropriate advice brochures, seminars, software and so forth. These educational programs, learning techniques and tools supply applicable methods, at the same time projecting new potential forms of being. Their aim is to make 'optimizing' the self seem desirable. Creativity training demands and supports a liberation of creative potential, without addressing existing social conditions that might pose an impediment. On the one hand, then, creativity shows itself to be the democratic variant of genius: the ability to be creative is bestowed on everyone. On the other hand, everyone is required to develop her/his creative potential. The call for self-determination and participation no longer designates only an emancipated utopia, but also a social obligation. The subjects comply with these new relations of power apparently by free will. In Nicolas Rose's terms, they are 'obliged to be free' (Rose, 1996: 17), urged to be mature, autonomous and self-responsible. Their behavior is not regulated by a disciplinary power, but by 'governmental' techniques grounded in the neoliberal idea of a 'self-regulating' market. These techniques are intended to mobilize and stimulate, rather than discipline and punish. As contingent and flexible as the 'market' is, the new labor subjects shall be.

The requirement or imperative to 'be creative', to fit yourself into the market, relates to the very traditional understanding of the artistic production, as an artist's income is conditioned on the sale of products in the art market (a myth that receives vehement reinforcement today). But at this point an important difference in the field of the managerial discourse comes into play. For failure in the labor market is not comparable to failure in the field of art. The artist who fails can still fall back on other subject positions and recuperate this failure by transforming it. The unrecognized or undiscovered artist can be mobilized in every moment of loss, because the absence of success can still be legitimated with rationalizations such as 'the time is not yet ripe', 'quality will out', and 'recognition takes time', (it may even come after you are dead). But this myth of the unrecognized, unsuccessful but still-talented, if misunderstood, artist cannot be easily integrated into the managerial discourse. We may have to wait some time for an enterprise that would become the object of scientific inquiry only years after its death-by-bankruptcy. That hyper-motivated, super-flexible and mobile person who just did not land a job in the labor market is not likely to get a retrospective in the MOMA, with a coffee table book and a place in the hall of fame… after his or her death.

Still the subjectivity of non-recognition is integrated into the self-representations of immaterial laborers at large. The artist as a model for the self-representation of the new flexible labor force can be found in several recent studies of the Germany business world, and the media and IT field in particular. A study of T-Mobile Germany showed that the humiliation of a time-limited or badly paid job was interpreted by many employees as a transition, a short-term experience that would soon be overcome, once the desired job is secured. The path to that job may be difficult, but the goal is clear. Contingent subjectivities are forming here, for which failures in the free market can be reinterpreted as positive individual experiences, and privatization and structural transformations in the social, political and economical fields can be treated as personal challenges.

Moreover, the mythology of the artist continues to project the image of a particular metropolitan lifestyle, where living and working are done in the same place – in a café or on the road – with the further illusory possibility of the added enjoyment of 'leisure'. As Elisabeth Wilson has shown in her *Bohemians: The Glamorous Outcasts*, the notions of flexibility and mobility emerge historically from the tradition of the 'drop-out' established by generations of artists who sought to resist modernism's dictums of discipline and rationalization (Wilson, 2000). The social status and cultural capital attached to the image of the 'artist' thus also points to a higher, indeed a more ethical form of work; this form of labor has discarded the coercion of disciplinary regimes and is destined for something 'better'. The artist's studio or 'loft' became a symbol for the convergence of labor and leisure in everyday life and for innovation and the diversity of ideas. In this way, neoliberal ideology acquires the aesthetic dimension it needs for full realization, as can be seen in office design and living spaces, now become 'habitats'. Subjects are placed in new environments; associated lifestyle opportunities proliferate. Shared aesthetic experience, then, becomes an instrument of initiation.

The style of living and working originally attributed to the artist promises new 'urban living experiences' throughout Europe. Today the term 'loft' no longer refers only to an artist's studio in an abandoned industrial space, but is applied to almost all the attic conversions and building extension projects fashionable in Switzerland and Germany in the late 1990s. Since then, driven by the competition for geographic advantages in the global market, European labor markets have been revamped and city districts enhanced with a culturalized vocabulary. Meanwhile, budget cuts in the social and cultural fields are legitimized under the paradigm of the 'self-reliance' of cultural producers as entrepreneurs (the core concept of the creative industries ideology) in this notion of economy based on 'talents' and self-initiative.

Figures of Resistance

These discourses have not been marginal. Moreover, they have consequences for society as a whole. Meanwhile the conditions of production are disguised in the surviving remnants of industrial production, as well as in art and design and in other precarious jobs in the service sector. Despite their economic crash, the IT and media industries, which referred constantly to the image of the 'artist', have become as influential a model of labor as the Taylorist and Fordist car industry once was. As shown in the spurious emulation of bohemian lifestyles by the IT industry, among other sectors, much remains to be learned about a discourse on labor suffused with 'cultural language' – namely, about the everyday circulation of this discourse, its effects on the formation of subjectivity and the relation between adjustment, failure and resistance. So far the erosion of the old paradigm of production, along with the new working conditions and their reference to 'artistic practice', have been analyzed almost exclusively from within the logic of 'industrial work' or in relation to stable labor biographies oriented toward white males, the so-called breadwinners of western societies. With only a few exceptions, there have been few attempts to address the cultural rationale and effects of these phenomena, and little attention to the motives and desires of the actors involved. The real relations of production involved in the construct of 'creative' production (self-employed artists, media workers, and multimedia, sound, and graphics designers) have been neglected or idealized in these optimistic discourses.

With this in mind, I initiated a series of collaborative studies or projects centered on interviews with cultural producers of different backgrounds. My investigation began in Zurich in 2002, while I was still engaged at the Institute for the Theory of Design and Art, with a focus on cultural labour in the self-organized design and multimedia sector and its agents. In its cultural and qualitative methods, the study attempted not so much to review the political discourse about the transformation of wage-labor as to approach it in a new and different way. This seemed necessary, in order to develop a theory of social constitution that is clearly distinct from the notion of 'accumulative' productivity familiar from the materialist tradition. Instead of seeking to prove how life is economized, I tried to find out how cultural actors in a specific place are attempting to develop tactics or strategies for resisting the common discourse.

So in the spring of 2002, I initiated discussions about contemporary relations of production at 'Atelier-/Büro-Blocks', a complex of studio and office spaces in which the norm is a hybrid cultural production combining art, graphics, journalism, photography, multimedia and music. Moreover, I myself have participated in production projects there. The building belonged to a SWISSCOM company before it was sublet at the end of the 1990s to different groups of cultural producers. Most of the discussions took place on a floor-level of the complex that was leased collectively in the late 1990s by a group of artists, journalists and electronic musicians who called themselves 'k3000', an appropriation of the name of Swiss supermarket chain that had gone out of business but had been known for low-priced goods. The k3000 collective sublet the floor to various producers including multimedia and graphic designers, sound and visual artists, and social scientists. In one office space, called 'labor k3000', media equipment was used and knowledge shared collectively. The group Labor k3000, of which I am also a member, has been active in critical artistic practices and cultural production since 1997. In the late 1990s the division between the artists and the designers was still quite marked. In the last five years it has become more and more common for critical artists, together with activists and theorists, to produce web projects, mailing lists, newspapers, videos, project exhibitions, actions and events. In this case, such collaborative production is only made possible by the spatial and social fabric of the Atelier-/Büro-Blocks, which maintains openings for the participation, ideas and skills of friends and colleagues from other fields of production.[1]

My research led me to revise several of my earlier assumptions about transformations in the conditions of production. I had assumed that the fields of design would perfectly exemplify the culturalization of economy – even more than would critical art practices. But here I had to correct myself, because those working in the field of design had work-biographies as freelancers and self-employed 'creatives' that already revealed very different results, and very different kinds of exit. And these transformations cannot be attributed solely to the economic situation following the crash of the 'e-economy'.

First of all, the interviews showed that the concepts and imaginaries involved in office and studio production spaces have already undergone a high degree of mixing. In Zurich's graphic design and art scene, after twenty years of personal computer culture, it is primarily the studio, rather than the office, that survives as a model of independent production. The people I spoke with had by the mid to late 1990s all been very active in producing multimedia applications for multinational companies or in enterprise branding. It was astonishing to see that this situation had shifted a few years later into a common agreement on the 'floor', that one should try to avoid working in this field of image production in general and that clients, whoever they may be, should no longer be invited into the building, even for signing contracts and so forth.

While multimedia producers and graphic designers shifted their orientation towards the 'studio', the artists in contrast used terms like 'laboratory' or 'office' in their attempts to describe a more collective and multimedia-oriented mode of production. As both groups shared the same building, the divergence in language seems to have been the result of strategic decisions on the part of each group. Moreover, my discussions with diverse producers showed, to my surprise, that temporary, collective networks were no longer typical among graphic and multimedia designers engaged in the production of corporate images. The production on the 'floor' did not function as a 'factory' at all, contrary to what Maurizio Lazzarato claims in his canonical text on 'immaterial labor' (Lazzarato, 1996). Lazzarato lays great stress on the links between the new conditions of production under post-Fordism and artistic-cultural work. He assumes that the characteristics of the so-called post-industrial economy, with regard both to its mode of production and to the relations of living in society as a whole, are condensed in the classical forms of 'immaterial' production. Even if these appear in fully realized form in the areas of the audio-visual industries, advertising and marketing, fashion, computer software, photography, and in artistic-cultural work in general, and even if artistic-cultural workers appear as agents and representatives of 'the classical forms of immaterial labor', the results of my study suggest that it is important to draw out their implicit potentials for resistance and emphasize everyday tactics in opposition to processes of economization.

The self-employed designers in the Zurich scene functioned more as an 'alternative economy' dependent on alternative cultural spaces; in these spaces they earned their small but quite adequate incomes. In discussions they presented themselves as enclosed studio monads who consciously resist cooperation with the 'branding' and 'marketing' systems. They cooperated – and this point makes it even clearer – only when in urgent need of money and doing a 'job' to pay the rent or fund a holiday trip. This group has no political strategy. They did not discuss unions or the transformation of society and the conditions of labor in general. Instead, they invented a way to make their living through self-organized, partially freelance relations.

In the interviews, almost all of them claimed that they did not reject a 9-to-5 job solely because this regimentation of time seems paternalistic to them, but also because they could not bear either business culture and its social dynamics or the idea of having to subordinate themselves to a hierarchical working relationship. Multimedia and graphics jobs – as I found out in the discussions – also made it possible for (mostly) young men to move up in class position. However, these jobs do not seem to enact noteworthy transformations in the gender dynamics, even if this is repeatedly postulated in labor market policy assumptions. This aspect could have something to do with the traditional relationships of women and men to technology. On the other hand, it could also be influenced by anachronistic assumptions about the 'artist' as solitary male genius.

Moreover, the graphic-designer's self-image increasingly aligns with that of the artist (as single author) to this day, allowing him or her to discard the image of the designer as a success-oriented craft-worker who following the demands of the client. Such self-images are to be found in the art-scene as well, where many actors do not appropriate the image of the artist in hopes of economic gain but much more with regard to social status and a possibility of dorm of social mobility not bound solely to money exchange. In the graphic art scene, the drift toward the artist's self-image even draws from the polar opposite of economic success – from the tradition of the failed and misunderstood artistic subject and its sub-cultural variations, with scant regard for whether that subject is desirable to capital.

The motifs of bohemian life come up not only in the discourses of labor market policies and economic success, but also in the field of applied art, where it is used as a social value to distinguish oneself from business as usual. Among this specific group of 'young creatives' as well, precarious working conditions are not determined solely by business. In every case I encountered, a way of living was deliberately chosen. In other words, freelancing or working independently, rather than in a position of permanent employment, corresponds to the desire for an enjoyable way of life that is not structured by others – a life that is precarious and will never lead to great riches or the social status of international fame but which may still lead to a comfortable living. This seems a great privilege that most of the people globally do not share, and that even some of us over-stressed theorists do not share.

This cultural 'niche economy' only exists because of a still-existing alternative cultural scene – alternative networks of institutions which it was possible to establish in the wake of riots in Zurich and other cities. It exists because unemployment money is still available in Switzerland for young people who have just finished their education, and also because a network of cultural producers relates to this alternative world of cultural spaces, bars and clubs, political initiatives, temporal teaching jobs and self-initiated projects. Within these networks, people always find ways to generate small incomes and involve other people from the 'floor' or their buildings in their small but real streams of money. Here the niche economy must be described as a key factor in cultural policy and the specifics of localities.

Even if the self-understanding and self-organization of an 'artistic subject' constituted as a kind of historical citation seem to correspond to the fantasies of labor market redevelopers and creative industries apologists, making this form of subjectivation 'productive' for economic processes, still the success of this conjunction remains questionable in both theoretical and epistemological perspectives. Artistic ways of living and working contain forces that cannot fully be controlled because they not only engender but also always take part in the dissolution of their own conditions. Furthermore, myths of artistic ways of life are not at exclusive disposal of human resource managers. These myths can also be used by social groups that would otherwise be silenced within existing power relations. Historical quotation of the artistic subject and aesthetic ways of living cannot serve as a source of the measurable data required by economic discourses because the production of a context of equivalency between the economical and specific forms of life is a reduction of the inherent complexities and antagonisms. In its functioning as ideology, however, it effectively obscures this shortcoming.

Notes

1   On projects such as MoneyNations, Be Creative, Transit Migration and MigMap, see www.k3000.ch.

11

Chanting the Creative Mantra: The Accelerating Economization of EU Cultural Policy

Raimund Minichbauer
language edited by Aileen Derieg

That the creative industries are high on the European Union's cultural political agenda has been evident in recent EU presidencies – the United Kingdom, Austria and now also Finland have given it a prominent place in their work programs.[1] They organized a series of conferences starting with 'The Creative Economy Conference' in the UK,[2] followed by 'Content for Competitiveness – Strengthening the European Creative Industries in the Light of the i2010-Strategy' in Austria,[3] and 'creativity.online.fi – European Content and Copyright Policy' in Finland.[4] The series was continued in the course of the German presidency.[5] Central issues in the conferences were intellectual property rights and copyright policies, with a special focus on online communication/distribution.

And creative industries has a prominent place not only in the context of these presidencies: The European Council's work plan for culture 2005/2006 lists this topic in first position, with plans including a study to be organized by the European Commission 'on ways in which creativity, creative industries, and public-private partnerships in the cultural sector already contribute to European economic, social and cultural potential and thereby to the achievement of Lisbon targets' (Council of the European Union, 2004b: 31). An invitation to participate in an online consultation organized by the Directorate General Education and Culture (DG EAC) in autumn 2006 explicitly mentions the cultural industries when defining the stakeholders as 'in particular, organizations and individuals active in the cultural sector, including cultural industries'.[6]

This chapter analyzes an economistic approach that has become increasingly predominant, is in danger of becoming a paradigm of cultural policies as a whole, and moreover contributes to the predominance of the paradigm of creativity in post-Fordist production contexts in general.

I begin with an introduction to the structural setting, within which creative industries policies in the EU context are situated, and then analyze current developments. Three topics in particular are elaborated: the Lisbon strategy as a root; the shift from a policy largely oriented to support for creative production (for example, regional policy) to a policy of 'hard law' regulations (such as those pertaining to copyright). The final section analyzes the interconnection between two contradictory relations: economic and cultural aspects on the one hand, and political competences on European and national levels on the other.

Policy Network

The aforementioned conferences are interventions in a very heterogeneous policy field. EU policies have a relatively long history in specific sectors; for example the EU flagship policy field within cultural industries – audiovisual policy – goes back to the early 1980s.[7] Policy strategies explicitly relating to 'creative industries' or 'cultural industries' as a global concept, however, have been developed only since the second half of the 1990s. Yet this did not lead to a common definition and consistent common policy, but took the form of a highly heterogeneous kind of policy network.

A working paper by Ellen Huijgh and Katie Segers (2006) gives an overview of the developments in European and international policies in that field. The authors describe EU policies on cultural industries as something that was introduced relatively late, as mainly being pragmatic, and – due to the lack of a common definition[8] – as an 'amalgam of policies' (Huijgh and Segers, 2006: 7). 'The documents of the European Parliament, European Commission and European Council', the authors observe, do not leave any doubt about the fact that cultural industries contribute to the global economic and cultural interests […]. Besides this, one never mentions explicitly whether the cultural industries are considered as an economic service or a service of global cultural interest […]. Due to the lack of consensus on the concept cultural industries the EU institutions seem not to be able to adjust their policies to apply the existing laws to the cultural industries. (Huijgh and Segers, 2006: 8)

What Huijgh and Segers evidently have in mind is a traditional policy setting, which departs from a discussion about the economic and cultural aspects, leading to clear definitions, on the basis of which a consistent policy can be developed. Several EU documents also refer to such a policy setting, asking for a clear definition of cultural industries and/or a coherent policy. However, they do not develop definitions themselves and sometimes tend to 'put the responsibility on the others' (Huijgh and Segers, 2006: 6).[9]

This is no mere insufficiency. Culture in EU policy is a cross-sectional matter.[10] To a much greater extent than in traditional cultural policy – regarding contemporary arts and cultural heritage – in the broader field of creative industries this seems to be an everyday reality. Audiovisual and media policy, regional policy, art policy, competition policy, internal market policy, including policies on intellectual property rights etc., all intervene in this field.[11] The different Directorate Generals and other political actors analyze the sector from their own perspective and intervene in that field according to their own logic. A network-like structuring of policy fields can have various consequences. In the present case it appears to be very important to the proponents of economization that the possibilities for action are not constrained by binding definitions and valuations, but to leave these interventions to a free play of forces.

Let us look, for example, at the conclusions drawn from their conference by the Austrian presidency:

Creativity is an important source for competitiveness in a knowledge-based society, and the application of ICT for content production and dissemination is a key factor for the promotion of growth and employment. It is important, however, not to see culture and the market, creativity and competition as contradictory. On the contrary, creativity and innovation need to be present in all policy areas. (Rat der Europäischen Union, 2006: 4)

There is obviously no interest in differentiating between economic and cultural aspects. The striking point about this quote is, in my view, not only that the existence of a contradiction between economic and cultural aspects is denied, but that this denial is combined with a reference to the cross-sectional policy approach and implicitly to the heterogeneity of the policy field. The free play of forces integrates the sector into the general trend in EU-policy to an ever increasing market liberalization.

The Lisbon Strategy as a Root

Reading the current EU-documents which deal with creative industries or aspects of the sector and looking at which other policy objectives they refer to, one always ends up with the Lisbon strategy – either directly, or indirectly through other EU documents.

The Lisbon strategy, as is well known, was formulated in the year 2000 with the aim of making the European Union 'the most competitive and dynamic knowledge-based economy in the world' by 2010 (Council of the European Union, 2000 and 2001). Due to the fact that the economic perspectives at the end of the 1990s were quite positive and most of the EU member states had social democratic governments at that time, the first formulation of the Lisbon strategy not only focused on competitiveness in the world markets, but also made reference to higher job quality, social cohesion, and sustainable development.

Some years later it became clear that the EU was behind schedule, and it became obvious that it would not be possible to reach the aspired aims by 2010. An interim report criticized mainly the inconsistent implementation of the strategy (namely on the part of the member states), and that the aims were too complex to be reached.[12] There was no critical appraisal of the underlying neoliberal principles. Instead, 'the European Commission and the Council adhered to the basic neoliberal conception and tried to implement it in its pure form – liberated from all ecological and social aspirations' (Huffschmid, 2006: 73). In 2005 a new start of the Lisbon process was proclaimed, with growth and jobs as the two main targets and with a tendency to eclipse all other aims, while reaffirming at the same time that social cohesion and ecological sustainability must not be attenuated.[13]

There is some insistence behind this new start. This is evident for example in the strategic guidelines on cohesion, which state that the policy mix in a regional strategy may vary according to the context, but the Commission's governing principle when negotiating the different regional and national programs will be their contribution to the 'Growth and Jobs Strategy' (Council of the European Union, 2006: 7). Or, even virtually in a tone of exhortation:

> In this context, it is important for the key stakeholders at national, regional and local level to rally behind the reform agenda so that resources are genuinely concentrated on promoting growth and jobs and put in place the necessary partnership networks to that effect. (Council of the European Union, 2006: 7)

There are several links between the Lisbon Strategy and cultural/creative industries. One link is the jobs in this sector. Interestingly, DG Employment seems to have been the first EU institution that became interested in 'cultural industries' as a global concept. A broader debate was started with a study which was published in 1998. (Huijgh and Segers, 2006: 5-6) This paper stresses the high job potential of the sector, and it at least also mentions the high degree of precariousness and uncertainty of many jobs in this sector.

In later studies and documents both aspects are repeatedly mentioned, with an increase in the sheer number of jobs as the main aspect for policy intervention (even though this aspect often seems to be more evoked in a way that is hardly scientifically coherent, than actually based on facts). The aspect of uncertainty and precariousness is either simply taken for granted, or possible solutions are sought in current neoliberal so-called empowering strategies – education, training, including workshops on how to become self-employed.

The contradiction between high job potential and the lack of social security has at least led to some demands in studies – that statistics should not just count the sheer number of jobs, but also collect data about income, and whether people can live from their jobs, and so forth, and also calls for an employment strategy for the cultural sector.

But these are only very small steps. It may be expected that the topic of employment in the creative industries will be even more strongly emphasized against the backdrop of the renewed Lisbon strategy.

However, taking into account the general tendency of this renewal – the attenuation of aspects which go beyond improvement of growth and jobs in sheer numbers – the policy approach is not likely to change substantially.

The second link, which is stressed frequently, is the role of creativity in the knowledge and information economy. A few years ago, this was not a main topic in EU cultural policy. In the Commission's proposal for the 'Culture 2007' program, for example, which was published in July 2004, the terms 'Lisbon', 'information society' or 'knowledge economy' do not appear at all (Commission of the European Communities, 2004). This might be due to timing; the proposal was finalized some time before the new start of the Lisbon strategy was officially launched. It may also have to do with content: the program's main aim has been to support non-profit arts and cultural heritage projects. Various attempts on the part of special interest groups to enforce the implementation of an additional (beyond audiovisual policy) support program for the cultural industries (or a budget line within 'Culture 2007') were either forestalled or did not materialize.[14]

In contrast to this, the Lisbon Strategy has an important place in the mentioned invitation of autumn 2006 to participate in the DG EAC consultation. This is also apparent in the questionnaire: 'Do you see a role for culture as a stimulus for creativity in Europe and as a catalyst for innovation and knowledge? If so, please indicate how this role should be supported at European level?'[15] Another current document, the Commission's proposal to make 2008 the European Year of Intercultural Dialogue, gives one possible answer to this question. It states that intercultural dialogue contributes toward achieving a number of the Union's strategic priorities, among others: 'by including the renewed Lisbon strategy, for which the knowledge-based economy requires people capable of adapting to changes and benefiting from all possible sources of innovation in order to increase prosperity' (Commission of the European Communities, 2005b).

What appears to be manifested and reinforced here in conjunction with the Lisbon strategy is a process that is also generally described in relation to cultural policy developments as a transition from policy concepts relating to 'cultural industries' to policy concepts relating to 'creative industries':

Further developments towards a wider context of application led to a shift from the concept of cultural industries to the notion of creative industries, the understanding of the creativity concept itself moving from the activities having a strong artistic component to 'any activity producing symbolic products with a heavy reliance on intellectual property and for as wide a market as possible'. (Marcus, 2005: 3)

In recent developments on the EU level, there seem to be two more aspects in addition to this general description. There is the threat that this development will not be restricted to creative industries but shape cultural policies as a whole (Gleibs and Schmalfeldt, 2005). And there is a tendency to go beyond the realm of symbolic products to become the predominant paradigm in post-Fordist production contexts in general.

From 'Soft Law' to 'Hard Law'

It seems that in the current discussion on creative/cultural industries, references to regional policy are quite rare. For example in the programs and materials of the three conferences mentioned at the beginning, there are a few minor references to the 'regional', but nothing substantial. In the 'i2010' strategy paper, regional policy is referred to, but only in a passage about technical infrastructure and Internet broadband access, with the task of ensuring equal technical standards in all regions (Commission of the European Communities, 2005a).

This is a bit surprising – not just in terms of the general fact that the major portion of creativity discussions, which are inspired by authors like Richard Florida, and the cluster theories mainly refer to location, but also in terms of the historical function of regional policies in EU politics with an impact on the cultural sector.

As early as the late 1980s the EU already abandoned the concept of regional policies that understands solidarity among regions in the sense of a direct compensation/balancing between richer and poorer regions. Unlike Thatcher's regional policy in the UK, for example, the EU basically maintained the aspect of solidarity, but it has been a model of solidarity based on the concept of competitiveness: a poor region gets support with the aim of making it competitive, so that it can participate in the overall competition between regions. EU cultural policy and cultural support on regional levels have been part of this, and I think that in the context of EU policies this was a primary instrument for turning economic aspects into an influential point of view in cultural policies (Minichbauer, 2004).

Seen against this background, it is remarkable that the connection between the current discussion and regional policies seems quite weak. My interpretation so far is that regional policy has contributed to making creative industries approaches an acknowledged part of cultural policy at the regional level and is now an everyday reality. At the same time, leading EU policies have moved to different levels: from being space oriented to the internet, from regional to pan-European, to some extent from content to infrastructure and hardware,[16] and seemingly also from so-called 'soft-law' (enabling through support-programs) to 'hard-law' regulations, for example about intellectual property rights.

Proposed restrictions in the field of intellectual property rights imply a certain tendency to criminalize media users and especially people who actively promote the free flow of information. The question arises as to whether such a development as has been briefly sketched here may signal an indication of a transition in neoliberalism from a mainly liberal to a more repressive stage (Raunig, 2005).

These kinds of displacements and re-compositions of policy fields also imply the threat that certain policy styles and basic attitudes could be transferred into other sectors. This might be similar to developments in the mid-1990s, which Christina Holtz-Bacha (2006) has described: the increasing convergence of audiovisual media policy and policy in the field of digital communication infrastructure led to an import of the 'spirit of deregulation and liberalisation', which had been omnipresent in EU action in the telecommunications sector.

Identity/Economy

The aforementioned invitation to the cultural sector to participate in the online consultation in preparation of the 2007 Communication on Culture of the European Commission mentions two 'main sets of objectives': 'developing active European citizenship, respecting cultural diversity, promoting intercultural dialogue, while fostering a sense of "European identity" complementary to other identities' and 'the economic and social objectives of the Lisbon agenda, and the role of creativity in enhancing the competitive edge of Europe'.[17]

Condensed into core aims, this means: identity politics and the economic aspects of the cultural sector. Both have been among the main objectives in EU cultural policy since the early 1980s[18] at the latest. In a cultural policy, which has become more and more pragmatic,[19] these core aims – including the economic aims – are increasingly becoming overwhelming today.

Identity

At the centre of EU cultural policies are still the national cultural identities and at the same time the aim of propounding a European cultural identity on the basis of a diversity of these national cultural identities (Kaufman, 2003). This forms the foundation for cultural action at the EU level in two respects: in the allocation of competences within the multilevel political system, and as an ideological grounding.

In the EC treaties cultural competences have not been mentioned at all for a long time. At that stage, legal and political competences for culture (at all levels, including the international) automatically belonged to the member states, apart from a few first initiatives such as the European Cultural City. In the Treaty of Maastricht (1992) an article on culture was included. The main competence, however, stayed with the member states, whereas only a supplementary competence is granted at the European level – in a complementary manner and only in connection with a European added value.

Gudrun Quenzel has analyzed the ideological grounding – the constructions of Europe – as laid down in the legal documents of the EC. She states that 'the conception of a shared European culture and different national cultures are not found in explicit contradiction to one another anywhere within the legal documents' (Quenzel, 2005: 138). She thus concludes:

> In summary, it is initially evident that the Council presumes homogeneous cultures and attributes a territorial foundation to them. In the legal documents cultures correspond to peoples and/or nations, or they coincide with the borders of these: either nations are the same as cultures, or they have a culture. In addition, the field of cultural and artistic production is regarded as a representation of nations and/or cultures. […] In terms of the integration of national identity into a shared European identity, the Council thus pursues the strategy returning cultural diversity to a diversity of antecedent European culture. The subjects are appealed to as members of their nation, and at the same time the nation is defined as an equal part of Europe. Through this process, in the appellation as national citizens there is

155

simultaneously the echo of an appellation as Europeans, and national identity becomes part of a European identity. (Quenzel, 2005: 159-60)[20]

In this context, Quenzel points out the practical problems that in this approach the phenomenon of migration is totally neglected and that the EU can comprehend states such as Russia or Turkey only as national and cultural entities, which are as a whole either European or not.

In general, the concept of national and European identities is completely inadequate in terms of serving as a basis for the development of political concepts able to deal with the processes of social re-composition that are currently taking place (Nowotny, 2003). And although it is evident that the European identity that the European Union aims at, is not of a comparably totalitarian nature as the classical political identity that the European nation-states developed, the model still is one of a territorially defined cultural identity, which conforms quite well to the political reality of a 'fortress Europe', which increasingly closes its borders and tightens laws.

It is not possible to develop a really transnational cultural policy on the basis of this ideological foundation, thus the attempts to this until now have been quite weak and undetermined.

Economy

In this policy setting, the convergence between economic and cultural aspects is a clear objective. Reaching these kinds of convergences, or at least making them plausible, seems to be especially easy once the 'cultural aspects' have been simplified to essentialist cultural identities. Examples for these kinds of convergences include the European cities of culture, which are supposed to contribute to building a European cultural identity and at the same time have considerable economic impact.[21] Also exemplary are the minimum quotas for European productions in the television directives, in which the arguments concerning a European identity converge with the arguments about raising market shares against the superiority of American movies.[22]

Yet on the other hand, these convergences are also not always so easy to achieve, so tensions between economic and cultural aspects remain present as a topic – either in the form of a critique of economistic cultural policies, or in the neoliberal denial of the contradictory nature of this relation.

Partly due to the allocation of competences (culture as a competence of the member states vs. for example internal market as a competence of the Union), contradictions between economic and cultural aspects often take the form of conflicts between member states and the Union, especially the European Commission.[23] An example here is the audiovisual and media policies of the EU, as analyzed by Christina Holtz-Bacha (2006). In the early 1980s there were attempts to set up a European TV-channel – arising mainly in association with the European Parliament. After these experiments failed, primarily because there were no proper solutions developed to deal with the many languages involves, the EU completely changed its policy, mostly due to urging from the European Commission. TV broadcasting was then recast as a service, and largely negative integration followed from deregulation. Holtz-Bacha's account of the subsequent developments documents the contradiction between the member states and their public broadcasting organizations bringing up cultural arguments, program quality, and so on, on the one hand, and the European Commission on the other, which argues economically in the sense of a free market policy in general, and also takes in the arguments of the private broadcasters.

Cases like this seem to confirm the allocation of competences and the cultural competence of the member states (which might be true for certain aspects of TV policy), but should not be generalized to a setting: nation states defending culture vs. the neoliberal Commission. But what we can see at the same time is that the practical realization of the member state's cultural competences – in the sense of actually enforcing decisions and rules – is much more challenged in this contradiction between economic and cultural aspects than it is in the relation national and European identities. And this challenge is all the more obvious if we take into consideration what was said earlier about the policy network.

In the conclusion of a study, which was commissioned by the Austrian Presidency as preparation for their 2006 conference, the authors argue that ascribing cultural competency to the member states in the European Treaty on a practical policy level does 'not say much, since […] content is a cross-sectional matter, which in many ways and respects falls within the competence of the community legislators' (Holoubek and Damjanovic, 2006: 153). They see the new television directive and the developments in the field of intellectual property rights as steps in the right direction and conclude:

> A European content policy that is more than the sum total of the individual member states' policies must be clearly identifiable as such. European primary law would be the right place for embodying democratic and cultural policy guideline principles for a special European market model covering important parts of the content sector. The 'cultural article' in its present form [...] does not appear to live up to this challenge. [...] If, in an open and proactive approach a culture-oriented European content policy is sought that preserves and promotes the global competitiveness of Europe's content industry, the community must be equipped with the necessary regulatory competences in the field of cultural policy. (Holoubek and Damjanovic, 2006: 150)

In the neoliberal discourse that accompanies these developments, there is also a tendency to incorporate arguments that were considered part of the 'cultural aspects' in functions that are ascribed to the market or economic policies. Thus, it is no longer a 'logic of the market' versus 'broad access to culture', but rather 'the market provides broad access to cultural goods'. Equally, there is no longer a juxtaposition of the 'logic of competitiveness' versus 'cultural diversity', but rather 'competition policy basically supports cultural diversity, because it aims to prevent the emergence of monopolies'.

As it has not been possible – nor even really attempted – to go beyond the concept of national cultural identities and develop a genuinely transnational cultural policy, there is a certain likelihood that in the near future the only path in this direction will follow the concepts of creative industries. But then it will not be realized as a cultural policy oriented to content/structure, but as a cultural policy that is to be shifted to form part of a free market policy.

Conclusion

The economization of the cultural sector, basically a long-term trend in EU policies, has been clearly intensified in recent years. One of the driving forces of the actual developments is the Lisbon strategy with its 'jobs and growth strategy' and concepts of information and knowledge economy. In terms of practical policy, three fields can be identified in which the EU is especially active: audiovisual, digital communication, and copyright policies.

'Cultural industries' or 'creative industries' as a global concept have also been part of the discussion at the EU level. While there have been rapid developments in certain sectors, the impact of the global concept was rather limited – at least until recently. In recent years, however, the terms 'creativity' and 'creative industries' (or even 'creative economy') seem to be proliferating in EU cultural policy. At the moment, it seems to be a set of terms that has no clear outline, but exists mainly to link the fields mentioned here, in which concrete policy is developed on the one hand, and the global concept of the Lisbon strategy or knowledge economy on the other. And this corresponds with the general process of the increasing economization of the cultural sector.

Accordingly, I don't think it would be useful to put the term 'creative industries' at the center of the development of counter-strategies against the increasing economization in EU cultural policy. This term should rather be seen as merely one element among others. Counter-strategies can mainly relate to concrete developments in certain sectors. For example, copyright policy has already led to broader resistance. And the tensions between economic and cultural aspects, which are not so easily resolved, open up possibilities for intervention. As far as the term 'creative industries' is concerned, it will be important in the near future to observe whether and how far the proliferation continues and which performative effects deriving from this become apparent at the EU level.

Notes

1 I would like to thank Therese Kaufmann for discussions that inform this chapter, which is the result of a research collaboration between FRAME and eipcp.

2 See http://www.creativeeconomyconference.org/. All web links in this text were accessed in October 2006.

3 The conference-website (http://contentconference.at) was taken offline after the conference. A print-publication about the conference by the Arts Division of the Austrian Federal Chancellery has been announced. Press releases on different panels/topics of the conference are available in German on the website of the Austrian EU Presidency

(http://www.eu2006.at/de/Meetings_Calendar/Dates/March/0203Conten
tforCompetitiveness.html), including a few texts in English. Holoubek and
Damjanovic, 2006, is a study commissioned by the Arts Division in
preparation for the conference.

4   See http://www.minedu.fi/OPM/Tapahtumakalenteri/2006/07/creativity_
    online.html.

5   The Conference 'Kultur- und Kreativwirtschaft in Europa – Kohärente
    Politik in einer globalen Welt' was held in Berlin in 2007; see
    http://www.european-creative-industries.eu/.

6   The invitation appeared on the European Commission's Culture website:
    http://ec.europa.eu/culture/eac/communication/consult_en.html.

7   Two other fields in which the EU is especially active are digital
    communication and copyright policies. For an overview of the
    developments in EU media and audiovisual policy, see Holtz-Bacha, 2006.
    The early 1980s marked the start of audiovisual media policy, while first
    regulations in the field of film production were already determined as early
    as the 1960s (Holtz-Bacha, 2006: 68, 258).

8   Huijgh and Segers note the problem that different political actors use the
    same terms and so seem to refer to the same subject, but in fact interpret
    the terms quite differently. Beyond this, the terms 'creative industries' and
    'cultural industries' are only used to a certain extent. For example, the terms
    do not occur at all in many relevant documents on current programs for
    regional and structural funding. (See for example Commission of the
    European Communities, 2006.) The Austrian Presidency in their
    conference, while using also the term 'creative industries' to a certain extent,
    focused their inquiry/argumentation on the term 'content' – in its neoliberal
    meaning which effectively and lastingly dissociates cultural contents from
    societal, political and communicative contexts and makes it utilizable for
    economic exploitation beyond creative production, including information
    services. Cf. Holoubek and Damjanovic, 2006: 20.

9   They go on to write:

    [The] European Parliament doesn't want to formulate a definition for
    the cultural industries on its 'own initiative' (European Parliament,
    12/05/2003, 22/04/2003, 14/07/2003). But in its resolution of the
    4th of September 2003 on the cultural industries the Parliament
    requests the European Commission to come up with a definition
    (European Parliament, 04/09/2003: point (1)). Meanwhile the
    European Commission's opinion group on cultural industries stresses
    that it did opt for not defining the cultural industries (European
    Commission, 28-29/01/2004: 1). (Huijgh and Segers, 2006: 6)

10 Clause 4 of Article 151 of the Treaty asserts: 'The Community shall take cultural aspects into account in its action under other provisions of this Treaty, in particular in order to respect and to promote the diversity of its cultures'. For an analysis of Article 151, see Kaufmann and Raunig, 2003: 18-23. Also important in the context of increasing economization of the cultural sector is the impact of this regulation on the level of practical fundraising for cultural projects: interest groups and networks in the cultural sector had claimed for a long time that the inadequate budget for the predecessor funding programs of 'Culture 2000' should be significantly increased. This demand was not met, and in this context Clause 4 had the effect of increasingly pushing cultural operators to apply for funds in other – much more economically oriented – programs, especially in regional and structural funds.

11 This is also evident in the questionnaire which was used by DG EAC for the consultation mentioned above:

> In your opinion, which are the Community policies and their specific aspects that have the greatest impact on the activities of the cultural sector at European level or to which the cultural sector could make an important contribution? How are you affected by these policies, which developments in these policies could contribute to the development of your sector and its cross-border activities, what might this contribution consist of, serving which specific aims and with which partners? Have you identified any concerns or difficulties in relation to these policies? Which European developments could facilitate the involvement of your sector?

> Please rank the policies or policy areas in decreasing order of priority and indicate, if necessary, their specific aspects (max. 500 characters): Agriculture, Audiovisual and Media, Civil Society, Competition, Culture, Customs Union, Economic and monetary union, Education and Training, Employment and Social affairs, Enterprise and Industry, Environment, Freedom, security and justice, Information Society, Internal Market, Maritime Affairs, Regional policy, Research, Development, Technology and Innovation, Sport, Taxation, Trans-European networks, Transport, Youth, Development, Enlargement, European Neighbourhood Policy, External assistance, External trade, Foreign policies.

> The questionnaire is online at http://ec.europa.eu/culture/eac/communication/pdf_word/questionnaire_en.doc.

12 See the report of the High Level Group, chaired by Wim Kok (Council of the European Union, 2004a).

13 'The European Council took on the core issues of this proposal, which does not contain any new economic policy ideas, for the spring summit in March 2005. It neutralized these issues, however, by indicating several times in its final communiqué that the new priorities for growth and employment must not lead to an attenuation of social cohesion and ecological sustainability. Nevertheless, this is seriously misleading; attenuation is indeed the core of the recommendations from the Kok report and the Commission paper. Growth and employment are the aim and nothing else. The Council accepted both documents and undermined them at the same time with attenuations, but without putting a different economic policy conception in their place. The "Conclusions of the Presidency" document neoliberal helplessness' (Huffschmid, 2006: 85).

14 From this former broader coalition, it is mainly the music industry that keeps up lobbying. See for example the website of the 'European Music Office': http://www.musicineurope.org/presentation/objectives.html.

15 See 'The 2007 Communication on culture', online at http://ec.europa.eu/culture/eac/communication/comm_en.html.

16 Several EU documents, for example Commission of the European Communities, 2005, give the impression that the main focus of European policy is the development of communication infrastructure, and in a second step, European content is required in order to enable the attainment of full economic returns.

17 See footnote 15 above.

18 'The presentation of the European documents by E. Colombo and H.-D. Genscher in 1981 marks the beginning of a third, not yet completed phase, the main characteristic of which is the start of a genuine cultural action founded on economic argumentation moving closer to a redefinition of cultural identity, but limited to the audiovisual sector and the field of education.' (Dumont, 1994: 126)

19 This is also evident when comparing the 'Culture 2000' program and its successor 'Culture 2007'. See Minichbauer, 2005.

20 Quenzel also speaks of a 'split of national identity into a potentially European part and another that is pushed into the background and cannot be integrated' (2005: 138).

21 Quenzel, 2005: 270. The European Capital of Culture program was started in 1985, and the cities chosen as capital of culture in the first years were cities that already had an international profile as cultural cities, like Athens or Paris. But in 1990 the UK made Glasgow European Capital of Culture, based on an argumentation referring to urban development, cultural

tourism, the context of public-private partnerships etc. Glasgow led to a reversal in trend, and these arguments became hegemonic in later discussions and decisions about cultural capitals.

22 But this cannot be interpreted as a convergence in a broader picture – taking into account the whole television directive –, since deregulation and commercialization suggest that the broadcasting corporations should work with the financially more competitive US products. See Dumont, 1994: 127.

23 The EU has developed political procedures for these kinds of contradictions. There have been processes of permanent negotiations for a long time, and it seems that the implicit tendency of this is that compromises between free market policies and essentialist identity politics are being developed, while other political/societal aspects of the cultural sector are being marginalized in political discourse at the same time.

PART FOUR: CULTURE INDUSTRY

12

Culture Industry and the Administration of Terror

Gene Ray

'Enjoy your precarity!'[1] This is the command behind the bubbling ideological re-descriptions and compensating revalorizations of the so-called creative industries. The contributors to this volume show this well, through analyses in various critical modes and keys and with regard to various national contexts. If such a command is to stick, it needs appeal, allure, mystique. The figure of the artist as creative rebel, dusted off and shined up, seems to do the trick. In the new imaginaries of post-Fordist cognitive capitalism, the old categories of autonomy and creativity are jolted back to life and luster. On the subjective level, it's all about moods, fantasies and libidinal investments. Self-exploitation can be hip, if deep knee-bends are performed to an appropriate sound track. It really is possible to find freedom in unfreedom, correct living in the false, if only you look for it in the new and approved ways. How much potential for resistance comes with these shifted productive relations and this readjusted subject of labor is a matter of some dispute, even between the covers of this book.

In any case, trends in the labor market, characterized by a painful intensification of precarity, dependency and demoralization, are evidently a firmly established aspect of the contemporary social process, even if claims about post-Fordist production arguably are more applicable to certain sectors in the Global North than generalizable as capital's new avant-garde.[2] Such shifts clearly have a material basis, not least in the dominant position capital has for decades held in the global force field. Neo-liberalism may be more than ever exposed by the current economic and biospheric meltdowns. But whatever legitimation crisis it suffers as a result, the social processes this hegemonic ideology was shaped to cover and justify are proceeding apace; with regard to policy and state interventions, this aggressive, offensive posture in the class war against labor has ceded hardly any momentum at all. In Europe in 2010, misery is advancing under the sign of an 'austerity' aiming to protect finance capital and mop up the remnants of organized labor-power. 'There is no alternative' is still the official mantra of the day.

How are we to explain this remarkable intransigence of capital in its neo-liberal posture? The classical balance of forces framework offers a sobering optic. It suggests that capital can go on wreaking such havoc because labor as an organized counter-power has been decomposed and pulverized. The reasons for this de-organization are debatable. Is it due to decisive defeats and co-optations – the result of a cumulative overpowering? Or is it rather attributable to deep shifts in the organization of social production, shifts in which labor has actively participated, by its selective resistance and exodus? But even the latter appears more and more as another form of defeat today, as the real and continuing costs of labor-power's weakness in relation to capital relentlessly come to light.

Back to Benjamin and Adorno then, back to the melancholy of impasse? Old school, no doubt, but a measure of Frankfurt pessimism is bracing corrective to an optimism become foolish. It is a willful gaze that can take in the last century and still see progress. Such a return would not be unproductive in this context, either, for as several authors in this volume remark, the discourse of creative industries is premised on a neutralizing appropriation of Adorno's critical category of 'culture industry'. This category certainly poses the problematic of subjectivity. But it also gives heavy weight to the dominant tendencies of objective reality. It is this second aspect that is sometimes discounted in even critical responses to the celebration of creative industries. Over the course of the 1950s and 1960s, Adorno came to see 'administration' and 'integration' as the decisive immanent tendencies of late capitalism. Both, it will be shown, are inseparably bound up with the category of terror, which has to be a part of any adequate account of the global social process that dominates life today.

The Stakes of Culture Industry

Discussions of culture industry typically begin with the famous chapter from Horkheimer and Adorno's *Dialectic of Enlightenment*. There, the tendencies and processes engulfing 'culture' – 'tendencies which turn cultural progress into its opposite' (2002: xiii) – are registered across 'philosophical fragments' emplotting 'the tireless self-destruction of enlightenment' (2002: xiv; 2003: 1): Enlightenment, the dream suicided by society. The liberation of man from a dominating 'nature' is converted into the class domination of man by man, and this dialectic takes catastrophic and genocidal turns under late capitalism, as the nets of the social whole tighten. The rationalized production of cultural commodities for mass consumption reinforces culture's affirmative ideological functions in a vicious spiral. Spaces for critical autonomy tend to be squeezed out and critical capacities atrophy, leaving conformity and resignation as the paths of least resistance. In a hostile takeover and permanent occupation of leisure time, the exploitative social given advertises itself unceasingly. Mass culture, as Adorno puts it in the continuation of the chapter, becomes 'a system of signals that signals itself' (Adorno, 2001: 82).[3] Culture industry denotes the dominant logic of cultural 'goods' that are impressively varied and apparently free of direct censorship, but which nevertheless exhibit a strong tendency toward uniformity. In this they mirror the logic of the global social process, that persistence in domination that Adorno in 1951 described vividly as 'the ever-changing production of the always-the-same' (Adorno, 1976: 13-14; 1992: 23; cf. Adorno, 2001: 100).

The culture industry chapter of *Dialectic of Enlightenment* was only a preliminary formulation of this thesis, however. Adorno offered some important elaborations of the argument in the 1960 essay 'Culture and Administration' and 'Culture Industry Reconsidered', from 1963. Additional glosses and remarks in passing can be found throughout his texts of the 1950s and 1960s. Moreover, the published book chapter represents only the jointly edited first half of a longer manuscript drafted by Adorno; in the 1944 mimeograph edition circulated to Frankfurt Institute members, the chapter ends with the line 'To be continued.' The unedited remainder was published posthumously in 1981, under the title 'The Schema of Mass Culture'.

The additional writings do not greatly change the argument and certainly do not retract the conclusions. But the clarifications and elaborations they offer get in the way of writers wishing to dismiss those conclusions too easily, on the grounds that changes since have made them obsolete. In the new preface to the 1969 edition of *Dialectic of Enlightenment*, Horkheimer and Adorno acknowledge that time does not stand still; processes change as they unfold. But they insist that the tendency they pointed to continues to hold:

> We do not stand by everything we said in the book in its original form. That would be incompatible with a theory which attributes a temporal core to truth instead of contrasting truth as something invariable to the movement of history. The book was written at a time when the end of the National Socialist terror was in sight. In not a few places, however, the formulation is no longer adequate to the reality of today. All the same, even at that time we did not underestimate the implications of the transition to the administered world. (Horkheimer and Adorno, 2002: xi; 2003: ix)

The general tendency or immanent drift of the global process has not changed, because the capitalist logic that grounds and generates it remains in force. This general tendency is the essence of capitalist modernity, which unfolds through all the dynamic processes that are its concrete appearance-forms. It holds, so long as the social world is a capitalist one.

In 'Culture Industry Reconsidered', Adorno recalls that he and Horkheimer chose the term 'culture industry' not only to express the paradoxical merger of an at least quasi-autonomous tradition with its opposite. They also aimed to critique the concept of 'mass culture', with its implication of an authentically popular culture: 'The customer is not king, as the culture industry would have us believe, not its subject but its object.' (Adorno, 1973: 60-1; 1991: 99) Adorno does not hesitate to reaffirm the tendency at work. The production and consumption of commodified culture 'more or less according to plan' tends to produce conformist consciousness and functions in sum as 'a system almost without gaps': 'This is made possible by contemporary technical capacities as well as by economic and administrative concentration.' (1973: 60; 1991 98)

The term 'industry', then, refers to the market-oriented rationality or calculus that drives all aspects of the processes involved. It registers the fact that there *is* a master logic, operative through technical developments and shifts in particular processes:

> Thus, the expression 'industry' is not to be taken too literally. It refers
> to the standardization of the thing itself – such as that of the Western,
> familiar to every movie-goer – and to the rationalization of distribution
> techniques, but not strictly to the production process. (Adorno, 1973:
> 62-3; 1991: 100)

The production processes themselves often still involve the input of
individuals who have not been entirely severed from their means of
production and who may be celebrated as stars – or today's 'creatives'.
But their contributions are still integrated according to the logic of
valorization and accumulation that dominates commodified culture:

> It [culture industry] is industrial more in a sociological sense, in the
> incorporation of industrial forms of organization even when nothing is
> manufactured – as in the rationalization of office work – rather than in
> the sense of anything really and actually produced by technological
> rationality. (Adorno, 1973: 63; 1991: 101)

It is no refutation of the culture industry thesis, then, simply to point to
this or that aspect of the cultural field today and note how aged and out
of date those old examples from the 1940s have become. If micro-
enterprises are the norm in today's creative industries, this means little if
their very existence is an effect of technology and 'economic and
administrative concentration'. The internet feels like freedom, but
Google and Verizon can still decide together how they will undo the
principle of net neutrality.[4] Nor will it suffice to point to counter-
tendencies, local or not, if these do not displace the master logic; over
time, generally if not in every case, the dominant tendency wins out, so
long as it is dominant.

To refute the argument, it would be necessary to show that the
overall drift or tendency no longer holds – or never did. The issue at
stake is manipulation: the restriction, impoverishment and seduction of
consciousness. Are the gaps, in which autonomous subjects can emerge
and from which practices of critical resistance might produce real
effects, still closing? Or are these gaps of autonomy expanding now, as
some claim, indicating a reversal of the trend? How are autonomous
subjects formed, anyway? What are the conditions of their formation
and, if they are to be considered as 'actors' in a cultural field, what
freedom of action is actually theirs?

Here, of course, the argument of culture industry clashes with theoretical orientations firmly established in academe in the wake of 1968. Rejecting Frankfurt pessimism, the new disciplinary hybrid of cultural studies took aim at the manipulation thesis. The dominated classes are not the passive objects of manipulation, it was countered; even as consumers, they find ways to express their resistance to control and exploitation. From one angle, scholars such as Edward Thompson, Raymond Williams and Stuart Hall insisted in Marxist terms on the existence of cultures of popular resistance, even within the forms of dominant culture. In a different vector, Michel Foucault, Gilles Deleuze and Félix Guattari, and Michel de Certeau became new reference points for an end-run around the manipulation problem that rejected the Marxist conception of social power; in this approach, the forms or modes of subjectivation constituted by specific relations of power gain priority over macro structures of exploitation and direct repression.

How far do such retorts and re-conceptions really come to grips with Adorno's dialectic of subjectivation and the dominant objective tendency? In answering this question, we need to avoid caricatures and straw-arguments. Whatever the rhetorical hyperbole of certain formulations, Adorno does not argue that the consumers of mass culture are merely passive slaves invariably doomed to eternal reification. He is careful to acknowledge that gaps and openings for critical autonomy still exist. The argument is that the dominant process is systematically reducing such gaps and that the constriction is well advanced; those critical and autonomous subjects who do emerge are increasingly blocked from any practice *that could change the dominant trend or aim radically beyond it*. In this sense, the system is 'totalizing'.

But totalizing does not and cannot mean *totalized*, as in actualized with an exhaustive completeness that would, once and for all, eliminate every gap and permanently block critical subjects from ever emerging again. This is a basic point of Adorno's 'negative dialectics' and of his critique of Hegel. Social systems tend toward closure, but they can only actualize closure through the final solution of genocidal integrations and subsumptions; the once-and-for-all of *global closure* would simultaneously eliminate the conditions of the system itself, which cannot do without the subjects it needs to activate, mobilize and control. The catastrophic aspect of late capitalism is that techno-power and so-called Weapons of Mass Destruction make the literal suicide of enlightenment a real historical possibility for the first time – this is where terror will have to come in, and will do later in the essay.

The point about subjectivation, however, is that *there are chains* – there are objective constraints that function as obstacles to subjective autonomy and limit what subjects can do with their autonomy. The problem is not exhausted in the question, why do people choose their own chains (or: give their consent to the hegemonic culture). Some may do so as the result of an economic calculation, or a specific fear, or the compensatory enjoyment of more unconscious repressions. But the high stakes of the culture industry argument are in the claim that the objective tendency reaches far back into the processes by which subjects are formed. 'Pre-formed' subjects begin to emerge, who no longer even recognize this choice – yes or no to their chains:

> The mesh of the whole, modeled on the act of exchange, is drawn ever tighter. It leaves individual consciousness less and less room for evasion, *pre-forms it more and more thoroughly*, cuts it off a priori as it were from the possibility of difference, which is degraded to a nuance in the monotony of supply. (Adorno, 1976: 10; 1992: 21, translation modified, my italics)

The modes and processes of subjectivation are a proper focus, then, for the forms and qualities of subjectivity are precisely what are at stake. But these modes and processes of formation are themselves shaped and constrained in ways that cannot be avoided or dismissed: 'Society precedes the subject' (Adorno, 1975: 132; 1995: 126). Subject-centered approaches are premised on the possibility of intervention into the modes of subjectivation. This entails the freedom and autonomy required to refuse an imposed or offered form of subjectivity, for example by withdrawing from a specific relation of power and domination. But how free are existing subjects? Are they masters of destiny who can do what they want, regardless of objective factors and forces? That hardly seems likely, and if they are not, then there is no reason to think Adorno has been answered or refuted.

Some post-structuralist approaches to subjectivation risk one-sidedly discounting the headlock of the objective – the constraints imposed by prevailing structures, conditions and tendencies. There is an implicit voluntarism in the assumption that subjects can simply refuse and leap out of every subjugating relation of power or de-link themselves at will from the forms of dominated subjectivity that correspond to such relations. (If they could, things would presumably be much different.) Adorno is clearly arguing against such voluntarism. But it would be a distortion of Adorno's position to attribute to him some version of absolutized passivity and servility. For him, critical autonomy is the necessary subjective vector of emancipation. Critical subjects can still emerge, but only through the hard mental work of self-liberation – against the processes and dominant tendencies of which the culture industry is an ideological mediator. This becomes increasingly improbable as critical capacity is systematically attacked, undermined, blocked and repressed. Unlikely but still possible: Adorno also insists it cannot be excluded. Individual subjects can through their own efforts break the spell and see through the mirages of social appearance. While the conditions of autonomy objectively dwindle, its subjective condition remains the subject's own desire for liberation.

Consider the ending of the full, extended version of the culture industry chapter:

> The neon signs that hang over our cities and outshine the natural light
> of the night with their own are comets presaging the natural disaster of
> society, its frozen death. Yet they do not come from the sky. They are
> controlled from the earth. It depends upon human beings themselves
> whether they will extinguish these lights and awake from a nightmare
> that only threatens to become actual as long as men believe in it.
> (Adorno, 1991: 96)[5]

Taken out of context, these lines could even leave an impression of idealistic voluntarism. But there is too much continual emphasis elsewhere, indeed throughout, on the objective domination of the global social process to warrant any such precipitous reading. The aporia is not that subjects cannot, here and there, break the spell, but rather that the conditions for *a critical mass* of such subjects, and thus for a passage to strategic social transformation, are evidently blocked.

Relative Autonomy, Resistance and Struggle

The problem with the culture industry argument is that, even if it reflects a sober and basically accurate estimation of social forces and tendencies, its pathos of pessimism threatens to become paralyzing. It tells us why there is less and less space for resistant subjects and practical resistance, without telling us what can be done about it. We are called to stand firm and seek whatever vestiges of critical autonomy are left to us, but at the same time we are told why this cannot possibly alter or transform the status quo. If critical theory does no more than reflect the given double-bind, then it too fosters resignation and contributes to the objective tendency it would like to critique. The heliotropic orientation toward praxis in late Frankfurt theory has wizened too much. The resistant subject (even qua object of exploitation and target of manipulation) cannot be less stubborn and intransigent than the agents of its systemic enemy.

One way out of the theoretical impasse opens up by pushing the notion of autonomy – not the mystified autonomy that returns in the discourses of creative industries, but the potential that is actually ours. Pure autonomy, we can agree, is a myth. For 'autonomy' we have to read 'relative autonomy'. The culture industry subverts artistic autonomy and tends to absorb it, but never does so entirely. Relatively autonomous art, holding to its own criteria and to the historical logics of its own forms, goes on – and insofar as it does, it remains different from the merely calculated production of cultural commodities. Such an art shares the social guilt and is always scarred by the dominant social logics it tries to refuse. Still, by its very attempts at difference, it activates a relative autonomy and actualizes a force of resistance. In comparison, the culture industry has less relative autonomy; there capital holds sway much more directly. But even in the culture industry, there is *some* relative autonomy to claim and activate. Even Adorno acknowledges as much in his discussion of individual forms of production in 'Culture Industry Reconsidered'. Although certain cultural commodities are produced through technical processes that can properly be called industrial, there is still a 'perennial conflict between artists active in the culture industry and those who control it' (Adorno, 1973: 63; 1991: 101).

Absolute autonomy is a sublime mirage. But so is its opposite. The absence of autonomy is slavery. But its utter absence, the elimination of even potential autonomy, would be absolute, totalized slavery – a closure impossible, short of global termination. Relative autonomy, then, is both the condition of resistance and the condition that actually obtains most of time. What varies – in the specifics of place, position and conjuncture – is the extent and kind of relative autonomy. This granted, we regain a focal point for possible practices of resistance. The culture industry, we can now see, may operate according to a dominant logic, but the operations of this logic cannot exclude all possibilities for resistance. The culture industry is not utterly monolithic, any more than the capitalist state is. It too is fissured by the tensions and antagonisms that plague any hierarchical system; it too mediates and condenses the social force-field, as a 'crystallization' of the forces in class struggle, as Nicos Poulantzas would have put it. To continue this analogy, the culture industry is neither an object-instrument of capital with zero autonomy nor a neutral, domination-free system in which actors can do anything, without regard for the power of capital. Obviously the institutional nexus of culture industry is also very different from the nexus of the state, but that difference can also be thought of as a difference in kind and degree of relative autonomy.

Such a focus brings back into view the class war of position and reopens the struggle for hegemony. It is compatible with the Frankfurt account, remembering the latter's caveats about the impossibility of full systemic closure. And in re-posing the linkage of resistant practices and radical aims, it goes beyond Frankfurt pessimism, without lapsing into a naïve voluntarism or pretending that there are no grounds for worry. The project of subjective liberation is bound to the liberating transformation of the objective whole, the global process. For that aim, the unorganized league of impotent critical subjects is clearly inadequate. Even within spheres of relative autonomy, individual or cellular micro-resistance remains merely symbolic and token, if it cannot organize itself as a political force capable of gaining and holding a place in the balance.[6] In the current weakness, the need is to recompose, reorganize and link struggles, through practical alliances and strategic fronts. Easier said than done, but concrete aims stimulate the search for strategies. Pessimism may be justified but need not freeze us: even in the culture industry, there is always something to be done.

Terror, Culture and Administration

For Adorno, 'integration' and 'administration' named the two linked tendencies of the late capitalist global process. Integration is the logic of identity and the subsumption of particulars, and Adorno traced its workings in social facts and cultural appearance-forms, from philosophical positivism and empirical sociology to astrology columns and Walt Disney cartoons. Administration, or techno-power concentrated in specialized institutions, is congealed as the instrumental logic of entrenched and expanding bureaucracies. Social subjects are not left untouched by processes of integration and administration; in fact, these processes reach into and shape the conditions for possible forms of subjectivity. Adorno emphasizes this point in 'Culture and Administration':

> Administration, however, is not simply imposed upon the supposedly productive human being from without. It multiplies within the person himself. That a particular situation in time brings forth those subjects intended for it is to be taken very literally. Nor are those who produce culture secure before the 'increasingly organic composition of mankind'. (Adorno, 1991: 122; 2003: 137)[7]

The objective tendency, produced by subjects and only transformable by subjects, nevertheless constricts the forms and modes of subjectivation: this dialectic, precisely, generates the perennial catastrophe. And as already noted, these tendencies do not stop short before the physical reduction and liquidation of actual subjects. 'Genocide is the absolute integration' (Adorno, 1975: 355; 1995: 362).[8] Genocide, then, cannot be dismissed as a deviation from the rule of law and humanist norms, for it belongs to the immanent drift of the global process. And after the demonstrations of Auschwitz and Hiroshima, we must live in a social world in which the final integration – the global termination of systemic logic that would at the same time terminate all life and the conditions of all systems – has become objectively possible. Exit, ruined, the myth of progress.

Terror and late capitalism, then, go together. What begins as the pressure of conformity and the market – today, the terrors of precarity and the miseries of austerity – tends toward the logic of exterminism. In the last pages of 'The Schema of Mass Culture', Adorno elaborates the connection between the 'anxiety, that is the ultimate lesson of the fascist era' and techno-power in the hands of administration:

> The terror for which the people of every land are being prepared glares ever more threateningly from the rigid features of these culture-masks: in every peal of laughter we hear the menacing voice of extortion and the comic types are legible signs which represent the contorted bodies of revolutionaries. Participation in mass culture itself stands under the sign of terror. (Adorno, 1991: 96)

The conformity and resignation fostered by a system of cultural uniformity is connected, through the mediations of an unfolding master logic, to the defeats of radical struggles and the triumphs of capitalist war machines. State terror, resurgent today, declares the bogus 'war on terror'.

Enjoyment and Enforcement

Another way to think about subjectivation is through Jacques Lacan's notion of *jouissance* or enjoyment. I began by détourning the title of a book by Slavoj Žižek (1992). Other Lacanian theorists have produced stimulating recent work on the problem of 'commanded enjoyment', a term introduced by Todd McGowan (2004) and helpfully elaborated by Yannis Stavrakakis in his *The Lacanian Left* (2007). Enjoyment, a form of pleasure that does not necessarily exclude pain, displeasure or even terror, compensates for impotence. The subjective investment in fantasmatic object choices and identifications is not experienced as a conflict with objective reality because enjoyment as it were flies under the radar of conscious reason. This embodied return on investment offers a compelling, if partial, account of our social 'stuckness' – our inability to resist our addiction to social processes we know, on another level of awareness, to be self-threatening. The notion of commanded enjoyment acknowledges that the repressed also returns, however, as the hidden cost, the element of unfreedom and compulsion. However indirectly, terror haunts enjoyment issued as a social imperative.

If enjoyment is one side of the coin, then, what we can call enforcement is the other. Enforcement, as I have developed this concept elsewhere (Ray, 2010), is the irreducible element of violence in capitalist reproduction. What begins as the asymmetry of antagonistic productive relations is channeled and intensified, through market competition and imperialist rivalries, into a global process that requires and culminates in war and state terror. The concentration of executive power and the rise of the national security-surveillance state, with its nuclear arsenals of mass destruction and rapidly expanding squadrons of terminator drones – these social processes mutating the capitalist state and hollowing out the carcass of democracy are the continuing condensations of what Adorno called integration and administration. As an unfolding master logic, capitalism has proved to be a self-driving terror machine. We know who and what it drives over.

In this light, coercion and the paradigm of discipline and punish have not been superseded so much as driven deeper into the structures of everyday subjectivity. Demonstrations of terror, from water-boarding and the dirty war technics of disappearing enemies to the 'shock and awe' of spectacular weaponry, show what is done to those who rebel or directly oppose the system. Absorbing the lesson in their bodies, spectators do not need to think twice about it. Terror pre-forms subjectivity and saturates labor relations within the cultural sector as everywhere else, but also circulates as the shadow or reflected presence, as insidious as it is demoralizing, of the real war machines globally in perpetual motion.

Moreover, the celebratory discourses of the creative industries, countersigned by the smirks of pseudo-bohemians, are giving cover to cultural trends that are alarming indeed. Hiroshima had already demonstrated the tendency for science and war machine to merge under the administrations of dominant states. What can be seen today, in company with the politics of fear and the increasing militarization of everyday life, is the merger of war machine and culture industry. Deployments of state terror are accompanied every step of the way by machines of image and spin; these sell the wars that never end by rendering them supremely enjoyable. More and more often, their operators are 'creatives' co-opted from the culture industry. The big-money world of bellicose computer gaming – dominated by the Pentagon-funded *America's Army* and its commercial rival, *Modern Warfare 2* – is one case in point.[9] The career of Adrian Lamo, the convicted ex-hacker turned snitch for Homeland Security, is another: in 2010, Lamo informed on US Army Private Bradley Manning, who allegedly had leaked a damning video of a 2007 massacre of civilians by US forces in Iraq.[10] The first case indicates the addictive power of enjoyment; the second, the corrupting effects and reach of enforcement.

Theories of subjectivation that do not give due weight to the objective factor of a dominating global logic risk lapsing into voluntarism. Those that do will have to face and grapple with the tendencies Adorno pointed to. Strategic resistance begins by assessing the preconditions for its own actual effectiveness. Unhappily, developments since *Dialectic of Enlightenment* have not yet refuted its case. But if we cannot make our history just as we like, oblivious to inherited constraints, we can always transform our pessimism by organizing and aiming it, as both Benjamin and Gramsci counseled at the dawn of the new terror.

Notes

1   This chapter comes from Ray, 2010b, a longer exploration of these issues
     for a *Brumaria* special issue on revolution and subjectivity.

2   As we now know, processes of 'new enclosure' in China and India have
     actually resulted in a massive increase in the size of the planet's industrial
     proletariat. These new 'direct producers' of commodities work in factories
     and sweatshops that combine elements of Fordist and pre-Fordist (in fact
     nineteenth-century) forms of organization and discipline. Evidently, the
     new ideal-typical worker is a young or teenage woman who has been
     separated from her family and social networks for the first time and who
     sends home the bulk of her earnings. These vulnerable workers, who may
     be charged with pay cuts for talking on the work floor or socializing off-
     hours with members of the opposite sex, clearly do not fit the model of
     post-Fordist virtuoso. Moreover, their terms of employment are precarious
     in the extreme; they have been largely stripped of representation and
     Fordist securities and can be fired at will. For a chilling glimpse into the
     new factory, see David Redmon's 2005 documentary film *Mardi Gras: Made
     in China.*

3   This formulation brings out the proximity of the culture industry argument
     to Guy Debord's later category of 'spectacle'. Both denote systematic and
     totalizing organizations of manipulation and social control.

4   In August 2010, corporate giants Verizon Communications and Google
     published detailed proposals for lawmakers regarding regulation of the
     internet. These proposals included provisions purportedly intended to
     protect net neutrality, the principle that Internet Service Providers and
     governments should not transform the structure of access and services in
     ways that favor certain users and contents over others, thereby introducing
     indirect forms of censorship. Critics have argued that the Verizon-Google
     proposal would in fact put in place the conditions for a two-tiered or class-
     inflected internet, with high-speed connections and access for corporate
     content providers and low-speed access for other providers. For analysis
     and assessment, see Electronic Frontier Foundation, 2010.

5   The scintillation of these lines begs comment. The alignment of ad-
     saturated pop culture (neon signs) with mystification (comet reading, or
     astrology) becomes a negative evocation of arcing V-2 rockets and aerial
     bombing – a prefiguring echo of the famous first line of Thomas Pynchon's
     Gravity's Rainbow ('A screaming comes across the sky.') While I will not
     remark it further, the oblique allusion to terror will be relevant to the last
     two sections of the essay.

6   Some tendencies within autonomist theory have had trouble acknowledging this. Indeed, autonomy-oriented approaches are pulled between the claims of subjective empowerment and the instrumental demands of struggle. See Ray, 2009.

7   This formulation is remarkably close to the kind of internalized discipline and governmentality analyzed by Foucault, who must have had such passages, as well as *Dialectic of Enlightenment*, in mind when he offered his disarmingly candid endorsement of Frankfurt critical theory in a 1978 interview: 'Perhaps if I had read those works earlier on, I would have saved useful time, surely: I wouldn't have needed to write some things and I would have avoided certain errors. At any rate, if I had encountered the Frankfurt School when young, I would have been seduced to the point of doing nothing else in life but the job of commenting on them' (Foucault, 1991: 119-20).

8   The passage continues: 'It is on its way wherever people are leveled off [*gleichgemacht werden*] – 'polished off' [*geschliffen*], as they called it in the military – until one exterminates them literally, as deviations from the concept of their utter nullity. Auschwitz confirmed the philosopheme of pure identity as death' (Adorno, 1975: 355; 1995: 362).

9   On the merger of war machine and culture industry, see Der Derian, 2001; on *America's Army* and computer gaming, see Singer, 2010. I discuss both and analyze the dialectic of enjoyment and enforcement in Ray, 2010a.

10 The video was famously posted by WikiLeaks, online at http://wikileaks.org/wiki/Collateral_Murder,_5_Apr_2010. See also Greenwald, 2010.

13

Add Value to Contents: The Valorization of Culture Today

Esther Leslie

Culture and Value

In Britain today, as elsewhere, culture is the wonder stuff that gives more away than it takes. Like some fantastical oil in a Grimm fairytale, this magical substance gives and gives, generating and enhancing value, for state and private men alike. Culture is posited as a mode of value-production: for its economy-boosting and wealth-generating effects; its talent for regeneration, through raising house prices and introducing new business, which is largely service based; and its benefits as a type of moral rearmament or emotional trainer, a perspective that lies behind the 'social inclusion' model, whereby culture must speak to – or down to – disenfranchised groups. Culture is instrumentalized for its 'value-generating' spin-offs. To exploit maximum benefits the value-producing output, culture, needs to be produced industrially. Hence, the 'culture industry', about which Adorno wrote scathingly, has been promoted with redoubled force as 'cultural and creative industries', affirmed as such by various bodies, from governments to supra-governmental forms, NGOs and private initiatives. The discourse of 'creative and cultural industries' penetrates at both national and supranational levels. Supranationally, UNESCO, which describes itself as 'a laboratory of ideas and a standard-setter to forge universal agreements on emerging ethical issues', insists that 'cultural industries', which include publishing, music, audiovisual technology, electronics, video games and the Internet, 'create employment and wealth', 'foster innovation in production and commercialization processes' and 'are central in promoting and maintaining cultural diversity and in ensuring democratic access to culture'.[1] UNESCO pushes the industrial analogy further in the insistence that cultural industries 'nurture creativity – the "raw material" they are made from'. In short, they 'add value to contents and generate values for individuals and societies'. Contents are apparently without inherent value, or enough value, before the magic wand of industry touches them. In addition, creative industries mysteriously make values – out of nothing, out of themselves. Value is a gift of industry, not a quality of artifacts themselves.

Many policy documents reference 'cultural value'. In such documents value has become a debased term, conceivable only from the perspective of quantification, as in, for example, visitor numbers with statistical breakdowns of type, in order to monitor social inclusion and provide data for advertisers or sponsors. As such value is easily subsumed into economic value. The value that is more valuable than all others is monetary. Tate Modern's fifth anniversary report from 2005 is one of many thousand examples. Here the former government Culture Secretary Chris Smith crows about culture's magical powers of wealth generation, asserting that 'Creative industries amount to well over 100 billion pounds of economic value a year, employ over a million people and are growing at twice the rate of growth of the economy as a whole'. (Tate Modern, 2005) Culture's marketability must be assured: culture is valuable only if it contributes to 'the economy'. Culture is quantified – witness the graphs on the UNESCO site of world imports and exports of cultural goods. This point is banal. Of course an industry, in a capitalist world, produces commodities. This particular industry produces art as commodity variously. Art-buying is commodified for broader layers by the encouragement of well sponsored and marketed 'affordable art' fairs, which generalize ownership of small art objects. Art experience is commodified through exhibition sponsorship by corporations and in policy-makers' quantification of social benefits derived from exposure to culture. And the art institution markets itself as commodity. Art galleries are reinvented as 'for profit' space, where the expertise of art workers is leased out to business and education; and merchandise is offered at every opportunity, including gift shops and digital reproductions for download. Tate is innovative here, licensing its strategically developed 'brand' Tate Modern to household paint and home improvements retailer B&Q. Another joint venture is with telecommunications provider BT. Specially commissioned artworks emblazoned on 'limited edition' BT vans support BT and Tate's joint rationale to bring 'art to all' by 'literally taking art out on to the streets'.[2] Art is conceived as an abstract quantity, another product, like baked beans, but the language of limited editions emulates the exclusivity inherent to art. This is art as commodity, another option on the supermarket shelf, conveniently delivered to your door or at least past it. It wants art to be a special, bonus-providing, life-enhancing substance, and, at the same time, it wants it to be on 'the streets', utterly accessible, completely everyday, so that its benefits might be widely distributed, along with those purported to stem from BT's private phone network.

Corporate partnership in culture – like the Public-Private Partnership in health, education and transport sectors – is part of *désétatisation*, a French term situated between 'privatization' and the public sector in the world of cultural provision. Crucial aspects of *désétatisation* include 'divestiture', free transfer of property rights, the change from state to independent organization, contracting-out of cleaning and catering, use of volunteers, private funding, individual patronage and corporate sponsorship. As in other state sectors (for example health and utilities), the shift in cultural policy sunders cultural institutions from the state and pushes them to attract private money. Artworld privatization (where economic rationale is central) is combined with a devolution of power that offers some autonomy as well as accountability to local managers.

In a paradox typical of neoliberalism, the rise of privatization and the inclusion of private industry as sponsors in the art sector has been accompanied by the subjection of culture to government and state intervention, under the name of cultural policy. The corollary of 'creative industries' in the private and especially the state sector is 'cultural policy'. Culture-making is a crucial industry in today's global battle for tourist cash. As such, like any other industry, it is subject to government policy. Cultural policy bears the same relationship to cultural criticism that the culture industry bears to culture. It is its commodification without counter-measure. The rhetoric of much cultural policy is, at best, propagandistic hot air or consolatory compensation, and, at worst, partner to the economic remodeling of the cultural front, akin to neoliberal IMF restructuring of economies. What is remarkable is that cultural policy has been pushed by the very same forces that once engaged in cultural criticism, in the guise of cultural studies and theory. If the ideology of privatization needed to promote the industrialization of culture and its annexing to the production of values, monetary and other, various cultural theorists were willing ideologues for this refunctioning.

Value Added: Theory as Policy

Cultural policy has a broad remit, from the banal to the fatal. Such scope did not prevent Tony Bennett, the leading Australian proponent of Cultural Studies, insisting, back in 1992, that Cultural Studies turn practical, engaging in policy, advising managers and governments rather than moaning on about ideological effects. Cultural Studies' long-standing promotion of cultural populism segued into the rhetoric of choice, which presents itself as anti-elitist. The irony is that theorists who once professed to adhere to some type of Marxism now promote culture as the benevolent and ameliorating face of capitalism. How did this happen? Cultural Studies observed a lack in the Marxist theories of culture that first impelled them. Marxism – according to cultural studies theorist Stuart Hall, 'did not talk about or seem to understand [...] our privileged object of study: culture, ideology, language, the symbolic' (Hall, 1992: 279). Note here that culture is subsumed into the intangible, non-material or simply 'cognitive'. Labor, the role of production, slips away as theorizable component of practice. This animus against production is reinforced with the focus on audiences and consumption. The labor of cultural production disappears.

After getting to just 'within shouting distance' of Marxism, as Hall termed it, Cultural Studies bifurcated. One wing headed for a sociology of culture that traffics in popular cultural practices. The other opted for style, surface, textuality and the allure of 'theory'. Precipitate of both was a shift in the understanding of ideology. Initially an Althusser-influenced delineation of ideology, and ideological state apparatuses conceived the state and its organs as producing contexts for thinking that serve class interests and the market as a force of control, an ideological justification of class oppression. This is replaced by an embrace of culture – or ideology – as authentic or post-authentic expression of subjectivity. Ideology is no longer a problematically inescapable effluent, but rather the very locus of pleasure, resistance, power and counter-power. Ideology is culture, and so culture is immaterial, purely *Geist*. This conceptualization made possible the remolding of Cultural Studies as Cultural Policy. It is culture's presumed immateriality, its symbolic accent that forwards the fixation on the consumer, who receives culture as adjunct to his or her identities, a marker of taste. Numerous cultural theorists reinvent themselves as wannabe policy makers in the 'cultural industries'. Still echoing terms from the cultural theory they absorbed, they marshal the language of market research and niche marketing, capitalism's tools for product placement in competitive industries (McGuigan, 2004: 139). John Holden, Head of Development at the think-tank Demos and a former investment banker with Masters degrees in law and art history, tells us in his essay 'The Cultural Value of Tate Modern', people attending Tate Modern, are not 'spectators' but 'actors' (Tate Modern, 2005). Here he adopts a version of Walter Benjamin's idea of the cultural auditor as producer. But the meaning is twisted into its contemporary parody. He goes on to claim:

> This [appearance of museum goers as actors] can be accounted for in marketing terms – people reinforcing their own coolness through their alliance with one of Britain's Coolest Brands, or it can be thought of as something loftier – forming identity and stretching the self through an interaction with what Tessa Jowell, the Secretary of State for Culture, has called 'complex culture'. (Tate Modern, 2005)

Adorno against Industry

Art is not only part of 'business as usual'. It is the universal grease relied upon to make the cogs of business turn better and the joints of society mesh smoother. Adorno's 'Culture Industry' concept – a yoking of the unyokeable – assumed that industry was anathema to culture. Industry signifies business, endless production. For Adorno, art is a placeholder for utopia, but this did not mean it had anything in common with technological utopias that imagined busy ways through and out of capitalism. Adorno posited utopia as a place for indolence, non-productivity, uselessness. Art likewise is not about ceaseless production, an industrial manufacturing of artefacts, values, by-products, outputs, outcomes and objectives – all necessary for grant applications and monitoring reports. Art is not even a place for manufacturing concrete alternatives: 'Like theory, art cannot concretize Utopia, not even negatively' (Adorno, 1984: 48). Adorno states:

> It is not the office of art to spotlight alternatives, but to resist by its form alone the course of the world, which permanently puts a pistol to men's heads. (Adorno, 1977: 180)

In its form art proposes something other than business as usual. Art holds a place for utopia, its form marking utopia's outlines. But it cannot represent it, instead figuring this future time negatively:

> We may not know what the human is or what the correct shape of human things is, but what it is not and what form of human things is wrong, that we do know, and only in this specific and concrete knowledge is something else, something positive, open to us. (Adorno, 1986: 456)

It is this negative imagining that impels art. But still it is possible to imagine – without concretizing – futures for and in art, as Adorno did when he wrote the following in *Aesthetic Theory*:

> While firmly rejecting the appearance of reconciliation, art none the less holds fast to the idea of reconciliation in an antagonistic world. Thus, art is the true consciousness of an epoch in which Utopia... is as real a possibility as total catastrophic destruction. (Adorno, 1984: 48)

Art might, because of its precarious, anomalous situation within commodity society, bear a non-concrete relation to Utopia. It marks the place of the 'idea' of utopia. In the face of cultural industry Adorno cleaves to art as utopia's only refuge, and our chance for another life. Adorno's clinging to art is correct enough, in that without the thought of art, just as without the thought of utopia, there would be no alternative to industry. But it goes only so far.

After Adorno: Cultural Policy as Aestheticization of Politics

Art cannot in itself recover from a situation intrinsic to industrial capitalism, whereby it has been made an adjunct of the political, for which read economic. It cannot separate itself off again into 'the aesthetic'. To deny its embroilment would only reinforce pre-critical ideas, as if Walter Benjamin, T.W. Adorno and Guy Debord had never existed. Art movements have fused with the business of politics in a number of ways. Politics has become an art of display. Walter Benjamin's closing statements to his Artwork essay, on 'the aestheticization of politics' and the 'politicization of art', have taken on a new validity. It is easy to observe an aestheticization of politics everywhere today. We live in a world of mediated political spectacle that enforces passivity and knee-jerk reactions. Politics is a show that we are compelled to watch and where the 'sides' on offer are simply divisions within the essentially identical. Benjamin's phrase indicates that beyond the aestheticization of political systems, figures and events is a more fundamental aestheticization (or alienation): the aestheticization of human practice. This amounts to an alienation from species-being, to the extent that we accept and enjoy viewing our own destruction. Benjamin discusses the issue of art's politicization in the context of human annihilation. War has become the ultimate artistic event, because it satisfies the new needs of the human sensorium, which have been remolded technologically. This was the completion *of l'art pour l'art*, or aestheticism, as seen in 1936, which means that everything is an aesthetic experience, even war. Humanity watches a techno-display of 'shock and awe' proportions, which amounts to its own torture. It revels in it. Genuine politics – the rational management of technologies, the democratic incorporation of the users of those technologies, revelations about the property-stakes that drive the system – require self-activity: authors as producers, audiences as critics, as Benjamin put it (Benjamin, 2005). Likewise the art that communism politicizes is not art as known and inherited (and reified for passive consumption), but rather, yet again, an opportunity for self-activity. This is a dialectical reversal not a negation. It might on the surface appear as if the politicization of art has been adopted in a widespread manner within the 'artistic community'. Exhibitions frequently draw attention to 'political' questions of poverty, gender, ethnicity, globalization, war. But this is not the victory of the Benjaminian idea of art's politicization. In fact, it is a further symptom of the aestheticization of politics. For what is produced by the real politicization of art is not that which we have become accustomed to in galleries – politically correct art that largely satisfies itself with and within the gallery and grant system, competing within the terms of the creative and cultural industries. Rather the politicization of art means a thorough rejection of systems of display, production, and consumption, monitoring and inclusion as well as elitism and exclusion, as art disperses into everyday practice and becomes political, that is, democratically available to all as practice and matter for critique.

Karl Marx notes that human activity constitutes reality through praxis, and truth is gained through the process of self-development. As he put it famously: the rounded individual of mature communism is a hunter in the morning, a fisherman in the afternoon, and a critical critic at night, without being defined socially as hunter, fisherman or critic. It is an unfreedom characteristic of class society that some people are charged with the task of being an artist, and bear that social role, while others are excluded from it. Conversely, marred by commodification, artistic practice today is a deformation of the sensuous unfolding of the self that indicates real human community. The reification of human activity into the separate realms of work and play, aesthetics and politics damages all and must be overcome. The aesthetic must be rescued from the ghetto of art and set at the centre of life.

What I mean finally to say is this: the critique of cultural and creative industries makes no sense unless you are prepared to criticize the capitalist industrial model as a whole, wherever it appears, for the manufacture of whatever ends. While Adorno may be right that art is a special type of labor, which reveals the critical pressure points of the system, in as much as it is industrialized, it has become effectively like all labor – shit to do, alienated and boring. This is where we should start – with the conditions of labor wherever they occur, not just the specific woes of artists. This means asking why 'social inclusion' is necessary in the first place, and why class society both needs and doesn't need art.

Notes

1   All quotations from UNESCO are taken from the UNESCO website, specifically the section on 'Culture, trade and globalisation'. See http://www.unesco.org/culture/industries/trade/.

2   The language of 'the streets' is used by BT's Head of Sponsorship on the BTPLC website and reproduced elsewhere in promotional competitions and the like.

14

Creative Industries as Mass Deception

Gerald Raunig
language edited by Aileen Derieg

The chapter from Max Horkheimer and Theodor W. Adorno's *Dialectic of Enlightenment* on the culture industry was entitled 'Kulturindustrie: Aufklärung als Massenbetrug' ('Culture Industry: Enlightenment as Mass Deception'). When Horkheimer and Adorno wrote their essay in the early 1940s, they were objecting to the growing influence of the entertainment industries, to the commodification of art, and to the totalizing uniformity of 'culture', especially in the country of their emigration, the USA. Their skeptical attitude toward the new media of radio and film moved the two authors to cover, in an eloquent style with cultural pessimistic undertones, a broad range of the cultural field with a concept that could hardly appear more alien in cultural spheres: they named culture as an industry.

For almost two decades, even after their return to Europe, Horkheimer and Adorno's theses remained more of an insider tip discussed only among the affiliates of the Institute for Social Research. Over the course of the 1960s, however, their impact began to develop, finally becoming fully established in the updated media critique of the 1970s: *Dialectic of Enlightenment* became a cornerstone of the literature not only on the ambivalence of the Enlightenment, but also and especially on the rigorous rejection of an 'economization of culture'. And in the cultural field, where the myths of genius, originality and autonomy are still significant factors, the term 'industry' is still regarded today, sixty years after the late publication of *Dialectic of Enlightenment*, as not much more than a dirty word. Thus the question arises as to how could it happen that with only a small shift from singular to plural, from culture industry to creative and cultural industries, this conceptual brand has now been reinterpreted as something like a promise of universal salvation not only for politicians, but also for many actors in the field itself.[1]

One possible explanation for this paradox arises from a closer look at the modes of subjectivation in the fields, structures and institutions that were and are described with the terms culture industry and creative industries. I will discuss these conditions of modes of subjectivation and the specific institutions in the field by analyzing four components of the concept of culture industry and then comparing them in reverse order from four to one with their updated counterparts within the creative industries today.

I

Adorno and Horkheimer's culture industry chapter was mainly about the growing film and media industries, especially Hollywood cinema and private radio stations in the US. In clear contrast to the writings of their colleague Walter Benjamin and also of Bertolt Brecht, who both had a more ambivalent idea of the opportunities and the problems engendered by mechanical reproduction, mass media and the manifold aspects of production and reception under new conditions, Adorno and Horkheimer took a thoroughly negative view of the culture industry: as an increasingly totalizing spiral of systematic manipulation and the 'retroactive need' to adapt more and more to this system: 'Films, radio and magazines form a system. Each branch of culture is unanimous within itself and all are unanimous together.' (Horkheimer and Adorno, 2002: 94; 2003: 128) In the interpretation of the Institute for Social Research, this unified form of culture industry is the institutional structure for modes of subjectivation that subjugate the individual under the power and the totality of capital.

The first component of the concept of culture industry, according to Horkheimer and Adorno, is that it totalizes its audience, exposing this audience to a permanently repeated, yet ever unfulfilled promise: 'The culture industry endlessly cheats its consumers of what it endlessly promises' (Horkheimer and Adorno, 2002: 111; 2003: 148). It is this eternal cycle of promise generating a desire and continually suspending this desire in an unproductive way that is at the core of the idea of culture industry as an instrument of mass deception. For Horkheimer and Adorno the products of culture industry are all designed in a way that they deny or even prevent imagination, spontaneity, fantasy and any active thinking on the part of the spectators. This ultra-passive form of consumption correlates to the tendency on the part of the culture industry to meticulously register and statistically process its audience: 'On the charts of research organizations, indistinguishable from those of political propaganda, consumers are divided up as statistical material into red, green and blue areas according to income group' (Horkheimer and Adorno, 2002: 97; 2003: 131).

The consumers appear as marionettes of capital, counted, analyzed, captured in the striated space of the culture industry:

> The consumers are the workers and salaried employees, the farmers and petty bourgeois. Capitalist production hems them in so tightly, in body and soul, that they unresistingly succumb to whatever is proffered to them. However, just as the ruled have always taken the morality dispensed to them by the rulers more seriously than the rulers themselves, the defrauded masses today cling to the myth of success still more ardently than the successful. They insist unwaveringly on the ideology by which they are enslaved. (Horkheimer and Adorno, 2002: 106; 2003: 141-2)

What is evident, of course, in the image of the consumers that have succumbed to the anonymous culture industry apparatus of seduction, is both the culmination and simultaneously the limitation of Horkheimer and Adorno's approach: the figure of the 'deceived masses' victimizes them as passive, externally determined, betrayed, and enslaved.

II

As a second component in Horkheimer and Adorno's concept of culture industry we also find a specific image of production: whereas the authors present the positions of producers and consumers as being clearly separated, this separation is not thought of as a dualistic figure of passive and active subjects of culture industry. Like the consumers, the producers also appear as subjugated, passive functions of the system. Whereas in Benjamin's theories of authorship and new media, authors are able to turn into producers by changing the production apparatus, and in Brecht's *Lehrstück* theory and practice of the early 1930s, in which there are inherently only authors and producers, instead of a consuming audience, Horkheimer and Adorno's rigid image shows only strangely passive producers trapped in the totality of the culture industry. Social subordination remains the only imaginable mode of subjectivation, even on the side of production. The most striking example in the chapter on culture industry shows the actors in radio broadcasts who are 'denied any freedom' as functions of the business:

> They confine themselves to the apocryphal sphere of 'amateurs', who, in any case, are organized from above. Any trace of spontaneity in the audience of the official radio is steered and absorbed into a selection of specializations by talent-spotters, performance competitions, and sponsored events of every kind. The talents belong to the operation long before they are put on show; otherwise, they would not conform so easily. (Horkheimer and Adorno, 2002: 96; 2003: 130)

In light of its updated version in Reality TV, docu-soaps and casting shows, in fact the image of extras that only appear to be protagonists seems more plausible today than ever. Looking at a broader idea of producers producing and presenting not only materialized goods, but also affects and communication, we see the picture of a totalizing system determining every move and every mood of the subject growing even darker. Horkheimer and Adorno anticipated this darkening, but in a strangely feminized form:

> The way in which the young girl accepts and performs the obligatory date, the tone of voice used on the telephone and in the most intimate situations, the choice of words in conversation, indeed, the whole inner life [...] bears witness to the attempt to turn oneself into an apparatus meeting the requirements of success, an apparatus which, even in its unconscious impulses, conforms to the model presented by the culture industry. (Horkheimer and Adorno, 2002: 136; 2003: 176)

The human-apparatuses correlate to the apparatus of the culture industry. Both consumers and producers appear as slaves of a totality and ideology, shaped and moved by an abstract system. As apparatuses they are cogs in a bigger apparatus; part of an institution called culture industry.

III

As an effect of this relationship between the apparatus and its cogs, the third component of the culture industry concept is that the actors, the cultural producers, are prisoners as employees of the institution(s) of culture industry. The institutional form, into which the culture industry developed according to Horkheimer and Adorno, is that of a gigantic music, entertainment or media corporation. Those who create find themselves enclosed within an institutional structure, in which their creativity is suppressed by the very form of dependent work. In *Dialectic of Enlightenment* this connection between creativity-constraining employment and social subordination is generally described in this way:

> Fundamentally, it is all about the self-mockery of man. The possibility of becoming an economic subject, an entrepreneur, a proprietor, is entirely liquidated. [...][T]he independent firm [...] has fallen into hopeless dependence. Everyone becomes an employee [...] (Adorno, 2002: 123, translation modified; 2003: 162)

Just as hopeless dependency and social control generally predominate in the world of employees, even the last resort of autonomy (and here there is an early echo of the romanticism of artistic autonomy in Adorno's later work, *Aesthetic Theory*,[2] the production of creativity is described as striated, structured and stratified, and the majority of its actors originally regarded as resistive are finally civilized as employees. According to the anthropological definition of institution, in return the institution is said to provide the employees with security and to promise a certain degree of control over irresolvable contradictions. Even if the specific institutions of the culture industry do not last forever, their apparatuses are intended to create this impression specifically because of their apparatus nature and to exonerate the subjects in this way. For Horkheimer and Adorno, however, even this notion itself is due solely to the effect that 'the managed provision of comradely care cultivation of comradeship, administered by every factory as a means of increasing production, brings even the last private impulse under social control' (Horkheimer and Adorno, 2002: 121, translation modified; 2003: 159).

IV

As the fourth and final component, according to Horkheimer and Adorno the development of the culture industry as a whole is to be seen as a delayed transformation of the cultural field catching up with the processes that had led to Fordism in agriculture or what is conventionally called industry. Nevertheless, Horkheimer and Adorno regard culture monopolies as weak and dependent in comparison to the most powerful sectors of industry – steel, petroleum, electricity, and chemicals. Even the last remainders of resistance against Fordism – and here again there is an echo of the formerly heroic function of autonomous art – are regarded as having finally become factories. The new factories of creativity (publishing, cinema, radio and television) conformed to the criteria of the Fordist factory. The assembly line character of culture industry consequently structured the culture industry production of creativity in a way similar to agriculture and metal processing before: through serialization, standardization, and the total domination of creativity. 'At the same time, however, mechanization has such power over leisure and its happiness, determines so thoroughly the fabrication of entertainment commodities, that the off-duty worker can experience nothing but after-images of the work process itself' (Horkheimer and Adorno, 2002: 109; 2003: 145). Thus according to Horkheimer and Adorno, the function of the factories of creativity is the mechanized manufacture of amusement goods on the one hand, and on the other – beyond conventional areas of production – the control and determination of reproduction, whereby reproduction increasingly becomes like working in a factory.

IV

Instead of regarding culture industry as something which replaced bourgeois art and the avant-gardes in the cultural field and translated a Fordist model that was developed elsewhere, outside culture, into the cultural field, the post-operaist philosopher Paolo Virno asks about the role that the culture industry assumed with relation to overcoming Fordism and Taylorism. According to his reflections in *Grammar of the Multitude*, the culture industry

> fine-tuned the paradigm of post-Fordist production on the whole. I believe therefore, that the mode of action of the culture industry became, from a certain point on, exemplary and pervasive. Within the culture industry, even in its archaic incarnation examined by Benjamin and Adorno, one can grasp early signs of a mode of production which later, in the post-Fordist era, becomes generalized and elevated to the rank of canon. (Virno, 2004: 58)

Here we find a fruitful inversion of the interpretation of culture industry as an industrialized field robbed of its freedom, as conceptualized by Critical Theory: whereas Horkheimer and Adorno call culture industry an obstinate latecomer in the Fordist transformation, Virno sees it as an anticipation and paradigm of post-Fordist production.

For Horkheimer and Adorno the institutions of culture industry formed modern culture monopolies, but also at the same time the economic area in which some part of the sphere of liberal circulation is able to survive, along with the corresponding entrepreneurial types, despite the process of disintegration elsewhere. Although some small spaces of difference and resistance still emerge within the purported totality of the culture industry, of course this difference is quickly reintegrated in the totality of culture industry, as Horkheimer and Adorno do not hesitate to explain:

> What resists can only survive by fitting in. Once a particular brand of deviation from the norm has been noted by the culture industry, it belongs to it as does the land-reformer to capitalism. (Horkheimer and Adorno, 2002: 104, translation modified; 2003: 140)

In this description, difference serving to achieve new levels of productivity is nothing but a vestige of the past, which is cast off in the general Fordization of the culture industry as a remnant. From Virno's perspective,

> it is not difficult to recognize that these purported remnants (with a certain space granted to the informal, to the unexpected, to the 'unplanned') were, after all, loaded with future possibilities. These were not remnants, but anticipatory omens. The informality of communicative behavior, the competitive interaction typical of a meeting, the abrupt diversion that can enliven a television program (in general, everything which it would have been dysfunctional to rigidify and regulate beyond a certain threshold), has become now, in the post-Fordist era, a typical trait of the entire realm of social production. This is true not only for our contemporary culture industry, but also for Fiat in Melfi. (Virno, 2004: 59)

From the view of post-operaist theory, the old culture industry is not only a weak and late-coming industry in the process of Fordization, but also a future model and anticipation of the wide-spread post-Fordist production modes: informal, non-programmed spaces, open to the unforeseen, communicative improvisations that are less a remnant than the core, less margin than centre.

III

The culture industry media and entertainment corporations, according to Horkheimer and Adorno, prove to be an institutional structure for subjugating the individual to the control of capital. Hence they are sites of pure social subjugation. Even if we accept this one-sided structuralist view for early forms of the culture industry, it seems that something has changed here since the mid-twentieth century. On the one hand, this change may be grasped with terms developed by Gilles Deleuze and Félix Guattari in the 1970s: the point here was primarily the insight, further explained below, that a second line develops beyond social subjection, which emphasizes active involvement and modes of subjectivation in addition to structural factors. In contradistinction to social subjection (*assujettissement social*), Deleuze and Guattari call this second line 'machinic enslavement' (*asservissement machinique*) (1987: 456-60). In addition to this problematization at the terminological level, the question can also be raised with regards to today's phenomena about which modes of subjectivation are arising in the new institutional forms of the creative industry. For what is now called 'creative industries', not only by neoliberal cultural politics and urban development, differs substantially in form and function from the old-school culture industry.

Turning to the third component that involves the institutional form, in particular, it is obvious that the arrangements labeled as creative industries are no longer structured in the form of huge media corporations, but mainly as micro-enterprises of self-employed cultural entrepreneurs in the fields of new media, fashion, graphics, design, pop, conceptualized at best in clusters of these micro-enterprises. So if we ask about the institutions of the creative industries, it seems more appropriate to speak of non-institutions or pseudo-institutions. Whereas the model institutions of culture industry were huge, long-term corporations, the pseudo-institutions of creative industries prove to be temporary, ephemeral, project based.

These 'project institutions'[3] seem to have the advantage of being grounded in self-determination and the rejection of the rigid order of Fordist regimes. In the last two sections of this article, I will question how convincing this argument is. At this point, however, and in reference to the previously described function of the institution as a manager of contradictions with an exonerating effect, I want to stress that the project institutions of the creative industries conversely promote precarization and insecurity. In fact, it is clear that a glaring contradiction is evident in the idea of 'project institutions': on the one hand the desire for long-term exoneration that the concept of the institution implies, and on the other a distinct time-limit implicit to the concept of the project. Following again from another motif from Paolo Virno's *A Grammar of the Multitude* and relating to the phenomenon of the 'project institution', the contradictoriness of the institution as a project inevitably leads, as Virno described, to the complete overlapping of fear and anguish, relative and absolute dread, and ultimately to a total diffusion of this concern throughout all the areas of life. (Virno, 2004: 32)

Horkheimer and Adorno still lamented the fact that the subjects of culture industry as employees lost their opportunities to become freelance entrepreneurs, it seems that in the present situation this problem has been completely reversed. The freelance entrepreneur has become mainstream, no matter whether s/he is floating as a part-time worker from project to project or building up one micro-enterprise after another. And even the successors of the twentieth-century culture industry, the major media corporations, conduct a policy of outsourcing and contracting sub-companies under the banner of entrepreneurship. In these newer media corporations with their convergence from the field of print to audiovisual media all the way to the Internet, all that remains for permanently employed workers in many cases – and this applies even to public service media – are only a few core functions of administration. In contrast, most of the people labeled as 'creatives', work freelance and/or as self-employed entrepreneurs with or without limited contracts. Somewhat cynically one could say that Adorno's melancholy over the loss of autonomy has now been perversely realized in the working conditions of the creative industries: the creatives are released into a specific sphere of freedom, of independence and self-government. Here flexibility becomes a despotic norm, precarity of work becomes the rule, the dividing lines between work and leisure time blur just like those between work and unemployment, and precarity flows from work into life as a whole.

II

But where does this universal precarization come from? Is the creative industry, like the culture industry, a system that enslaves its subjects, or is there a specific form of involvement of the actors within this process of precarization? To discuss this second component, the contemporary modes of subjectivation in the cultural field, I would like to take up Isabell Lorey's discussion of 'biopolitical governmentality and self-precarization' (Lorey, 2009). Lorey speaks of precarization as a force line in liberal governmentality and biopolitical societies. This force line that reaches far back into early modern times was actualized in a specific way by the living and working conditions that emerged in the context of the new social movements in the 1970s and the principles of the post-1968 generations: deciding for yourself, what and with whom and when you want to work; freedom, autonomy, self-determination, and in this context consciously choosing precarious living and working conditions. Here Lorey develops the term of self-chosen precarization, or self-precarization: people already had to learn to develop a creative and productive relationship to the self under liberal governmentality as well; this practice of creativity and the ability to shape one's self has been a part of governmental self-techniques since the eighteenth century. But what is changing here, according to Isabell Lorey's argument, is the function of precarization: from an immanent contradiction in liberal governmentality to a function of normalization in neoliberal governmentality, from an inclusive exclusion at the margins of society to a mainstream process. In the course of these developments, which also explain the transformation of the phenomena described by Horkheimer and Adorno into the current forms of the creative industries, the experiments of the 1970s to develop self-determined forms of living and working as alternatives to the normalized and regulated regime of work were especially influential. With the sovereignly imagined emancipation from spatially and temporally rigidly ordered everyday life, there was also a reinforcement of the line that allows subjectivation beyond social subjugation to be imagined no longer only in an emancipatory way:

> [I]t is precisely these alternative living and working conditions that have become increasingly more economically utilizable in recent years because they favor the flexibility that the labor market demands. Thus, practices and discourses of social movements in the past thirty to forty years were not only dissident and directed against normalization, but also at the same time, a part of the transformation toward a neoliberal form of governmentality. (Lorey, 2009. 196)

So here we are in the present: at a time when the old ideas and ideologies of the autonomy and freedom of the individual (especially the individual as genius artist) plus specific aspects of post-1968 politics have turned into hegemonic neoliberal modes of subjectivation. Self-precarization means saying yes to exploiting every aspect of creativity and of life.

This is the paradox of creativity as self-government: 'Governing, controlling, disciplining, and regulating one's self means, at the same time, fashioning and forming one's self, empowering one's self, which in this sense, is what it means to be free' (Lorey, 2009: 193). Here there is perhaps also an echo of the conceptual difference defining the distinction between the branding of the culture industry and the creative industries: whereas the culture industry still seemed to emphasize the abstract collective component of culture, a constant appeal to the productivity of the individual occurs in the creative industries. A distinction of this kind between the collective and the individual, however, only exists at the level of this appeal. What distinguishes the industries of creativity is that they traverse these dualisms.

I

Recalling now in conclusion the first component in Horkheimer and Adorno's concept of the culture industry, which totalizes the individual and completely subjugates consumers under the power of capital, an expansion of the horizon should become possible in conjunction with Isabell Lorey's theses: a shift of focus from the promotion of reductionist totality and heteronomy concepts in the direction of a focus on the specific involvement of practices of resistance against the totalization of creativity, which have in turn led to the present modes of subjectivation.

The culture industry generates 'role models for people who are to turn themselves into what the system needs'. (Horkheimer and Adorno, 2002; 2003) Even though it is logically contradictory, an ambivalence is suggested here – as in other places in *Dialectic of the Enlightenment* – which, if it does not quite conjoin self-active enslavement and externally determined subjugation through a totalizing system, at least places them next to one another on an equal level. For Deleuze and Guattari, enslavement and subjugation are simultaneously existing poles that are actualized in the same things and in the same events. In the regime of social subjugation, a higher entity constitutes the human being as subject, which refers to an object that has become external. In the modus of machinic enslavement, human beings are not subjects, but are, like tools or animals, parts of a machine that overcodes the whole. The interplay of the two regimes is particularly evident in the phenomenon of the creative industries, two poles that perpetually reinforce one another, whereby the components of machinic enslavement grow in significance due to a surplus of subjectivation. 'Should we then speak of a voluntary servitude?' ask Deleuze and Guattari. And their answer is no: 'There is a machinic enslavement, about which it could be said that it appears as re-accomplished; this machinic enslavement is no more "voluntary" than it is "forced"' (Deleuze and Guattari, 1987: 460).

From this perspective of the double movement of the subjugation to a social unity and the enslavement within a machine, we cannot adhere to Adorno and Horkheimer's idea of a system that works as a totality on the one side and the actors as passive objects of the system on the other side. Rather, the modes of subjectivation reconstruct totality over and over again; their involvement in the processes of social subjugation and machinic enslavement is neither voluntary nor forced. And here we also finally find an answer to the question raised at the beginning: how could it happen that this small shift from culture industry to creative and cultural industries became a brand of universal salvation not only for politicians, but also for many actors in the field? It happened precisely because the modes of subjectivation of machinic enslavement are conjoined with both desire and conformity, and the actors in creative industries interpret the appeal as meaning that they have at least chosen self-precarization themselves.

In this sense, and to return to the title of this text, in light of the involvement of the actors in the mode of machinic enslavement it is hardly appropriate to speak of 'mass deception' – and I would doubt that it was meaningful at any time. In the context of the creative industry it would thus be more apt to speak of a 'massive self-deception' as an aspect of self-precarization. And we could also add to this 'self-deception' the possibility of resistance, which is actualized in the plane of immanence of what is still labeled as creative industries today.

Notes

1 In the cultural political context, the most likely interpretation seems to be that in the course of establishing the term creative industries throughout Europe in the programs of cultural policies, the aim has increasingly been to shift state funding for art from support for critical/deviant positions to support for commercial enterprises.

2 Contrary to Adorno's substantialization of the autonomy of bourgeois art, however, it has long been asserted that specifically this has the effect of a total, heteronomizing and hierarchizing praxis, striating both the space of production and of reception: the four-stage production apparatus of bourgeois theatre, for instance, or the extreme discipline in classical orchestras correlates to the habits of reception in both fields.

3 See Stefan Nowotny's contribution to this volume, chapter one, above.

Bibliography

Adorno, T.W. (1975) *Negative Dialektik*, in *Gesammelte Schriften*, vol. 6, eds. R. Tiedemann et al. Frankfurt/Main: Suhrkamp.

Adorno, T.W. (1976) 'Résumé über Kulturindustrie', in *Ohne Leitbild: Parva Aesthetica*. Frankfurt/Main: Suhrkamp.

Adorno, T.W. (1976) *Prismen: Kulturkritik und Gesellschaft*. Frankfurt/Main: Suhrkamp.

Adorno, T. W. (1977) 'Commitment', in R. Taylor (ed.), *Aesthetics and Politics*. London: NLB.

Adorno, T.W. (1984) *Aesthetic Theory*. London: Routledge & Kegan Paul.

Adorno, T. W. (1986[1953]) 'Individual and organisation', in T.W. Adorno, *Gesammelte Schriften*, vol. VIII. Frankfurt/Main: Suhrkamp.

Adorno, T.W. (1992) *Prisms*, trans. S. Weber and S. Weber Nicholsen. Cambridge, MA: MIT Press.

Adorno, T.W. (1995) *Negative Dialectics*, trans. E.B. Ashton. New York: Continuum.

Adorno, T.W. (2001) *The Culture Industry: Selected Essays on Mass Culture*, ed. J.M. Bernstein. London: Routledge.

Adorno, T.W. (2003) 'Kultur und Verwaltung', in *Soziologische Schriften 1, Gesammelte Schriften*, vol. 8, eds. R. Tiedemann et al. Frankfurt/Main: Suhrkamp.

Allen, K. (2005) *Choosing Fame – Choosing a Self: Celebrity Culture, Performing Arts Education and Female Individualisation.* London: Goldsmiths, University of London.

Andrade, O. de (1990) *A Utopia Antropofágica.* São Paulo: Globo.

Arendt, H. (1977) *Between Past and Future: Eight Exercises in Political Thought.* New York: Penguin.

Arendt, H. (1998[1958]) *The Human Condition.* Chicago: University of Chicago Press.

Aristotle (1988) *The Politics,* trans. S. Everson. Cambridge: Cambridge University Press.

Artaud, A. (1958) *The Theater and Its Double,* trans. M.C. Richards. New York: Grove.

Baetens, J.D. (2010) 'Vanguard Economics, Rearguard Art: Gustave Coûteaux and the Modernist Myth of the Dealer-Critic System', *Oxford Art Journal,* 33(1): 25-41.

Bakhtin, M. (1975) *Questions of Literature and Aesthetics,* (Russian) Moscow: Progress Moscow.

Becker, H.S. (1982) *Art Worlds.* Los Angeles: Berkeley University Press.

Benjamin, W. (1978) *Reflections: Essays, Aphorisms, Autobiographical Writings,* trans. E. Jephcott. New York: Schocken.

Benjamin, W. (2005[1934]) 'The Author as Producer', in W. Benjamin, *Selected Writings, Volume 2, Part 1, 1927-1930.* Cambridge, MA: Harvard University Press.

Bennett, T. (1995) *The Birth of the Museum: History, Theory, Politics.* New York: Routledge.

Bollenbeck, G. (1999) *Tradition, Avantgarde, Reaktion: Deutsche Kontroversen um die kulturelle Moderne, 1880-1945.* Frankfurt/Main: Suhrkamp.

Boltanski, L., and È. Chiapello (1999) *Le nouvel esprit du capitalisme.* Paris: Gallimard.

Boltanski, L., and È. Chiapello (2000) 'Vers un renouveau de la critique sociale. Entretien réalisé par Yann Moulier Boutang', *Multitudes* 3; and online at http://multitudes.samizdat.net/Vers-un-renouveau-de-la-critique.html.

Boltanski, L., and È. Chiapello (2005) *The New Spirit of Capitalism,* trans. G. Elliott. London: Verso.

Bourdieu, P. (1984) *Distinction: A Social Critique of the Judgement of Taste* [1979], trans. R. Nice. Cambridge, MA: Harvard University Press.

Bourdieu, P. (1987) 'La révolution impressionniste', *Noroit*, 303(September-October): 3-18.

Bourdieu, P. (1996[1992]) *The Rules of Art*, trans. S. Emanuel. Stanford: Stanford University Press.

Brombert, B. (1996) *Edouard Manet. Rebel in a Frock Coat*. Chicago: University of Chicago Press.

Butler, J. (1997) *The Psychic Life of Power: Theories in Subjection*. Stanford, CA: Stanford University Press.

Cachin, F. (1995) *Manet, The Influence of the Modern*. London: Thames and Hudson.

Caillebotte, G. (1883) 'The Will', in K. Varnedoe (2000) *Gustave Caillebotte*. New Haven and London: Yale University Press.

Callen, A. (2000) *The Art of Impressionism*. New Haven: Yale University Press.

Chomsky, N. (1991) *Linguaggio e problemi della conoscenza (Language and Problems of Knowledge: The Managua Lectures)*. Bologna: il Mulino.

Clark, L. (1997) 'L'homme structure vivante d'une architecture biologique et cellulaire', in M. J. Borja Villel and N. Enguita Mayo (eds.) *Lygia Clark* (exhibition catalogue). Barcelona: Fundació Antoni Tàpies.

Clark, T.J. (1984) *The Painting of Modern Life. Paris in the Art of Manet and His Followers*. London: Thames and Hudson.

Collins, R. (2005) 'Foreword', in G.R. Azarian *The General Sociology of Harrison C. White*. New York: Palgrave MacMillan.

Commission of the European Communities (2004) 'Proposal for a decision of the European Parliament and of the Council establishing the culture 2007 programme (2007-2013). COM(2004) 469 final', Brussels: EU. Online at http://ec.europa.eu/prelex/ detail_dossier_real.cfm? CL=en&DosId=191537.

Commission of the European Communities (2005a) 'i2010: a european information society for growth and employment. COM(2005) 229 final'. Brussels: EU. Online at http://europa.eu.int/ information_society/eeurope/i2010/docs/communications/com_2 29_i2010_310505_fv_en.pdf.

Commission of the European Communities (2005b) 'Proposal for a decision of the European Parliament and of the Council concerning the European year of intercultural dialogue. COM(2005) 467 final'. Brussels: EU. Online at http://eurlex.europa.eu/LexUriServ/site/en/com/2005/com2005_0467en01.pdf.

Commission of the European Communities (2006) 'Community strategic guidelines on cohesion [COM(2006) 386 final]'. Brussels: EU. Online at http://ec.europa.eu/regional_policy/sources/docoffic/2007/osc/com_2006_0386_en.pdf.

Corsani, A. (2004) 'Wissen und Arbeit im kognitiven Kapitalismus: Die Sackgassen der politischen Ökonomie', in T. Atzert and J. Müller (eds.) *Immaterielle Arbeit und imperiale Souveränität: Analysen und Diskussionen zu Empire*. Münster: Westfälisches Dampfboot.

Council of the European Union (2000) 'Lisbon European Council 23 and 24 March 2000, presidency conclusions'. Brussels: EU. Online at http://www.europarl.europa.eu/summits/lis1_en.htm.

Council of the European Union (2001) 'European Council Göteborg 15 and 16 June 2001, conclusions of the presidency'. Online at http://www.europarl.europa.eu/summits/pdf/got1_en.pdf.

Council of the European Union (2004a) 'Facing the challenge: the Lisbon strategy for growth and employment'. Online at http://ec.europa.eu/growthandjobs/pdf/kok_report_en.pdf

Council of the European Union (2004b) 'Press release, 2616th council meeting, education, youth and culture, Brussels, 15-16 Nov. 2004 (14380/04 (Presse 310)'.

Council of the European Union (2006) 'Proposal for a council decision on community strategic guidelines on cohesion. COM(2006) 386 final'. Online at http://ec.europa.eu/regional_policy/sources/docoffic/2007/osc/1180706_en.pdf.

Csíkszentmihályi, M. (1997) *Creativity. Flow and the psychology of discovery and invention*. New York: Harper.

Csíkszentmihályi, M. (1999) 'Implications of a systems perspective for the study of creativity', in R.J. Sternberg (ed.) *Handbook of Creativity*. Cambridge: Cambridge University Press, 313-339.

(DCMS) The Department for Culture, Media and Sport (2001) *Culture and Creativity*. London: DCMS.

(DCMS) The Department for Culture, Media and Sport (2004) *Government and the Value of Culture*. London: DCMS.

Deleuze G., and F. Guattari (1980) *Mille Plateaux: Capitalisme et Schizophrénie*. Paris: Editions de Minuit.

Deleuze G., and F. Guattari (1987) *A Thousand Plateaus: Capitalism and Schizophrenia*, trans. B. Massumi. Minneapolis: University of Minnesota Press.

Denvir, B. (1993) *The Chronicle of Impressionism*. London: Thames & Hudson.

Der Derian, J. (2001) *Virtuous War: Mapping the Military-Industrial-Media-Entertainment Network*. Boulder: Westview Press.

Dippel, A. (2002) *Impressionismus*. Cologne: DuMont.

Diserens, C., and S. Rolnik (eds.) (2005) *Lygia Clark, de l'oeuvre à l'évènement: Nous sommes le moule, à vous de donner le souffle* (exhibition catalogue). Nantes: Musée des Beaux-Arts de Nantes.

Distel, A. (1990) *Impressionism: The First Collectors*. New York: Harry N. Abrams.

Dumont, H. (1994) 'Die Zuständigkeiten der Europäischen Gemeinschaft auf dem Gebiet der Kultur', in N. Dewandre, and J. Lenoble (eds.) *Projekt Europa: Postnationale Identität: Grundlage für eine europäische Demokratie?* Berlin: Schelzky & Jeep.

Electronic Frontier Foundation (2010) 'A review of Verizon and Google's net neutrality proposal'. Online at http://www.eff.org/deeplinks/2010/08/google-verizon-netneutrality.

Florida, R. (2002) *The Rise of the Creative Class: And How It's Transforming Work, Leisure, Community and Everyday Life*. New York: Basic Books.

Florida, R. (2010) *The Great Reset: How New Ways of Living and Working Drive Post-Crash Prosperity*. New York: Harpers.

Foucault, M. (1991) *Remarks on Marx: Conversations with Duccio Trombadori*, trans. R.J. Goldstein and J. Cascaito. New York: Semiotext(e).

Foucault, M. (1997) 'Cours du 28 janvier 1976' in M. Foucault *Il faut défendre la société. Cours au Collège de France (1975-1976)*. Paris: Seuil.

Foucault, M. (2004a) *Geschichte der Gouvernementalität I: Sicherheit, Territorium, Bevölkerung*. Frankfurt/Main: Suhrkamp.

Foucault, M. (2004b) *Naissance de la biopolitique: Cours au Collège de France (1978-1979)*. Paris: Seuil.

Foucault, M. (2010) *Manet and the Object of Painting*, trans. Matthew Barr. London: Tate Publishing.

Freud, S. (1960) *Jokes and Their Relation to the Unconscious* [1905], trans. J. Strachey. New York: Norton.

Galenson, D., and R. Jensen (2007) 'Careers and Canvases: the Rise of the Market for Modern Art in Nineteenth-Century Paris', Current Issues in Nineteenth Century Art, *Van Gogh Studies*, 1: 137-166. Amsterdam: Van Gogh Museum.

Gardner, H. (1993) *Creating minds. An anatomy of creativity seen through the lives of Freud, Einstein, Picasso, Stravinsky, Eliot, Graham, and Gandhi*. New York: Harper.

Gehlen, A. (1985) *L'uomo: La sua natura e il suo posto nel mondo*. Milan: Feltrinelli.

Giuffre, K. (1999) 'Sandpiles of Opportunity: Success in the Art World', *Social Forces*, 77(3): 815-818.

Gleibs, H.E., and T. Schmalfeldt (2005) 'EGKS: Europäische Gemeinschaft für Kreativität und Selbstinitiative', *Kulturrisse*, 4: 26-29.

Greenberg, C. (1993) 'Modernist painting' [1960], in *The Collected Essays and Criticism*, Vol. 4. Chicago: University of Chicago Press.

Greenwald, G. (2010) 'The strange and consequential case of Adrian Mole, Bradley Manning and WikiLeaks', for *Salon.com* (18 June). Online at http://www.salon.com/news/opinion/glenn_greenwald/2010/06/18/wikileaks.

Habermas, J. (1985) *Der Philosophische Diskurs der Moderne: Zwölf Vorlesungen*. Frankfurt/Main: Suhrkamp.

Habermas, J. (1987) *The Philosophical Discourse of Modernity: Twelve Lectures*, trans. F. Lawrence. Cambridge, MA: MIT Press.

Hall, S. (1992) 'Cultural studies and its theoretical legacies', in L. Grossberg et al. (eds.) *Cultural Studies*. New York: Routledge.

Hall, S., and T. Jefferson (eds.) (1976) *Resistance Through Rituals*. London: Hutchinson.

Hauser, A. (1989) *The Social History of Art. Volume IV: Naturalism, Impressionism, The Film Age*. London: Routledge.

Heinich, N. (2005) *L'élite artiste: Excellence et singularité en régime démocratique*. Paris: Gallimard.

Herbert, J.D. (1998) 'Impressionism', in M. Kelly (ed.) *Encyclopedia of Aesthetics*, Vol. II. Oxford: Oxford University Press.

Holmes, B. (2002) 'The Flexible Personality: For a New Cultural Critique'. Online at http://transform.eipcp.net/transversal/1106/holmes/en.

Holoubek, M., and D. Damjanovic (eds.) (2006) *European Content Regulation: A Survey of the Legal Framework*. Vienna: Austrian Federal Chancellery and Vienna University of Economics and Business Administration, Institute for Austrian and European Public Law.

Holtz-Bacha, C. (2006) *Medienpolitik für Europa*. Wiesbaden: VS Verlag für Sozialwissenschaften.

Horkheimer, M. and T.W. Adorno (2002) *Dialectic of Enlightenment: Philosophical Fragments*, trans. E. Jephcott. Stanford: Stanford University Press.

Horkheimer, M. and T.W. Adorno (2003) *Dialektik der Aufklärung: Philosophische Fragmente*. Frankfurt/Main: Fischer Verlag.

Huffschmid, J. (2006) 'Mailand, Maastricht, Lissabon: das Scheitern der neoliberalen Integrationsstrategie', in Attac (ed.) *Das kritische EU-Buch*. Vienna: Deuticke.

Huijgh, E., and K. Segers (2006) 'The Thin Red Line: International and European Tensions between the Cultural and Economic Objectives and Policies Towards the Cultural Industries'. Online at http://www.re-creatiefvlaanderen.be/srv/pdf/srcvwp_200601.pdf.

Kaufmann, T. (2003) 'What is wrong with "cultural diversity"?' Online at http://eipcp.net/policies/dpie/kaufmann1/en.

Kaufmann, T., and G. Raunig (2003) 'Anticipating European Cultural Policies'. Online at http://eipcp.net/policies/aecp/kaufmannraunig/en.

Lazzarato, M. (1996) 'Immaterial Labour', trans. P. Colilli and E. Emory, in P. Virno and M. Hardt (eds.) *Radical Thought in Italy*. Minneapolis: University of Minnesota Press.

Lorey, I. (2007) 'Vom immanenten Widerspruch zur hegemonialen Funktion: Biopolitische Gouvernementalität und Selbst-

Prekarisierung von KulturproduzentInnen', in G. Raunig and U. Wuggenig (eds.) *Kritik der Kreativität*. Vienna: Turia + Kant.

Lorey, I. (2009) 'Governmentality and Self-Precarization: on the Normalization of Cultural Producers', in G. Raunig and G. Ray (eds.) *Art and Contemporary Critical Practice: Reinventing Institutional Critique*. London: MayFly.

Marcus, C. (2005) 'Future of creative industries: implications for research policy'. European Commission – Foresight Working Document Series. Online at http://www.creativeeconomy conference.org/Documents/Future_Of_Creative_Industries.pdf.

Marx, K. (1975) *Early Writings*, trans. R. Livingstone and G. Benton. New York: Vintage.

Marx, K. (1988) 'Productive und unproductive Arbeit', in *Ökonomische Manuskripte, 1863-1867*. *Marx-Engels-Gesamtausgabe (MEGA)*, Part II, vol. 4.1. Berlin: Dietz.

McGowan, T. (2004) *The End of Dissatisfaction?: Jacques Lacan and the Emerging Society of Enjoyment*. Albany: SUNY Press.

McGuigan, J. (2004) *Rethinking Cultural Policy*. Maidenhead: Open University Press/McGraw-Hill Education.

McRobbie, A. (1994) *Second Hand Dresses and the Role of the Ragmarket in Postmodernism and Popular Culture*, 2nd edition. London: Routledge.

McRobbie, A. (1998) *British Fashion Design; Rag Trade or Image Industry?* London: Routledge.

McRobbie, A. (2002) 'Club to Company', *Cultural Studies*, 16(4): 516-532.

McRobbie, A. (2004) 'Everyone is Creative?', in T. Bennett and E. De Silva (eds.) *Contemporary Culture and Everyday Life*. London: Routledge.

Menger, P.-M. (2005a) *Les intermittents du spectacle: sociologie d'une exception*. Paris: EHESS.

Menger, P.-M. (2005b) *Profession artiste: Extension du domaine de la création*. Paris: Textuel.

Minichbauer, R. (2004) 'Regional strategies: on spatial aspects of european cultural policy'. Online at http://eipcp.net/policies/minichbauer1/en

Minichbauer, R. (2005) 'Pure policy: EU cultural support in the next 10 years', in M. Lind and R. Minichbauer (eds.) *European Cultural Policies 2015*. Vienna: eipcp.

MY Arts Inc. (2011)*Production My Arts Inc.* (www.productionmyarts.com/arts-et-marche/100-oeuvres-fr.htm)

Nancy, J.-L. (2002) *La création du monde ou la mondialisation*. Paris: Galilée.

Nord, P. (2000) *Impressionists and Politics. Art and Democracy in the Nineteenth Century*. London/New York: Routledge.

Nowotny, S. (2003) 'Answering the question: Are cultural policies part of democratic policies?' Online at http://eipcp.net/policies/dpie/nowotny1/en.

Précaires Associés de Paris (2003) 'Elements de propositions pour un régime solidaire de l'assurance chômage des salaries à l'emploi discontinu'. Online at http://eipcp.net/transversal/0704/precaires/fr.

Pühl, K., and B. Sauer (2004) 'Geschlechterverhältnisse im Neoliberalismus: Konstruktion, Transformation und feministisch-politische Perspektiven', in U. Helduser et al. (eds.) *Under Construction? Konstruktivistische Perspektiven in feministischer Theorie und Forschungspraxis*. Frankfurt/Main and New York: Campus.

Quenzel, Gudrun (2005) *Konstruktionen von Europa: Die europäische Identität und die Kulturpolitik der Europäischen Union*. Bielefeld: transcript.

Rat der Europäischen Union (2006) 'Stärkung der europäischen Kreativwirtschaft: ein Beitrag zu Wachstum und Beschäftigung – Schlussfolgerungen des Vorsitzes/Gedankenaustausch [8954/06 – CULT 44 / AUDIO 14 / TELECOM 41]'. Online at http://www.eu2006.at/de/News/Council_Conclusions/KreativwirtschaftDE.pdf)

Raunig, G. (2005) '2015', in M. Lind and R. Minichbauer (eds.), *European Cultural Policies 2015*. Online at http://eipcp.net/policies/2015/raunig/en.

Raunig, G., and G. Ray (eds.) (2009) *Art and Contemporary Critical Practice: Reinventing Institutional Critique*. London: MayflyBooks.

Raunig, G., and U. Wuggenig (eds.) (2007) *Kritik der Kreativität*. Vienna: Turia + Kant.

Ray, G. (2009) 'Antinomies of autonomism: on art, instrumentality and radical struggle', *Third Text* 100, 23(5): 537-46.

Ray, G. (2010a) 'Beyond enforcement: traversing state terror and the politics of fear', in *Terror and the Sublime in Art and Critical Theory*, 2nd edition. New York: Palgrave Macmillan.

Ray, G. (2010b) 'Limits of terror: on culture industry, enforcement and revolution', *Brumaria*, Special Issue on Revolution and Subjectivity.

Rewald, J. (1961) *The History of Impressionism*. New York: Museum of Modern Art.

Rolnik, S. (1998a) 'Anthropophagic subjectivity', in P. Herkenhoff and A. Pedrosa (eds.) *Arte Contemporânea Brasileira: Um e/entre Outro/s* (exhibition catalogue of the XXIVth Bienal Internacional de São Paulo). São Paulo: Fundação Bienal de São Paulo.

Rolnik, S. (1998b) 'Schizoanalyse et anthropophagie', in E. Alliez (ed.) *Gilles Deleuze: Une vie philosophique*. Paris: Les empêcheurs de penser en rond.

Rolnik, S. (2005a) 'Life for sale', in A. Pedrosa (ed.) *Farsites: Urban Crisis and Domestic Symptoms*. San Diego/Tijuana: InSite.

Rolnik, S. (2005b) 'Zombie anthropophagy', in I. Curlin and N. Ilic (eds.) *Collective Creativity*. Kassel: Kunsthalle Fridericianum.

Rolnik, S. (2006a) *Cartografia Sentimental: Transformações contemporâneas d o desejo*, Second Edition. Porto Alegre: Sulina.

Rolnik, S. (2006b) 'Politics of flexible subjectivity: the event-work of Lygia Clark', in T. Smith, N. Condee and O. Enwezor (eds.) *Antinomies of Art and Culture: Modernity, Postmodernity and Contemporaneity*. Durham: Duke University Press.

Rose, N. (1996) *Inventing our Selves: Psychology, Power, and Personhood*. Cambridge: Cambridge University Press.

Schlesinger, P. (2007) 'Creativity: from discourse to doctrine?', *Screen* 48(3): 377-387. Online at 10.1093/screen/hjm037.

Sennett, R. (2005) *The New Culture of Capitalism*. Cambridge, MA: Harvard University Press.

Sfeir-Semler, A. (1992) *Die Maler am Pariser Salon 1791-1880*. Frankfurt/New York: Campus.

Singer, P.W. (2010) 'Meet the sims… and shoot them: the rise of militainment', *Foreign Policy*, 178: 91-5.

Spinoza, B. (1883) *Ethics*, trans. R.H.M. Elwes. Online at http://frank.mtsu.edu/~rbombard/RB/Spinoza/ethica-front.html.

Stavrakakis, Y. (2007) *The Lacanian Left: Psychoanalysis, Theory, Politics*. Edinburgh: Edinburgh University Press.

Tate Modern (2005) 'Tate modern: the first five years'. Online at http://tate.org.uk/modern/tm_5yearspublication.pdf.

Thomson, B. (2000) *Impressionism: Origins, Practice, Reception*. London: Thames and Hudson.

Thornton, S. (1995) *Club Culture*. Cambridge: Polity.

Vaisse, P. (1993) *La Troisième République et les peintres*. Paris: Flammarion.

Valéry, P. (1978) *Monsieur Teste*. Paris: Gallimard.

Virno, P. (1994) *Mondanità. L'idea di "Mondo" tra Esperienza Sensibile e Sfera Pubblica*. Rome: Ed. Manifestolibri.

Virno, P. (2003) 'Virtuosity and revolution', trans. E. Emory. Online at http://makeworlds.org/node/34.

Virno, P. (2004) *A Grammar of the Multitude: For an Analysis of Contemporary Forms of Life*, trans. I. Bertoletti, J. Cascaito and A. Casson. New York: Semiotext(e).

Virno, P. (2005a) *Grammatik der Multitude: Öffentlichkeit, Intellekt und Arbeit*, trans. K. Neundlinger. Vienna: Turia + Kant.

Virno, P. (2005b) *Grammatik der Multitude: Untersuchungen zu gegenwärtigen Lebensformen*, trans. T. Atzert. Berlin: ID-Verlag.

Virno, P. (2005c) *Motto di spirito e azione innovativa. Per una logica del cambiamento*. Turin: Bollati Boringhieri.

Voß, G.G., and C. Weiß (2005) 'Ist der Arbeitskraftunternehmer weiblich?' in K. Lohr and H.M. Nickel (eds.) *Subjektivierung von Arbeit: Riskante Chancen*. Münster: Westfälisches Dampfboot.

Walser, R. (1986) *Poetenleben*. Frankfurt/Main: Suhrkamp.

Watson, P. (1992) *From Manet to Manhattan: The Rise of the Modern Art Market*. London: Hutchinson.

Weitzenhoffer, F. (1986) *The Havemeyers: Impressionism Comes to America*. New York: Yale University Press.

White, H.C. (1992) *Identity and Control: A Structural Theory of Social Action*. Princeton: Princeton University Press.

White, H.C. (1993) *Careers and Creativity: Social Forces in the Arts*. Boulder: Westview.

White, H.C., and C. White (1993[1965]) *Canvases and Careers: Institutional change in the French painting world*. Chicago: University of Chicago Press.

White, H.C. (2008) *Identity and Control: How Social Formations Emerge*. Princeton: Princeton University Press.

Wijnberg, N.M., and G. Gemser (2000) 'Adding Value to Innovation: Impressionism and the Transformation of the Selection System in Visual Arts', *Organization Science*, 11(3): 323-329.

Wittel, A. (2001) 'Towards a Network Sociality', *Theory, Culture and Society*, 18(6): 51-77.

Woolf, V. (2004) *A Room of One's Own*. London: Penguin.

Žižek, S. (1992) *Enjoy Your Symptom!* London: Routledge.

Zola, É. (1867) 'Exposition universelle, 1867. Nos peintres au Champ de Mars', in É. Zola (1959) *Salons*. Paris: Drouz.